THE
ROMAN
TRIUMPH

by
ROBERT PAYNE

Illustrated with
photographs
and line drawings

ABELARD-SCHUMAN, LTD.
London   New York   Toronto

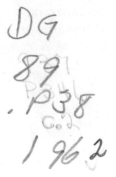

London	New York	Toronto
Abelard-Schuman, Ltd.	Abelard-Schuman, Ltd.	Abelard-Schuman, Ltd.
8 King Street	6 W. 57 Street	896 Queen St., S.W.

Printed in the United States of America

LAWRENTIO CLARK POWELL
in honorem

CONTENTS

Insert of Illustrations Opposite Page 128

THE ROMAN TRIUMPH

THE STRONGEST POISON EVER KNOWN
CAME FROM CAESAR'S LAUREL CROWN.
WILLIAM BLAKE, *Auguries of Innocence.*

INTRODUCTION

FOR over a thousand years Roman conquerors returning from the wars enjoyed the honour of a triumph. For a whole day, sometimes for many days, the Roman people were presented with a vast and tumultuous parade celebrating the glory of the returning general. In the procession came trumpeters and musicians and strange animals from the conquered territories, together with carts laden with treasure and captured armaments. The conqueror rode in a triumphal chariot, and the dazed prisoners walked in front of him. In imperial times the conqueror was crowned with a laurel wreath and wore a purple tunic embroidered with palms under a purple toga embroidered with stars. Sometimes his children, robed in white, stood with him in the chariot, or rode the trace-horses. A slave stood behind the conqueror, holding a golden crown over his head, and whispering in his ear a warning that all glory is fleeting.

The Roman triumph was a sacramental rite, and every detail of the procession and of the sacrifices performed at the culminating moment of the mystery was prescribed by law. From time to time there were changes in the order of the procession brought about by the pressure of historical events, or new symbols were introduced, but the general nature of the procession was fixed from a very early age. Yet in the most subtle ways there were changes of emphasis, sudden alterations in texture, curious permutations of grandeur. The nature of the conqueror changed, as the nature of conquest changed; and the triumph, while celebrating its inflexible and unchanging purpose, suffered from the inevitable infirmities which descend upon any religious rite which has endured over a long period of time. Repeatedly it was corrupted, and repeatedly it rallied. Even when the Romans no longer believed in their gods, the momentum acquired by the triumph was so great that it continued to be the greatest and most desirable spectacle known to the Romans.

There were excellent reasons for the survival of the triumph, and perhaps the most pressing of all was the Roman need for it. That strange barbaric procession, born out of many accidents, answered to a deep-felt longing for security, for the sense of the common mystery. An observer in Rome, watching the procession pass by, might be pardoned if he thought the Roman people were celebrating the conqueror: in fact they were celebrating themselves. They rejoiced in their victory, incarnate in the figure of the conqueror, and they saw in this earthly procession intimations of divine blessing.

We shall never know the excitement that passed through the crowds or the happy agony enjoyed by the conqueror as he contemplated his own majesty in the triumph, himself arrayed like a god on the eve of presenting himself to a god. Our own agonies and joys have different origins. We cannot put ourselves in the minds of the Romans, but we can study them at a safe distance with the help of the immense number of books and inscriptions they left behind. They never troubled to document the triumph, and so we are compelled to piece together the scattered observations that fell from the lips of the historians, orators, letter-writers, poets and theologians. And what is strange is that whenever they come to discuss the triumph, however briefly, we are nearly always made aware of a catch in the voice, a momentary uneasiness, as though they could hardly bring themselves to speak aloud about something so magnificent, or so terrible.

The Romans seem to have been awed by the triumph because it was the most solemn of their mysteries, the one closest to the ethos of the nation: a blinding thing, with many facets, and each facet illuminated some strange corner of the Roman soul. There is a sense in which all Roman history revolves around the festival of triumph. There, if anywhere, was to be found the *raison d'être* of the Roman people, that small body of men determined to rule the world so that all men should become like the Romans. Just as the *triumphator* saw the procession as the celebration of a man in his greatest glory, his utmost power and most perfect achievement, so the Romans saw the triumph as the apotheosis of their pride. Because the triumph spoke to them of their safety, of riches pouring into Rome from all the corners of the earth and of the vigour of the nation mysteriously renewed and increased by the intervention of divine powers, it was inconceivable to them that there was any blessing greater than this. They saw themselves as the celebrants of a mystery, which was for them the central mystery of the universe.

We shall never understand the Romans unless we understand the triumph. Myths, superstitions, strange religions from abroad, traditions so old that no one knew their origin, customs so ancient that men could barely understand why they existed, a thousand fantasies worked upon the triumph and subtly influenced it. The Romans themselves were sometimes ignorant of what it was about. All kinds of terrors and deluding images were aroused by the sight of the procession, and they knew, as we know, that vast unconscious forces were being released. Sometimes they wondered whether the procession was not a kind of mirage, as empty as the air, as evanescent as the incense which often hid the *triumphator* from sight.

Sometimes indeed the glittering Roman triumph streaming across centuries of history, thundering with the march of the legions, reminds us of nothing so much as the sad triumphal procession of the Indians after the trial of Dr. Aziz in *A Passage to India*. The procession, it will be remembered, petered out. No one ever knew how it came into being. "It was a victory, but such a queer one," one of the characters exclaims. "Where was the procession going?"

We do not know where the triumph was going, but we know that it went where the Romans wanted it to go. Afterwards they would invent legends to explain why the Capitol was the most sacred site in Rome and speak of a long-buried head still bleeding when they dug it up—Capitol, they said, meant *Caput Auli,* but no one knew very much about Aulus, and no one cared. They invented legends to explain why Jupiter Capitolinus replaced Jupiter Feretrius, to whom the spoils were originally dedicated, and sometimes they did not trouble to invent legends at all. The triumph *was*. It was a thing that baffled their imaginations, as sometimes it baffles ours.

A hundred perturbing questions haunt the student, as he watches the triumph vanishing into the distance. Why were the prisoners sometimes killed secretly, while the white oxen were sacrificed publicly? Did the *triumphator* smear his face with red paint in order to look more war-like or in order to resemble more closely the great god in the temple, or in order to screen his blushes? More precisely, did the *triumphator* paint his face at all? All references to the painting of his face derive from late sources, suggesting that it was a late addition to the ceremony. What is the significance of the *tunica palmata* and *toga picta*? What hymns and invocations were sung at the sacrifice?

There are no simple solutions to these problems, and we cannot entirely trust the Christian apologists. The Christian author Minucius Felix wrote that "every Roman triumph introduced a new impiety, and every successful war involved a new spoliation of the gods". He believed that the Romans became a great power only because they committed innumerable acts of sacrilege, and at the heart of the Roman religion there was "the act of triumph over the trampled gods".[1] It is strange that a Christian writer should be so concerned to defend the pagan gods destroyed by the Romans, but he was following an established tradition. Virgil, too, spoke of the guilt which had descended upon the Romans. The Romans were perfectly aware of the crimes they had committed on the road to empire, and the old Roman curse, *Ultimus suorum moriatur,* seems to have been there from the beginning.

There is a sense in which the Roman triumph is an act of propitiation, a desolate gesture towards the gods to forgive the crimes committed in their name. It was a joyful procession, but also a melancholy one. The silent *triumphator,* gazing straight ahead for fear of languishing in his own pride, looking always towards the Temple of Jupiter Capitolinus where the ultimate sacrifice was to be performed, was himself a victim, almost a sacrificial victim. He knew, if others did not, that the burden was almost too great to be borne, that men cannot attain these heights without incurring the wrath of the gods, and that it is easier to walk a tight-rope high up in the sky than to receive the wild adulation of the mob and still remain sane.

The Romans, however, did not regard the *triumphator* as a victim: they saw him as the mediator between earth and heaven, as Jupiter incarnate, a man remote from mortal preoccupations, in whom for a brief period there flourished the virtues of the tutelary gods, and at the same time they saw him as a human being in danger of suffering from the sin of pride, and so they set a slave to whisper into his ear, hung phallic ornaments to avert the evil eye about his gilded chariot, and shouted obscenities as he passed. Their feelings towards him were always ambiguous. If he was god and man, then let the man beware and let the god be tamed so that he will live peacefully with them. Fear and adulation went hand in hand in the procession.

That strange procession becomes stranger the more we look at it. It is easy to understand the adulation, but why the intense fear which accompanied the *triumphator* throughout his progress? Perhaps Minucius Felix and St. Augustine were right when they suggested that Rome fell because there had been a tradition of bloodshed and crime and pride from the beginning. According to a late tradition, Romulus, the founder of Rome, murdered his brother and his two foster-fathers, continually exalted himself,

[1] Octavius, XXV, 6, 7.

dréssed in purple, saw visitors while reclining on a couch, and was
at last mysteriously murdered near a place called the Goat Marsh
on a day when, according to Plutarch, "sudden strange alterations
took place in the air, and the face of the sun was darkened, and it
was not a peaceable night, but one shot through with terrible
thunderings and winds from all quarters". There was a murder at
the beginning of Roman history: this we know for certain: the
echoes of the murder can be heard throughout her history. Rome
was built on foundations of blood and the Roman triumph was a
Roman sorrow: the more lands they conquered the more impossible became the hope of holding the empire. A remorseless destiny
ruled them. They must go on and on, conquering for the sake of
conquest, never finding any peace until for a brief while Augustus
Caesar threw the mantle of his imperial benevolence over the
world; but this peace lasted less than a life-time. Characteristically,
Augustus Caesar put an end to the triumph as a right to be enjoyed
by conquering generals: henceforward this right belonged to the
emperor alone.

There were triumphs before the Romans, but they seem to have
been simple affairs consisting of processions of soldiers leading
their prisoners and passing in review before their king. A relief
found in the palace of Sennacherib in Nineveh shows the triumphant return of Assyrian soldiers leading the bound prisoners of
war and the captured women and children. The triumphant
soldiers are seen holding the heads of their enemies high in the
air, while they march beside the Tigris beneath the high walls
of Nineveh. One of the manacled prisoners is about to have his
head struck off: he seems unconcerned. Later, as we know from
other reliefs, the heads will be formed into pyramids and a clerk
with a slate in his hand will count them as though they were so
many apples. Having captured the kings of Sidon and Cilicia, the
Assyrian King Esarhaddon wrote: "I hung the heads of Sanduarri
and Abdilkutte round the necks of the nobles to demonstrate to
the people the power of Ashur, my lord, and so I paraded them
through the main wide street of Nineveh while the singers played
on their harps."

In historical times the Greeks rarely, if ever, permitted themselves the luxury of formal triumphs. They speak of trophies and
ἐπινίκια, but never of anything corresponding to a triumphal procession. The classic Greek text is the one which Aeschylus puts
in the mouth of Eteocles when making a vow to the guardian gods:

If this city and all its citizens be saved,

Then will I sprinkle the altars with the blood of sheep,
And hang up trophies in the holy temples
From the spoils of the enemy armour conquered by spears.
                                    (*Seven against Thebes*, 275-278)

But these trophies were of a very rudimentary kind: suits of armour
were hung up, and then allowed to perish as the old evils faded in
the memory of men. The Greeks preferred to avoid the sin of
hubris: there must be no insolence, no maltreatment of the enemy
dead, no killing of prisoners. When the army entered an enemy
city, the soldiers sang a sacred hymn—θρίαμφος, from which the
word *triumphus* is derived.

La mort semble née à Rome, wrote Chateaubriand. "It seems
that death was born in Rome." And sometimes as we look upon
those stern, unpitying men, grown small through the telescope of
history, but still large enough to haunt us with the memory of their
fearful powers, it comes to us that the triumph was a kind of dance
of death, a ga e played on the edge of the abyss for a stake that was
never worth while. The highest honour open to a Roman was the
honour of a triumph: for this men fought, intrigued, suffered and
died. For the honour of a triumph immense sums of money were
expended, innumerable people were needlessly killed, vast
treasures were dissipated, and whole countries were laid waste.
The economy of Europe, Africa and Asia was mercilessly disrupted,
and a hundred cities and a hundred thousand towns were pillaged,
so that the conquerors could return laden with plunder to Rome
and show what they had accomplished. But the same battles had
to be fought over and over again, and when at last the Empire was
falling into ruins, the emperors were still inscribing *Pax Aeterna*
on their coins, when there was no peace, nor any hope of peace.

There are some evident lessons to be learned from the triumph.
We shall see how conquest inevitably engenders conquest, and
hatred breeds hatred, and how the ultimate crime lies in the self-
regarding mind of the conqueror, who discovers too late that
human pride shatters his humanity. In time the Romans became
aware of the dangerous pride of the *triumphator* and learned to
deride him while at the same time worshipping him; but these
jests seem to have been introduced only in the later days of the
Republic, and by then the harm was done.

In a preface to his history of the Civil Wars Appian explained
the reasons which brought him to write about an age remarkable
only for the extent of its lawlessness. He said he wrote in order
that future generations might learn "the measureless ambition of

men, their dreadful lust of power, their unwearying perseverance, and the countless forms of evil". In much the same spirit I have written this account of the triumph. I have told the story as a continuing history, beginning with a brief excursus in Etruria, sketching in the background in the hope that the *triumphatores* can be seen as real men against an authentic landscape. It has seemed preferable to write a reasonably short work rather than a vast compendium drowned in footnotes, if only because my purpose is to show the fire and colour of those vast and tumultuous processions in all their majesty and terror, and the pity of it.

I

THE ETRUSCAN SPLENDOUR

To THIS DAY no one knows where the Etruscans came from, though for a century the scholars have puzzled over their origins. They appear first in history in the eighth century B.C., their civilization already formed, their art already at the highest level it would ever reach, a gay pleasure-loving people who showed a wonderfully civilized face to the world. We do not see them going through the normal phases of a culture: they seem to have had no childhood, no adolescence: from the very beginning they demonstrated a strange maturity. They almost certainly came to Italy from the coast of Asia Minor about the time of the fall of Troy, and it is just possible that there were Trojans among the first Etruscan settlers who built their cities in the Po valley and spread over northern Italy. According to Cato, there was a time when nearly the whole of Italy was under their dominion.

When we see them first in the dawning of the Italian world, they are farmers and seamen, bearded and ruddy-faced, iron-smiths, masters of painting, possessors of pirate fleets raiding the Tyrrhenian and Ionian seas, with their own colonies in Elba, Corsica, Sardinia, the Balearic islands and the coast of Spain; their influence was felt in southern France and in North Africa. Their wealth came from raiding and from the possession of iron-mines; they exported iron to Phoenicia and Greece and in return received the luxuries which decorate their tombs.

Herodotus was the first to write at any length on the origin of the Etruscans. He says they came from Lydia in Asia Minor, emigrating because of a famine under their leader Tyrrhenos, the son of King Atys of Lydia, and they established themselves in regions previously occupied by the Umbrians; five hundred years later Virgil followed this tradition by writing indiscriminately of the Lydians and the Etruscans. But in Virgil's time not everyone believed in the Asiatic origin of the Etruscans. Dionysus of Halicarnassus devoted six chapters of the first book of his *Early History of Rome* to an examination of the problem, and came to the conclusion that they were a people "like no other people", speaking a language remote from any languages of Asia Minor, with their own religion and their own customs, and he developed the theory that "they did not come from outside, but were the native inhabitants of the place". This theory, however, seems to have been developed for the particular purpose of convincing the Greeks that their Roman conquerors had the same origin as themselves and were not descended from the outpourings of Asia. *"Asia Tuscos sibi vindicat,"* wrote Strabo. "Asia claims the Etruscans as her own." It is a belief that has long survived, and at this late date we have no reason to question it.

The Romans were continually bewildered and dazzled by the splendour of the Etruscans, long after they had defeated them in war and destroyed their cities. They were dimly aware of the long and heroic past enjoyed by the Etruscans, but though the Emperor Claudius wrote their history, now lost, and other histories were written, there seems to have been a conscious conspiracy to forget that the Romans owed their imperial traditions to a nation they had almost completely annihilated, while at the same time they re-membered vividly the great *lucumenes,* the priest kings, who ruled over the cities of Etruria and were always attended with immense panoply. In the words of Diodorus Siculus, the Etruscans were "the authors of that dignity which surrounds rulers", and this dignity together with all the ceremonies which went with it were borrowed by the Romans with no sense of impropriety, just as they borrowed many of the Etruscan gods. In all other matters they regarded themselves as superior to the Etruscans, but they saw a peculiar justice in purloining the alien gods.

When the *lucumenes* appeared in public, they rode in gilded carts drawn by four horses, wearing embroidered robes and tunics adorned with the palms which proclaimed their Asiatic origin. They were preceded by lictors who carried the *fasces,* the sharp double-headed axes which were the ancient symbols of sovereignty. They wore heavy gold crowns and gold breastplates, and from their necks dangled the golden orbs (*bullae aureae*) which were also symbols of their vast and portentous powers. Trumpeters heralded their approach, and when they descended from their chariots ivory stools were prepared for them, and they were attended by officers wearing togas with purple borders. Eagles were the standards of their armies, and when they won victories they held long pro-cessional triumphs, of which the details are unknown to us. To celebrate their triumphs they instituted games and gladiatorial displays. Deeply religious, passionately convinced that they pos-sessed mysterious powers granted to them by heaven, the *lucumenes* passed through life with the calm majesty of gods, aware that their least gestures possessed significance. All that was noble, powerful and divine seemed to be concentrated in those regal figures who were at once earthly rulers and high-priests of the sacred mysteries.

It would be a mistake to suggest that the Etruscans were a calm, wide-eyed people, interested only in the quiet purposes of living. They were ruthless fighters. They enjoyed bullfights, horse-races and gladiatorial contests, and seem to have performed human sacrifices. Surviving accounts of the wars between the Romans and the Etruscans all come from Roman sources, but the overwhelming impression derived from reading them is that they fought well and eagerly, were superbly equipped, and could usually hold their own. In 396 B.C., after a siege of ten years the Etruscan city of Veii surrendered, but the Romans were still fighting the Veientes a hundred and fifty years later.

The Romans were originally a small community living in the marshlands near the mouth of the Tiber, indebted to the Etrurians and the Greeks for nearly all the culture they acquired. What is surprising is how little the Romans adapted: they preferred to borrow outright. From the Etruscans they acquired their numerals, many gods, some of the days of the month, many festivals, the shape of the three-cell temple, their methods of worship and of questioning the divine will of the gods. The toga came from Etruria; so did the form of the Roman sandal.

The Romans never wearied of expressing their debt to Etruria. The historian Florus says the Romans borrowed from the Etruscans all the *impedimenta* of the triumph: *fasces*, robes of state, official chairs, rings, horse trappings, military cloaks, purple-bordered togas, the gilded chariot drawn by four horses, and the embroidered robes and tunics adorned with palms. Even the trumpets which preceded the procession were invented by the Etruscans, who built the great temple to Jupiter, Juno and Minerva on the Capitoline hill during the last days of the Etruscan royal dynasty ruling over Rome. In this temple there stood the terracotta image of Jupiter himself, naked and holding the thunderbolt in his left hand. The image was made by the Etruscan sculptor Vulca of Veii, who was summoned especially to Rome for this purpose.

So much of the triumph was derived from the Etruscans that we may wonder whether the Romans did not borrow it outright, even to the prayers offered at the sacrifice. From time to time, as we shall see, they discarded some elements of the original triumph, invented others, incorporated fragments of alien rites from abroad, deliberately recreating an image closer to their own conception of a triumph. It was as though a vast and glittering crown had been offered to them, and from time to time they removed some of the jewels, replacing them with barbaric ornaments, until at last the crown resembled one of those singularly powerful crowns worn by Gothic kings, all rusty iron and uncut emeralds. In the end the triumph belonged to them.

No description or representation of an Etruscan triumph has survived, and nothing is gained by attempting to recreate it. We know the *impedimenta* well—the two-headed axes, the lictors in their scarlet cloaks, the gilded chariots—but we cannot guess how they bore themselves in procession, or exactly how they fulfilled their vows to the gods. Though every day their relics are being dug up, they remain mysterious. We see them only in glimpses. Occasionally we observe the proud *lucumenes* riding in procession, and the Etruscan priests charging against the Roman lines with reckless courage, brandishing live snakes and naked torches; then the mist comes down. We do not know very much about them in the days when Romulus was setting out to carve out a little empire of hills, at the dawn of Europe.

Gods float in the azure air
Bright gods and Tuscan, back before dew was shed.
Light: and the first light, before ever dew was fallen.

2

THE ROMAN TRIUMPH

THE STORY of the founding of Rome is shrouded in so many layers of legend that we shall never know the name of the founder, or when it took place, or what tribes were conquered before the Romans were able to establish their precarious peace. Somewhere, very dimly discernible behind a veil of legends, we observe a familiar face—the face of Romulus. We see him gathering a band of dispossessed farmers and woodlanders, building wattle-and-daub huts on the slopes of a low hill and cunningly contriving to extend his dominion over the neighbouring hills and the surrounding marshes. We hear a recognizable voice, which is stern, unpitying, raucous, filled with the lust of conquest. And it seems perfectly appropriate that this mysterious forerunner of the Roman people should have disappeared one bright summer day when standing on the edge of the marshes in the Campus Martius, struck dead by a thunderbolt which appeared out of a cloudless sky. It is almost possible to believe the Roman legend that he was rapt up to heaven in a thunder-cloud.

All we know for certain about the founding of Rome is that at some distant time in the past a small group of desperate men abandoned their settlement on the shores of Lake Nemi, and led by a young hero, half warrior, half magician, reputed to be the son of the wolf-god Mars, they came to the Palatine hill and established themselves there, far from the highroads and the fertile plains inhabited by the Etruscans. They may have brought with them their flocks and herds, and they may have called the hill after Pales, the god who looked after shepherds, whose feast was celebrated on the same day as the day traditionally observed for the founding of Rome. Pales may have been Pan in his Roman disguise.

We can only guess how they lived and survived during the early years of the settlement. By day their flocks grazed in the hollows and along the slopes which were later to be called after the thick groves of trees which grew there—osiers, oaks, laurels and beeches. Scattered on the edge of the marshes and over the hill were the straw huts which can still be seen in the vineyards of the Campagna, where a man can sleep away the long drowsy afternoons:

25

four poles, a thatched roof weighted down with stones, the door secured by a stout wooden bar and the windows narrowed to prevent thieves from slipping in. At the beginning there were perhaps no more than thirty or forty determined men, living in a small isolated community, regarded by the neighbouring villagers as bandits or worse.

These original settlers had chosen well. Of the seven hills which stood on the banks of the Tiber, the Palatine was the only one which could be regarded as an ideal place for a settlement. It was close to the river; it was steep on all sides; it could be easily defended; and it had the further advantage of being central among the other hills and in no danger of being taken by surprise. No better base for military operations could be imagined.

At first the Romans seem to have had no intention of attacking the neighbouring settlements. They were too small a force, and too weak, to assume the responsibilities of war: their weapons were guile and cunning. The nearest villages were Caenina, Crustumium and Antemnae, and there were a number of other villages occupied by Sabines, a people believed to be of Lacedaemonian descent. Tradition relates that these villagers were invited during the harvest festival to come to the Palatine and celebrate the discovery of an altar to Consus, the god of the crops, found buried beneath the earth. At a signal from Romulus the Romans threw themselves upon the women, most of whom were Sabines, and sped off with them into the fastnesses of the hill. In the past their requests for women had remained unanswered; they now had as many women as they wanted; and they were prepared to take the consequences of breaking the laws of hospitality.

We have no reason to doubt the story of the rape of the Sabine women, but we may reasonably doubt that more than a handful were taken. The Mauretanian King Juba II, who became one of the most learned antiquarians of his time, believed that 683 virgins were seized: a more conservative tradition claims that there were no more than thirty. Whatever the number, the rape of the women was a cause for offence, and the loudest complaints came from the village of Caenina and its chieftain who bore the typically Greek name of Acron. There was war between Caenina and Rome, and with the defeat of Acron the Romans enjoyed their first triumph.

According to Plutarch, Romulus met Acron in single combat and killed him, and then went on to rout his army and capture the village. He had no desire to harm the villagers and ordered them to destroy their huts and accompany his soldiers back to Rome, where they would receive all the privileges of citizenship, being absorbed in the community. Before the battle he vowed to offer his adversary's armour to Jupiter Feretrius, whose dwelling place was the oak-tree always sacred to Jupiter and whose emblem was a flint stone. Plutarch believed that Feretrius derived from *ferire,* to smite; and Jupiter the Smiter was not an unlikely god to receive the worship of a guerrilla chieftain. Plutarch goes on to describe how Romulus carried out his vow:

> Thereupon Romulus, in order to perform his vow in a manner suitable to Jupiter and with an eye to pleasing the city, hewed down a great oak which he saw growing in the camp, trimmed it to the shape of a trophy and hung upon it the suit of armour belonging to Acron, and arranged it properly. Then girding his clothes about him and crowning himself with a laurel garland, his hair flowing gracefully, with the trophy resting erect on his right shoulder, he led the procession, singing songs of triumph, with the whole army marching after him; and all the citizens received him with cries of joy and wonder.
>
> The procession of this day was the origin and model of all the triumphs which came afterwards.
>
> *(Romulus,* xvi.)

Plutarch's account of the first triumph differs only slightly from the accounts left by Livy and Dionysius of Halicarnassus. Livy says the trophy was deposited on the Capitol and Romulus promised the god that for all future generations the trophies of slain kings would be deposited in his shrine, but it seems likely that the Capitoline hill was reserved for later triumphs under the Etruscan kings of Rome. Dionysius of Halicarnassus gives some details of the fighting, explicitly saying that Romulus took the army of Caenina by surprise and made himself master of their camp. If Romulus or any early chieftain of Rome carried the armour of his adversary on a tree stump, he was doing what the Greeks had done from time immemorial. There was nothing therefore essentially Roman in the custom. What was new was the solemn promise of Romulus to spare the enemy and to incorporate them in the settlement. The first triumph was peaceful. No prisoners were immolated, and no sacrifices were offered to the god, and there was no triumphal chariot—all these would come later. A long-standing tradition asserted that Romulus walked in the procession, and all the statues of Romulus in his triumph seen by Plutarch showed him on foot. Afterwards, when the triumph became a vast and majestic procession, when the conquering general was surrounded by all the insignia of pomp and majesty, people sometimes remembered the simplicity of the early triumphs and wished they could return to the past. But the triumph moved with its own momentum; obeyed a logic of its own; acquired a variety of symbolic meanings; and never recaptured its early simplicity.

Caenina has long since disappeared, and no one knows the site of the village which saw the beginning of the first triumph. Pliny relates that it had vanished in his own day, leaving no trace. Plutarch says it was "a Sabine town", and Diodorus Siculus reckons it one of the colonies of Alba. The memory of the obscure settlement persisted down to imperial times, for we find a *Sacerdotium Caeninense* mentioned in an inscription. Somewhere along the Via Salaria leading north-east from Rome we may one day find the site of the first battle fought by the Romans.

Romulus was credited with three triumphs, the second following close upon the first. There was a quick, short battle against the Antemnates, and once more there was a triumphal procession to celebrate the victory. Dionysius of Halicarnassus wrote that this triumph was accompanied by the first manifestations of those outward signs of glory which were to become so prevalent later. He wrote:

Romulus led his army home, bearing with him the spoils of the slain and the choicest portions of booty as an offering to the gods; and he offered many other sacrifices. Romulus himself came last in the procession, wearing a purple robe and with a wreath of laurels round his head, and in order to retain his royal dignity he rode in a chariot drawn by four horses.

As for the army, both infantry and cavalry, they came up in due order according to their several divisions, praising the gods in song and extolling the conqueror with improvised chants, while the citizens with their wives and children came out to meet them, lining the roads, welcoming them and congratulating them on their victory. Then when the army entered the city, they found wine-bowls filled to the brim and tables loaded with food set out before the most important houses so that anyone who pleased might take his fill.

Such was the victory celebration, marked by the carrying of trophies and concluding with a sacrifice, which the Romans called a triumph, as it was first instituted by Romulus.

(*Roman Antiquities*, II, 34.)

So Dionysius of Halicarnassus goes on, bewailing the lost simplicity, remembering the pomp and pageantry and displays of wealth which he had observed in triumphs of his own time, while describing an ancient triumph which already bears the marks of sophistication. Plutarch, wiser in the ways of the ancient Romans, asserts bluntly that Dionysius was wrong in believing that Romulus rode in a chariot—that honour was reserved for the first Tarquin, or perhaps for Poplicola. By implication Plutarch asserts that the entire description of a primitive triumph by Dionysius is merely a rhetorical fabrication. The original triumphs were rude, devoid of pageantry, no more than a procession of soldiers marching with their chief, with no need of any panoply, for it was enough to taste the heady wine of victory.

So far the wars and skirmishes had been fought against neighbouring tribes of Greek descent. The third battle involved a far more dangerous enemy—the Etruscans of the citadel of Veii, twelve miles from Rome and on the other side of the Tiber, standing on a high and rocky spur at the confluence of two branches of the Cremena river. The citadel was almost impregnable, but the Veientes made the mistake of sending their army to meet the Roman army in the plain; they were routed, pursued to the walls of the city and compelled to make peace, surrendering according to Plutarch their salt mines along the banks of the river, a large tract of land and sixty of their noblemen as hostages. Romulus celebrated his triumph over the Veientes by leading a procession of captives to Rome, among them the old general in command of their army, who wore a purple cloak and the gold *bulla*, symbol of his rank, attached to it. The memory of this doddering old man survived in a custom still followed in Plutarch's day, for after every triumph an old man would be led through the Forum and up the steps of the Capitoline hill, while the town-crier shouted: "Sardians for sale!" The Romans believed that Sardis, the capital of Lydia, was the original home of the Etruscans.

Tradition goes on to relate that soon after his victory over Veii Romulus died. In the last months of his life he had grown increasingly proud and capricious. He dressed in scarlet with a purple-bordered robe, gave audiences while lying on a couch of state, and surrounded himself with a bodyguard of young men bearing staves of office. When he died, Rome was still no more than a huddle of houses on the Palatine, but she possessed a powerful army, salt-mines, annual tribute from Veii, and a scattering of allies. The prayers to the she-wolf and the ditch were being answered.

Such are the legends concerning the handful of outcasts from Lake Nemi who established themselves on the Palatine and reached out to conquer the neighbouring settlements, and at some early date found themselves strong enough to make war on an Etruscan fortress on the southern frontiers of Etruscan territory. Henceforth the influence of the Romans would increase. Out of continual wars and skirmishes there would emerge a civilization which married the stern hillmen to the luxury-loving Etruscans. We call it Roman civilization, but in fact it was as much Etruscan as Roman. Nearly all that was delightful, highly coloured, ornate and feverish in that civilization can be traced to the Etruscans; to this the Romans added their brute strength and massive determination to spread out until they had encompassed the whole world.

First there was the ditch around the meeting-house, and then the furrow around the hill, and finally there was a third circle which embraced the universe.

But in the years following the attack on Veii, Rome was exhausted. There followed the long peaceful reign of Numa Pompilius, a Sabine elected to the chieftainship by virtue of his knowledge of magic and his towering presence. Where Romulus wears the garments of divinity, a god's son and himself a god (*deo prognatus deus ipse*), Numa Pompilius stands like a priest, blessing and being blessed, an aged autumnal figure, whose task, if we can believe legend, was to safeguard the sanctity of the Roman people. For himself he asked nothing; it was enough that the Roman people should endure in quietness and peace; and it was said of him that he especially worshipped the goddess of silence, Tacita, who always held a finger to her lips.

Numa fades into mythology: he wears no recognizable face, no recognizable speech comes from him. They say he was a student of Pythagoras and was the first to give names to the months and to divide the Roman people according to their trades. They say, too, that he inaugurated the religious code, appointing Pontiffs to preside over public worship, Augurs to listen to the will of heaven, Flamens to minister in the temples, Vestal Virgins to guard the sacred flame, and Salii to adore the gods while dancing in full armour. They say he built the Regia, on the walls of which it was long believed the lists of triumphing generals were first hung, and then inscribed. But there were no wars in his reign of nearly forty years, and he died very quietly in old age, "as though he had just fallen asleep".

Numa may have been legend, a figure invented to satisfy men's longing for a father image: the founder of the laws, the generous and compassionate prince of peace. He was succeeded by Tullus

Hostilius, a man of a very different stamp, war-like, fiercely superstitious, the first of the Roman rulers to wage war treacherously.
He fought against the people of Alba and Fidenae, and finally
against the Sabines, winning victories over all of them. He was the
pure savage. After treacherously seizing Mettius Fufetius, King of
Alba, he ordered him roped to two four-horsed chariots and then
whipped the horses in opposite directions until the King was torn
asunder. Tullus Hostilius died while attempting to perform some
magic rites, and having failed to perform them in the proper
manner he was struck down by an opportune thunderbolt.

His successor, the gentle Ancus Marcius, a grandson of Numa,
had no love for war, but was provoked into fighting against the
Latins. It is recorded that he celebrated a triumph with "immense
spoils" and transported the inhabitants of the conquered towns
back to Rome.

About this time a certain Demaratus of Corinth, who had held
high positions in the government, fled into exile as the result of
an uprising, and with a small band of his followers settled in
Tarquinii in southern Etruria. He married an Etruscan woman,
who gave him two sons. He seems to have become King of Tarquinii, and one of his sons inherited the kingship. The other grew
restless and set off for Rome, accompanied by his wife and a large
retinue. According to the legend he was on his way to Rome and
had already reached the Janiculum when an eagle removed his
hat, flew up in the air with it, and then dropped it back on the
young prince's head. He regarded the apparition of the eagle as
a sign of divine favour. His father had been tyrant of Corinth; he
would become tyrant of Rome.

So it happened, for on the death of Ancus Marcius the young
prince, by bribes and well-considered overtures, found himself
king of Rome, and gave himself the title of Lucius Tarquinius. A
born intriguer, brilliant and wayward, with a flair for Corinthian
luxury, he ruled with more panoply than any of the kings before
him. He seems to have made war for the joy of celebrating
triumphs. He attacked the Latin town of Apiolae, returning with
so much booty that the Romans were amazed; and they were
delighted by the elaborate games he offered in honour of his own
victory, the horses and boxers being for the most part imported
from Etruria. These games, the forerunner of the Roman games
which were continued for nearly a thousand years, seem to have
taken place in the open fields, with the people watching as best
they could, and the court officials and the knights sitting in improvised boxes consisting of rows of seats elevated about twelve feet
from the ground. The king was not completely pleased with these

arrangements, and gave orders for the construction of the circus which was later known as the Circus Maximus.

All the Roman historians are agreed that Lucius Tarquinius, the son of a Greek exile from Corinth, was responsible for introducing panoply to Rome. Strabo says he introduced from Tarquinii the hitherto unknown triumphal and consular ornaments: *fasces,* axes, trumpets, sacrifici᷂ ᷂᷂s, divination and all the music publicly used by the Romans. Zonaras says he was the first to wear magnificent garments, consisting of "the toga and the tunic, purple all over and shot with gold, a crown of precious stones set in gold, and an ivory sceptre". According to Zonaras he was the first to sit on the throne, to parade in a four-horse chariot and to keep twelve lictors for life. His greatest claim, however, on the affection of the Romans was the Temple to Jupiter Capitolinus, which he vowed during the course of a war against the Sabines. He laid the foundations of the temple, which was completed by his son.

Kings who delight in great magnificence live threatened lives and must continually guard against usurpers, especially the princes of a former dynasty. Lucius Tarquinius was no exception. His reign seems to have been marked by continual revolts, put down with great savagery. In the end, after a reign of forty-four years, he was killed by one of the descendants of Ancus Marcius. He had enjoyed three triumphs—against the Latins, the Etruscans and the Sabines—and he had left upon the Romans an impress they were never to forget. Henceforth the name of Tarquinius was to be associated with tyrannical majesty.

Exactly what happened in the confused and turbulent years following his death is unknown. Power seems to have fallen into the hands of his son, Gnaeus Tarquinius. The rebels under the command of Caelius and Aulus Vibenna of Vulci, two brothers from a distinguished family, challenged the power of the new king and defeated him in a battle which is depicted on one of the frescoes of the François tomb with the names of the combatants clearly indicated in the Etruscan tongue. Among the figures we see the mysterious Mcstrna freeing Caelius Vibenna from his bonds —presumably he had been captured by Tarquinius. It is a vivid battle. Blood pours from the dying king. There is a sense of violent movement, of desperate measures desperately accomplished, the daggers gleaming and the robes swirling. So, with the help of scattered fragments from Varro, Servius, Dionysius of Halicarnassus and the Emperor Claudius who engraved on two bronze tablets found in the sixteenth century in Lyons a short commentary on early Etruscan origins, we are enabled to fill in the details of the brief rebellion which put a temporary end to the rule of the Tarquins. Arnobius, the Christian theologian who lived during the reign of Domitian, supplies the information that the conspirators fell out, and in the end Mcstrna emerged as the sole victor after cutting off the head of Aulus Vibenna and burying it in the hill which henceforward bore the name of Capitol, from *Caput Auli*, the head of Aulus.

But nothing in all this is certain. A fitful light broods over the conspiracy. Suddenly the clouds part, and we come into the sunlight. Mcstrna, with his barbaric and unpronounceable name, vanishes, and in his place we have the king Servius Tullius, who is only Mcstrna in his Roman disguise. He is the first authentic historical figure in Roman history.

Servius Tullius seems to have been the son of an aristocratic woman kept in captivity in the court of Tarquinius. His mother came from Corniculum, one of the Latin cities conquered by Tarquinius. He was brought up in the palace, and as a child sleeping by the hearth-stone he was seen to have a radiance shining round his head. Tarquinius was impressed by the miraculous light surrounding the boy, treated him as a son, and secured for him the inheritance. He was known as a good king, especially concerned to improve the lot of the people, and he was credited with three triumphs, all against the Etruscans. His long reign came to an end when his daughter Tullia conspired with her husband, the son of Lucius Tarquinius, to murder him. He was stabbed to death and Tullia rode in her chariot over his dead body.

The tyrannical majesty of the first Tarquinius was only equalled by that of his son, who was so proud that he was ever afterwards known as Lucius Tarquinius Superbus. He was, however, a man of immense energy and resource. He abolished the rights conferred upon the people by Servius, but he brought Rome to a position of dominance as the head of the Latin confederacy. He waged war against the Volscians—the war was to continue intermittently for two hundred years—and celebrated the first of his two triumphs. With the booty amounting to forty talents of silver, he built the temple to Jupiter Capitolinus which had been vowed by his father. Livy records that when the workmen were digging for the foundations of the temple they came upon a human head which showed no signs of decay, and the priests pronounced the head to be the heaven-sent sign that this place was to become the head of a great empire.

This temple was to become the focal point of the Roman triumph, but its origins were essentially Etruscan. It was built by Etruscan workmen in an Etruscan style; the terracotta statue of Jupiter Capitolinus was modelled by an Etruscan artist, Vulca, from Veii. It was at first a small temple. According to Dionysius of Halicarnassus it was only fifteen feet long. It was to grow prodigiously. In 1919, when its pavement was at last uncovered after being hidden for centuries, it was found to be 203 feet long and 187 feet wide. In time the temple was to be faced with marble and roofed with gold plate, and men would speak of the *aureum Capitolium fulgens*—the golden and shining Capitol—but now there was only a small squat temple in the Etruscan style with a wooden entablature, with three rows of columns in front and four columns on each side. Inside there were three *cellae*. The middle *cella* contained the terracotta statue of Jupiter; that on the right contained the statue of Minerva, and that on the left the statue of Juno. All of them seem to have been Etruscan gods. Beneath the temple, in a stone chest, were kept the three sacred books of prophecy bought by the king from the Sibyl of Cumae.

The temple was still unfinished when a popular revolt, led by the king's son-in-law Lucius Junius Brutus, led to the sudden flight of the king and his exile in Cumae. Once more there is a period of confusion, with armies moving mysteriously against the city. Lucius Brutus emerged briefly as a dictator, having thrown off the disguise of madness which enabled him to plot the conspiracy under the eyes of the king. Plutarch described him as "a man like steel of too hard a temper, who never had his character softened by thought or study", and he was soon overthrown and replaced by Publius Valerius Poplicola, whose sobriquet meant that he cultivated the affections of the people. His military career—he triumphed twice in wars against the Sabines, and the people of Veii and Tarquinii—was rivalled by that of his brother Marcus, who was credited with the singular feat of achieving a victory over the Sabines in which the enemy lost 13,000 men without the loss of a single Roman! After this triumph Marcus was honoured with a house on the Palatine at the public expense—the house was provided with doors which opened outward into the street as a sign that public recognition was "continually making way for him".

Poplicola hoped to dedicate the temple of Jupiter Capitolinus, which had been vowed by the first Tarquin. But when the temple was finally completed, it was decided that the honour should fall on one of the two consuls, and so it happened that the honour fell to the obscure first consul, Marcus Horatius Pulvillus. Poplicola was not present when the temple was opened in 509 B.C. In a rage he went off at the head of his army to make war against the people of Veii.

In those early years Rome was surrounded by enemies; or so she thought. The disease of war had entered into her soul. She fought for honour, for prestige, for the glory of fighting and exercising her young muscles. There were small wars and large wars; there were wars fought for a purpose, and wars which were purposeless. No quarter was given. When the two Roman colonies of Cora and Pometia went over to the tribe of the Aurunci, the Romans attacked in force. Pometia was a very small town, hastily put in a state of defence. The Romans were about to storm the walls when the Pometians capitulated, hoping they would be pardoned. Instead the town was razed to the ground, the leaders beheaded, and all the inhabitants sold as slaves. The consuls, says Livy, obtained a triumph, "more because they had heavily avenged wrongs committed against the Romans than on account of the magnitude of the war so successfully brought to a conclusion." Many triumphs seem to have been granted for wars against villages.

The Roman temper was hardening, while the Roman state was shaken by political quarrels. Private armies were being organized by members of the nobility. Pestilence crept into the city. There were slave uprisings—one night 2,500 slaves and exiles seized the Capitol, and when the senators called upon the people to defend their gods they were rewarded with silence and hostility. The Capitol was saved only by the intervention of an army from the Roman colony of Tusculum. Increasingly the Romans became suspicious of their leaders. They protested bitterly against the rich, who imprisoned them for debt, and against the generals who ordered them into the army. Already there was the wide cleavage between the nobility and the people which was to lead in time to relentless and bloody civil wars.

The wars went on, on many fronts. There were wars against the Volscians, the Sabines, the Aequians, the Latins, the remnants of the Tarquinian armies. There were even wars against armies commanded by Roman generals, who had fled from Rome to the

greater safety of a foreign camp. The most dreaded were the
Volscians, who ruled over large areas south of Rome. In 494 B.C.,
after a particularly violent engagement with the Volscians which
led to the conquest of Velitrae, the returning general was awarded
a triumph. Then for the first time the *triumphator* was given the
distinction of a special place at the games, being entitled to
sit through the games on a curule chair. Henceforward the right to
a special place at the games was given to all *triumphatores*.

As Livy, who is our most reliable authority, discusses the
triumphs of these years, we are aware of hesitations and ambigui-
ties. The triumph was not an institution with a fixed set of rules:
each returning general would celebrate his triumph in his own
way. Thus when Lucius Lucretius Tricipitinus won a victory over
the Volscians and the Aequians—there was some dispute whether
he was entitled to a triumph—Livy notes as an unusual feature
that the booty was not carried in the procession, but exposed in
the Campus Martius for three days and the soldiers were invited
to take what belonged to them: what was left over was sold,
presumably for the benefit of the conqueror. Four years later, in
458 B.C., Cincinnatus was called from his plough to the dictatorship to deliver the Roman army from the perilous position in
which they were placed by the Aequians, and having won a victory,
he was commanded by the Senate to enter the city in triumph,
together with his soldiers. It was an important and memorable
triumph, and Livy describes how the captured generals were led
before the chariot. He speaks of the standards being borne on
ahead, referring presumably to the standards of the enemy, and
afterwards came the soldiers laden with booty. Tables were spread
before the houses, and "the troops feasted as they marched, singing songs of triumph and joking to their hearts' content as they
followed the chariot like revellers". It seems to have been a rather
rustic procession, not unlike the triumphal march of Romulus.
The booty belonged to the soldiers. In future times the booty was
to be separated by an immense distance from the military parade.
In these earlier triumphs we are aware of a feeling of close communion between the commander and his soldiers.

Romulus had killed Acron in single combat, and every Roman
general hoped to repeat the feat. Only two others accomplished it.
The second was Aulus Cornelius Cossus in 428 B.C. He was a strik-
ingly handsome man proud of his aristocratic lineage, and brave
to foolhardiness. In a war against the Etruscans he recognized the

enemy commander Lars Tolumnius, conspicuous in his royal robes
as he galloped up and down the lines. Cossus was on horseback;
he levelled his lance and rushed at the Etruscan, unhorsing him.
Then he leaped to the ground, and when the enemy attempted to
rise Cossus kept him down with the boss of his shield, and at last
pinned him with a spear to the earth. Afterwards it was a simple
matter to remove the royal robe and cut off his head. Brandishing
the head of Lars Tolumnius on a spear, Cossus led the advance
against the enemy, panic-stricken at the sight of the king's head.

Cossus, however, was not in command of the Roman army on
the Etruscan front; his rank was that of cavalry tribune, immediately below that of the commander of a legion. The honour of
the triumph therefore went to the dictator Mamercus Aemilius.
Livy offers a vivid picture of the dictator riding in procession,
while all eyes are turned on Cossus as he bears off the spoils of the
dead Etruscan king. The soldiers do not sing about the *triumphator*; they sing instead about the cavalry tribune, comparing him
with Romulus, who also brought the *opima* to the Temple of
Jupiter Feretrius. We know very little about this temple. We know
that there was an image of Jupiter and that he wore a wreath, and
there was kept in the temple the flint stone, which was the oldest
Roman representation of the god, and a sceptre, perhaps belonging to Romulus, on which every civil magistrate swore an oath on
entering office. More than two hundred years were to pass before
another gift of the *opima* was presented to Jupiter Feretrius.

There is some mystery about Cossus. In theory only a consul, a
king or a dictator was permitted to present the *opima* to the god.
According to the ancient annals kept in the temple of Moneta,
Cossus became consul seven years later. Perplexed, Livy consulted
the Emperor Augustus, who remembered having visited the temple
and examined the *opima,* and he discovered on the linen breastplate taken from Lars Tolumnius an inscription which said that
Cossus was consul at the time. It is possible that Cossus was an
honorary consul, but it is too late to inquire into his rank.

Meanwhile the bitter wars with the Latins continued; the
Volscians and Aequians continued to ravage the countryside; and
hardly a year passed without ferocious battles. Plague and pestilence swept through Rome, until the Romans could hardly endure
their fate. At last in 399 B.C. they decided to propitiate the gods by
inaugurating the strange ceremony of *lectisternium* at which the
statues of the gods were wrapped in gaily decorated robes, placed

on couches and solemnly fed. In the same year the Romans were
ordered to walk quietly, to make peace with one another, and to
pray for an end to the drought and victory in the coming wars.
The gods answered by sending another pestilence.

Veii was still the most powerful enemy. The city had resisted a
ten-year siege. Marcus Furius Camillus assumed command of the
siege. He was about fifty, a calm methodical man, noted for his
mildness and sudden fits of furious energy. Since all attempts to
break down the resistance of the enemy had failed, he decided to
employ a stratagem—he would construct an underground tunnel
and send his soldiers through it, and to prevent the enemy from
learning about the existence of the tunnel he continued to maintain sporadic attacks against the city. The ruse was successful. The
mine surfaced close to the Temple of Juno, the largest and most
important temple in Veii, and the Roman soldiers poured into
the city, which was sacked, only the great statue of Juno being
spared. No quarter was given to the defenders. Camillus was
awarded a well-deserved triumph. He had put a decisive end to a
war which had lasted with occasional intervals of truce for eighty-
six years.

The triumph was more brilliant than popular (*clarior quam
gratior*), according to Livy. For the first time the *triumphator* rode
in a chariot drawn by four white horses. Such pomp, customary
among the Etruscans, was reserved by the Romans for their ancient
kings and for Jupiter. It was widely believed that the general had
given way to overweening pride and considered himself equal to
the king of the gods and to Apollo, to whom he had vowed a tithe
of the spoils. Camillus fell into disfavour and went into exile, but
the memory of his triumph remained. In time all the *triumphatores* rode in chariots drawn by white horses.

The historian Florus speaks of the Veientes as "yearly enemies"
(*anniversarii hostes*), but the "day-to-day enemies" (*cotidiani
hostes*) had still to be fought. Among these enemies were the
Aequians, who came originally from central Italy and lived to
the south-east of Rome on the slopes of the Apennines. In 392
B.C., four years after the fall of Veii, an expeditionary force under
Lucius Valerius Potitus was sent against them. Livy says the
battle was "scarcely worth remembering" (*haud memorabile*).
Potitus went through them like a knife. There was an unremark-
able triumph, which Livy dismisses in two lines.

There were more important enemies than the Aequians. The

Romans had a healthy fear of the Gauls, tall men with flaxen hair who wore heavily embroidered robes which they threw off in battle. They poured over the Alps into Italy, conquered from the Etruscans the valley of the Po and were threatening Rome almost before the Romans were aware of being threatened. At the last moment an army was sent out to stop them. Romans and Gauls met on the Allia River twelve miles from Rome. It was all over in a few hours. The Romans panicked. At sunset on the same day the advance patrols of the Gauls entered Rome, and the following morning they came in force, to find the Senators and the *triumphatores* waiting for them, sitting on their thrones in the Forum, wearing their most colourful ceremonial garments, fearless and imperturbable. It was a memory which remained long afterwards to haunt the Roman mind—the empty Forum, the barbarians entering by the Colline Gate, and the old men waiting in indomitable defiance for death.

Only the Capitol could be defended. The long siege went on for seven months. Rome was a shambles under the occupation of the Gauls. Once they found a secret pathway up the slopes of the Capitol and would have captured the citadel if it had not been for the geese which gave the alarm, awakening Marcus Manlius who rushed his troops to the spot and fought off the attackers. The Roman watchman was flung from the cliffs for having allowed the Gauls to come so close.

At this time only one general possessed authority: this was Marcus Furius Camillus, who from his exile in Ardea had led an attack against a Gallic outpost and shown that he at least refused to be panic-stricken by the presence of the Gauls in Roman territory. He worked patiently. He collected and trained an army. On the road to Gabii he suddenly attacked the Gauls in force and routed them. Then, for having saved Rome, he was awarded in 390 B.C. a second triumph and given the titles "Father of his Country" and "Second Founder of the City". Afterwards Camillus ordered Capitoline games to be held in honour of Jupiter Optimus Maximus "who preserved the city".

The occupation by the Gauls was something the Romans never forgot. Above all their defeats this was the one that rankled most, and the moment the Gauls were out of the way, in a fury of injured pride they set about reconquering the lost territories and punishing the Etruscan settlements which had made common cause with the enemy. In 388 B.C., Camillus celebrated his triumph for victories in three separate campaigns. Most of the prisoners led before his chariot were Etruscans. From the money received in the sale of the prisoners the *triumphator* ordered three golden bowls inscribed with his own name, and these were solemnly laid at the feet of the statue of Juno in the Capitol.

The wars went on. The Romans were determined to punish their enemies. The Volscians, who lived on the southern plains of Latium near the coast in the direction of Campania, refused to submit. They were attacked, and in 385 B.C. Camillus triumphed for the fourth time. Meanwhile he had quarrelled bitterly with Marcus Manlius, and some supposed that he celebrated his triumph in an attempt to increase his influence over Marcus Manlius. "He gained more ill-will than glory from this triumph," says Livy. "People were murmuring that he earned it not on the battle-field but at home, not over the enemy but over a citizen: only one thing was lacking in his arrogance—he did not lead Marcus Manlius before his chariot." Shortly afterwards Camillus used his influence to have Marcus Manlius put on trial for the crime of high treason; and the man who had saved the Capitol and who had ordered the execution of the watchman on the night when the Gauls clambered up the slopes was himself thrown down from the Tarpeian rock.

The Gauls were still a force to be reckoned with. Livy speaks of six Gallic invasions and six triumphs over them in a period of forty years. There was a brief war against Praeneste, an ancient town of Latium, twenty miles south-east of Rome, won by Titus Quinctius who bore back with him in his triumph the statue of Jupiter Imperator, placing it between the shrines of Jupiter and Minerva on the Capitol, and writing an inscription on a tablet for all to see: "Jupiter and all the gods granted Titus Quinctius the dictator that he should take nine towns." One of the purposes of the Roman wars appears to have been the capture of the gods of the surrounding settlements.

Camillus was eighty-one when he celebrated his last triumph over the Gauls in 367 B.C. It was a signal victory, and the triumph was awarded by the Senate and the plebs acting together. After this final triumph—his fourth or his fifth, for there is some doubt whether he actually took part in the triumph of 385 B.C.—he passes out of history. He died of the pestilence two years later, to be remembered for his mildness of manner, his superlative generalship and his quiet, relentless pride. It was the kind of pride which terrified the Romans.

No one ever said of Camillus that he earned his triumphs by trickery, but it was charged against Caius Poetelius who celebrated a double triumph over the Gauls and the Tiburtes that he had simply stepped in and put an end to a battle between Gauls and Tiburtes, and then announced he had conquered them. The Tiburtes swore revenge, and promised to punish the Romans for their deceit. They were as good as their word. They crept up to Rome one night when everyone was sleeping and attacked in force. They had not counted on the superior equipment of the Romans, and were put to flight. Livy was horrified by the actions of Poetelius, but acclaimed a Gallic victory by a certain Caius Sulpicius in 358 B.C. "Since the time of Camillus," he writes, "no one ever deserved a victory so much." Sulpicius had captured a vast quantity of gold. This was solemnly dedicated to Jupiter Capitolinus and placed in a stone coffer in the Capitol.

By this time the theory of the triumph had been worked out in all its essential details. The *triumphator* must show that the war was necessary for the survival of Rome, or it must redound to the credit of Roman arms; he must return with prisoners and trophies, preferably the gods of the captured cities; he must obtain from the Senate permission to ride in a chariot through the streets of Rome and receive the acclamations of the people. Only *triumphatores* of unusual accomplishment were allowed to drive in a four-horsed chariot. It was not always necessary for the *triumphatores* to obtain the permission of the Senate. Livy records that in 356 B.C. Caius Marcius Rutilus was granted a triumph by the people without authorization of the Senate. Such triumphs, however, were rare, for the power of the Senate was still in the ascendancy.[1]

In those days the triumph still followed the primitive form. There were no musicians except trumpeters, no *tableaux vivants*, no gilt crowns offered by the municipalities, no *toga picta* emblazoned with stars, and we have no reason to believe that the *triumphator's* face was painted bright red, nor that a slave held a gold crown above his head and whispered into his ear: "Remember that you are mortal." All these came later, during more sophisticated ages. The Senators marched in front, or did not march at all. In front of the *triumphator* marched the prisoners in chains preceded by trumpeters and the spoils. After the *triumphator* marched the army. In his chariot the *triumphator* wore the red cloak which formed the battle-dress of a Roman general. He

---

[1] The first triumph granted by the people took place, according to Livy, in 449 B.C. The *triumphator* could, if he felt it necessary, enjoy a triumph without the approval of the Senate or of the people, either within the city or in later times on the Alban Mount, but in such a case he would have to defray his own expenses. A number of these triumphs seem to have taken place, but they were unofficial and not recorded in the archives.

did not yet regard himself as the equal of Jupiter: his office more clearly resembled that of a priest whose triumph was no more than the formal procession before the sacrifice, which took place at the Temple of Jupiter Capitolinus.

The meaning of the procession, however, was gradually changing. Camillus had introduced four white horses, and in so doing he had significantly altered the scope of the *triumphator's* role. Livy notes quite casually that about this time, following the Gallic wars, there was an influx of Etruscan dancers and flute-players in Rome, and it is probable that they took part in the triumphal processions. Gradually more and more prominence was to be given to the *triumphator,* and the procession itself was becoming more colourful.

For over forty years Rome was dominated by the forceful presence of Camillus. His successor in the affections of the Romans was a certain Marcus Valerius, a young and unknown army officer in 348 B.C. when he offered to fight in single combat against a Gallic chieftain. The slender Marcus Valerius found himself opposed by the thickset, towering Gaul. He had almost no hope of victory, but while they were grappling together a raven settled on the young officer's helmet and pecked fiercely at the Gaul's face and eyes. The Gaul, panic-stricken, was an easy prey. Marcus Valerius killed him, the raven flew off to the east, and the Romans succeeded in routing the Gauls. For this exploit Marcus Valerius received the name "Corvinus" (from *corvus,* a raven), ten oxen and a gold crown. In the following year he commanded an expedition against Satricum, a city in Volscian territory, and put it to the flames, saving only the temple of Mater Matuta, the goddess of birth and the dawn. When he rode in triumph, four hundred prisoners marched before his chariot. In character he resembled Camillus, outwardly mild, but capable of the greatest cruelties when roused. "He could win or lose without changing countenance," said Livy. "He had a passion for sharing the duties of the meanest soldiers, and was therefore wildly popular."

The Romans were in need of a great leader. Exhausted by war, they were determined to continue to fight for the conquest of Italy. They did not know, and could not have guessed, that three long and disastrous wars would have to be fought before they could assume hegemony over all Italy. The first war was fought against the Samnites, "a people powerful in arms and in resources," and lasted for fifty-three years. There followed the brief and desperate battles against Pyrrhus, King of Epirus, and the long-drawn epic struggle with Carthage which ended only in 146 B.C. When these wars were over the character of the Romans had changed, and their military might extended over most of the known world.

In the year 345 B.C., when the Samnite wars began, the Romans numbered perhaps no more than a hundred thousand men altogether in settlements spreading no farther than 50 miles from the city. They could count, according to Livy, almost more triumphs than years since the foundation of Rome in 753 B.C., but after waging war against half the tribes of Italy, they had little to show for their victories.

The Samnites were offshoots of the Sabines, a fierce, freedom-loving people who had taken to the hills. Today all traces of them have vanished except for the frescoes in pastel-colours, showing their young horsemen in white and many-coloured robes, and their young women mourning, which are preserved in the National Museum at Naples. Livy describes the opulence of their crested helmets, silver scabbards and gold sword-belts, and their horses with gold-embroidered saddlecloths. They were masters of guerrilla warfare. In 321 B.C. at the Caudine Forks between Capua and Beneventum they trapped a Roman army in a defile, closing it on both ends. The Romans surrendered their arms, their baggage and even their clothes except for a single garment, and were forced to pass under the yoke. It was a defeat as disastrous as their defeat at the hands of the Gauls.

The lives of the Romans were magnanimously spared, but they did not take defeat gracefully; nor did they agree to a perpetual truce with the Samnites. According to Livy, they were "on fire with wrath and hate" (*ira odioque ardens*). They were prepared to use all the weapons of treachery and cunning to wipe out the affront. Command was given to Lucius Papirius Cursor, an energetic general known for his astonishing capacity for food and wine and for his sternness towards his men. Once when his cavalry-men asked to be excused from performing some onerous duties, he answered: "I release you only from the duty of rubbing your backs when you dismount." It was claimed that he was the equal of Alexander the Great in generalship and would have defeated the King of Macedonia and Asia if he had ever dared to set foot in Italy.

Under the leadership of Papirius Cursor a series of punitive expeditions was sent against the Samnite strongholds. These expeditions were remarkable for acts of quite astonishing treachery on the part of the Romans. For his victories Papirius Cursor was awarded three triumphs, the last in 308 B.C. On this occasion the captured gilt shields of the enemy were distributed among the

silversmiths to decorate their shop-fronts on the Forum. It was a
significant addition to the *décor* of the triumph, and Livy observes
that the shields were henceforth hung outside the shops whenever the images of the Capitoline gods were carried in solemn
procession to the Circus.

About this time the Forum was acquiring some of the *mana*
previously reserved for the Capitol. Two equestrian statues of
triumphatores were erected there in 338 B.C. It was regarded as an
unusual honour. And while the Forum was becoming a focal
point in the triumphal procession, the triumph itself was beginning to assume the form it would have until the time of the
Emperors. For the first time in a speech delivered in 300 B.C., while
the Samnite wars were still being fought, we find unequivocal
references to the *tunica palmata,* the *toga picta,* the triumphal
crown, the laurel wreaths, and the spoils fastened to the walls of
the *triumphator's* house. Nothing is said about the red paint on
the *triumphator's* face, but it is distinctly stated that he rides in a
gilded chariot wearing the robes of Jupiter Optimus Maximus.
Significantly the words come in a speech made on behalf of the
plebs against the privileges of the nobility, and they were uttered
by Publius Decius Mus, a man who had every right to attack
entrenched privilege, for his father had deliberately offered himself as a sacrifice to the gods on behalf of the Roman state, and the
son was to do the same. It would appear that the triumph came to
maturity during the period between the Gallic invasion of 390 B.C.
and the concluding years of the Samnite wars. First from the
Etruscans and then from the Samnites the Romans learned the
arts of opulence.

Gradually the forces which had kept the Romans in check were
succumbing to the ferocious determination of a small group of
patrician generals who hoped by means of their victories to maintain their privileges. One by one the enemies of Rome were giving
ground. At the battle of the Vadimonian Lake in 309 B.C. Etruscan
power was finally extinguished, and fourteen years later at
Sentinum, where Publius Decius Mus gave up his life, the Romans
won the first of the two victories which put an end to Samnite
resistance. There followed in 293 B.C., the battle of Aquilonia,
where 20,340 Samnites were killed, 3,870 were captured and 97
military standards were taken. The Romans were heady with
victory even before the battle was joined, and the general vowed
to Jupiter Victor if he routed the enemy a good-humoured offering of a thimbleful of mead before drinking strong wine himself.

This general bore a well-known name. He was Lucius Papirius

Cursor, and he was the son of a still more famous father. His triumph in 293 B.C. was even more imposing than his father's triumph fifteen years before. The Temple of Jupiter and the Forum were heaped with the spoils, and there was so much booty that some of it was distributed among the allies and the neighbouring colonies to decorate their temples and public squares. Livy says that 2,533,000 pounds of bronze collected from the sale of the captives and 1,830 pounds of silver taken from the conquered cities passed in review during the triumphal procession, and all this money was solemnly deposited in the treasury to the annoyance of the people, who were forced to pay a war-tax for the upkeep of the soldiers when they had hoped to see the money spent on reducing their own taxes. Noble Samnites were led in the procession. The soldiers wore their decorations. Never in living memory had there been such an opulent triumph, or such a pervading sense that the war for Italy was coming to a conclusion. Immediately after the triumph the general set out at the head of a mopping-up expedition to capture the last remnants of the enemy in the hills.

In the following year there occurred at the games two innovacions which were to affect the triumph. For the first time soldiers who had been awarded crowns for gallant action in the field were allowed to wear them publicly, and victors in the games were awarded palms following the Greek fashion.

The last pockets of Samnite resistance were wiped out when Quintus Fabius Gurges captured their chief magistrate, Caius Pontius, and in 276 B.C. led him in triumph and shamefully beheaded him. The gods seem to have disapproved, for they sent a pestilence. The Romans were so troubled by the pestilence that they sent a fleet to the Greek city of Epidaurus to seek counsel from Asclepius, the god of healing. The fleet returned with a sacred serpent, which slipped ashore on the island of the Tiber, and there a temple was erected to Asclepius. Before the end of the century there were to be many more temples to foreign gods.

During the fifty years of constant warfare with the Samnites the Romans had celebrated thirty-one triumphs over an enemy who admitted defeat only when he was bled white. Rome was now saturated with Samnite opulence. For the first time the Romans began to mint silver coins. The Forum was beginning to be crowded with equestrian statues of victorious generals, all gilded. And on the roof of the Temple of Jupiter Capitolinus, visible sign for miles around of Roman dominance, there was now a statue of Jupiter riding in a four-horse chariot, while within the temple itself, according to Livy, Spurius Carvilius had fashioned a new statue of Jupiter made from the breastplates, greaves and helmets of the Samnite enemy.

Yet there was no peace, for by their very nature the Romans invited war.

The Greek colonies in southern Italy were appalled by the dictatorial methods of the Romans and the imminent threat of invasion. The citizens of Tarentum especially feared attack and summoned the aid of Pyrrhus, King of Epirus. Then for the first time the leader of a Mediterranean power set foot in Italy, and the war for the Mediterranean had begun.

3

THE TRIUMPH OVER CARTHAGE

FOR NEARLY a hundred and forty years, with varying success, Rome fought for supremacy over the Mediterranean, her most resourceful and powerful enemy being Carthage, a city founded by Phoenicians of Tyre in the second half of the ninth century B.C. The Carthaginians were skilled metal-smiths, merchants, bankers and colonists. They were a brave, hardy people with a settled form of government. They had colonized Sardinia, northern Sicily, large areas of Spain, and were in effective control of the western Mediterranean. Like the Romans they elected two consuls each year, who presided over the Senate; unlike the Romans they did not permit the consuls to exercise military command. It was a form of government which contrasted favourably with the Roman form; there were checks and balances; the oligarchy was tempered by an occasional referendum to the people. Only one danger threatened them—their wealth. They had come to the stage reached in time by all great civilizations when natural vitality is blunted by luxury. They were resting on their laurels.

Luxury indeed was the curse of that age in all the surviving empires on the Mediterranean. In Egypt, Syria and Macedonia the successors of Alexander the Great were slowly dying of luxury. Alexander had captured the gold hoards of the Persian and Indian kings; the children of the conquerors were revelling in the wealth obtained at sword-point by their fathers; and oriental luxuries imported into the west were giving men a taste for unsuspected comforts. Ptolemy had been a hard-bitten warrior, fighting beside Alexander the Great. His son, Ptolemy II Philadelphus was a gentle scholar with a talent for displaying the oriental magnificence of his wealth. When he became King of Egypt in 283 B.C. he celebrated the most splendid triumph that has ever been recorded.

As Callixenus of Rhodes tells the story in a long fragment preserved by Athenaeus, every device of luxury and ostentation was employed to celebrate the greatness of the king. There was, for example, a magnificent tent erected within the fortress of Alexandria for the king's repose, with immense scarlet hangings

and great sheets of strewn flowers on the floors. It was remarked
that the triumph took place in mid-winter and the flowers were
specially cultivated for the occasion. There were a hundred and
thirty golden couches for the banqueters arranged in a circle, and
innumerable golden tripods and silver lavers. There was an
enormous procession with everyone wearing golden crowns and
gowns made of the finest cloth, singing hymns to Dionysus. We
shall see later how parts of this procession were incorporated in
the Roman triumph. Here is Callixenus's description of the
Dionysus procession:

> First of all came the Sileni, whose task was to hold off the
> multitude of spectators, and they were clad in purple and scarlet
> robes. They were followed by Satyrs, who carried gilded lamps
> made of ivy wood. After them came images of victory with
> golden wings, and they bore in their hands incense burners six
> cubits high, adorned with branches of ivy wood and gold, and
> clad in tunics embroidered with figures of animals, and there
> was a good deal of gold ornament about them. After them
> followed an altar six cubits high, a double altar, all covered
> with gilded ivy leaves, bearing a crown of golden vine-leaves.
> And then there came boys in purple tunics, bearing frankin-
> cense and myrrh, and saffron on golden dishes. And then came
> forty Satyrs crowned with golden ivy garlands, their bodies
> painted—some purple, some vermilion, some in other colours.
> They wore golden crowns fashioned like vine-leaves and ivy-
> leaves. Then came the poet Philiscus, the priest of Dionysus,
> and with him all the artisans in the service of the gods, and
> afterwards came the tripods from Delphi to be given as prizes
> to the trainers of the athletes. There was one for the trainers of
> the young athletes—this was nine cubits high—and another for
> the trainers of men—this was twelve cubits high.
>
> Afterwards came a four-wheeled carriage fourteen cubits high
> and eight cubits wide, drawn by 180 men, and on it there was
> an image of Dionysus ten cubits high. He was pouring libations
> from a golden cup and wore a purple tunic reaching to his feet.
> Before him lay a Lacedaemonian goblet of pure gold, holding
> fifteen measures of wine, and a gold tripod with a golden incense
> burner and two golden bowls full of cassia and saffron; and
> there was a kind of sunshade over it, adorned with ivy and vine-
> leaves, and other green shrubs. To this were fastened chaplets
> and fillets, ivy wands, drums, turbans, and the masks of actors.
>
> There were many more carriages, and at last there came one

drawn by six hundred men. This carriage was twenty-five cubits long and fifteen broad. On this was a wine-sack holding three thousand measures of wine, fashioned from the sewn skins of leopards. The wine poured out of the sack and sprinkled the whole road.

(Athenaeus, *Deipnosophistae*, V, xxv.)

This was not all, for there followed an endless array of similar wonders. There were long columns of palace servants displaying the golden vessels of the king; twenty-four chariots, each one drawn by four elephants; twelve chariots drawn by antelopes, fifteen by buffaloes, eight by pairs of ostriches, eight by zebras. There were mules and camels, and twenty-four lions. At the end came a procession of troops, all superbly equipped. There were altogether 57,600 infantry and 23,200 cavalry.

This tremendous procession, a sophisticated and elaborate imitation of the triumph celebrated by the god Dionysus on his return from India, may have had the deliberate purpose of recalling the triumph of Alexander the Great. It will be remembered that Alexander made his way across Karmania in a strange drunken revelry, riding in a triumphal chariot made of two waggons roped together with a platform over them; and on this platform, beneath a canopy of green branches, the king and his companions drank from golden bowls and beakers, while his soldiers, crowned with flowers, danced and capered to the music of flutes and lyres with the harlots they had brought from Pura. Alexander was imitating the revels of Dionysus in all their drunken simplicity. Ptolemy II Philadelphus was staging a theatrical version of the revels aided by all the resources of his treasury.

The Romans were not yet affected by the vices of the East, and many years were to pass before the Roman triumph incorporated elements of the Dionysus procession. At this moment they were still putting down rebellions on the frontiers of their small empire and demanding the surrender of the Greek cities in southern Italy. The Tarentines summoned Pyrrhus to their assistance, and there followed a strange long-drawn-out war, interrupted by frequent exchanges of ambassadors between the Romans and the king of Epirus, who had lost a large number of the troops he had brought to Italy by shipwreck and was clearly hoping to win his battles by guile and diplomacy.

When Pyrrhus sailed into the harbour of Tarentum, he brought with him 3,000 cavalry, 20,000 foot-soldiers, 2,000 archers and 500 slingers. There were also 20 elephants. The first battle, fought near Heraclea, was indecisive. The Romans had never seen elephants before. "These savage animals with their strong odour and huge bulk" alarmed them, and having no name for them, they called them "grey oxen". The Romans might have fled if a legionary had not cut off an elephant's trunk with his sword, and so maddened the elephant that it plunged back into the Greek lines. The battle lasted a whole day. The Romans lost 15,000 infantry, 250 cavalry, and there were 2,000 prisoners in Greek hands. They also lost twenty-two standards. Pyrrhus had in fact won the day but his losses were so great that he was unable to claim a victory. There was a second battle on the borders of Apulia. This time the victory fell to the Romans, and Pyrrhus lent a ready ear to the invitations of the Greeks in Sicily to help them in their war against the Carthaginians: he was glad to escape the Romans. But the Carthaginian war proved to be as exhausting as the war with Rome, and he decided upon one final battle against an enemy who was threatening to destroy all vestiges of Greek influence in Italy. This third battle was fought near Beneventum. The Romans had now taken the measure of the elephants. They used fire-darts smeared with pitch and capped with barbed spurs, and flung them at the elephants, setting light to the towers on their backs, or else they pushed fire-darts up their hind-quarters. Pyrrhus lost 33,000 troops on the field, and a further 30,000 were captured. The victory was complete, and the Roman general Manius Curius Dentatus was awarded a triumph. For the first time elephants with towers on their backs padded softly through the streets of Rome. The historian Florus lived three hundred years later, but his description of the triumph seems to be based on documents written at the time.

Rarely has a fairer or more glorious triumph entered the city. Up to this time the only spoils you ever saw were the cattle of the Volscians, the flocks of the Sabines, the waggons of the Gauls and the broken weapons of the Samnites. Now, when you looked at the prisoners, you recognized Molossians, Thessalians, Macedonians, Bruttians, Apulians and Lucanians. Now, when you looked at the procession, you saw gold, purple statues, all the luxuries of Tarentum. But on nothing did the Roman people look with greater pleasure than upon those huge beasts, which they had feared so much, with towers upon their backs, now following the horses which had conquered them. The elephants came with their heads bowed low, and they were not wholly unaware that they had been captured.
(Florus, I, xiii.)

This was not the first triumph won by Manius Curius Dentatus —he was awarded a triumph in 290 B.C. after a victory over the Samnites—but it was his greatest. One day shortly after his second triumph that stern and frugal old warrior was reminded of the immense territory he had added to the Roman dominions, and thinking of the small acreage of land allotted to the people after the expulsion of the Tarquins, he answered testily: "Any man who thinks seven *jugera* of land are not sufficient should be regarded as a dangerous citizen." He retired to his farm in the country of the Sabines, and there some Samnite ambassadors came to him, bringing presents. They found him sitting over his hearth and roasting turnips. He rejected their presents and said mildly that he preferred conquering people who possessed gold, to possessing it himself.

Meanwhile the small border-wars against the Italian tribes continued unabated, and one of the strangest of all battles was fought against the Piceni, whose battle-standard was the woodpecker (*picus*) sacred to Mars. Orosius tells how the armies were already within spear-range when a violent earthquake so terrified the soldiers of both armies that for a long time they stood motionless. When they charged, it was with the fury of despair, for the gods had evidently spoken in the earthquake. Only a few Romans survived to enjoy their victory, but the commanding general Publius Sempronius Sophus was awarded a triumph.

Soon there would be an end to these small border-wars. Four triumphs for victories over obscure tribes are recorded for 266 B.C. Then for a period of twenty-two years the only triumphs are those won in battles over the Carthaginians. At long last the war against Carthage had been joined.

The first Carthaginian war tried the temper of the Romans to the utmost: there were phenomenal victories, and phenomenal defeats. Sicily was the stepping stone, and Messina the point of attack. There the consul Manius Valerius Maximus achieved a victory over the combined Carthaginian and Syracusan army. By this victory sixty-seven cities passed over to Rome, and the consul earned a triumph and the title of Messala, from the Latin name of Messina. For his triumph the consul arranged for an enormous painting representing his victory to be exhibited along the side of the Curia Hostilia. It was not the first time such paintings had been hung. Lucius Papirius Cursor, the hero of the Samnite war, had a picture of himself as *triumphator* painted for the temple of Consus, the god of secrets, in 272 B.C., and Marcus Fulvius Flaccus had a similar picture of himself put up in the neighbouring temple

of Vortumnus, the god of fruit and the changing seasons, in 264
B.C. But the significance of these paintings coming at a time when
the Romans were about to launch upon a vast imperial adventure
cannot be underestimated. Up to this time the *triumphator* had
been the possessor of priestly powers, the sanctified representative of the *mana* of the Roman army. In theory at least his triumph
was a representative triumph and the sacrifice at the temple of
Jupiter Capitolinus a representative sacrifice, shared by the
Roman people. But with the emergence of the paintings of the
triumphator there is a sudden insistence upon the individuality
and personality of the conqueror: the triumphs belong to him
alone.

Four years later, in 260 B.C., the Romans celebrated another
triumph and once more we are made acutely aware of the individuality of the conqueror as "the sole victor".

In the early spring of that year the Senate met to debate the
fortunes of the war. Everywhere the Romans found themselves
at a disadvantage when faced with the overwhelming sea-power
of the enemy. Accordingly the Senate gave orders for the building
of 100 quinqueremes and 20 triremes to be ready for the summer
campaigning season. The Senate also ordered the training of
recruits. The Romans never worked better than when they were
under strain, and within sixty days of the felling of the trees the
ships, which were probably built by captured Greek shipwrights
from the Roman colonies in South Italy and Sicily, and partly
modelled on a beached Carthaginian galley, were ready. Polybius
says they were "badly built and sluggish", but they were sea-
worthy.

Off Sicily it occurred to one of the naval commanders that the
fighting ability of the ships would be improved if they were provided with landing-boards, spiked at one end to grip into the
enemy vessel and provided with cranes and pulleys to enable them
to be dropped at the proper moment. This was done, and the
strange unwieldy-looking ships set off in pursuit of the Carthaginian fleet in Sicilian waters. They were sighted off Mylae. Hannibal, the son of Gisco, was in command in a seven-banked galley
which had once belonged to Pyrrhus. There were altogether 130
Carthaginian vessels. Caius Duilius, the Roman commander-in-
chief, immediately grappled with the enemy. The spiked landing-
boards proved to be surprisingly effective, and when the two sides
pulled clear, thirty-one of the enemy ships, including Hannibal's
immense galley, had been boarded and captured by the Romans.
There was a second engagement. The Carthaginians lost thirteen

more ships, and then fled. The Romans had won their first naval victory with their first fleet.

Caius Duilius was awarded the first naval triumph ever awarded to a Roman. To commemorate the victory off Mylae a *columna rostrata*, decorated with anchors and the beaks of ships, and surmounted by the statue of the victor, was raised in the Forum, with an inscription which has been preserved in a marble copy from the early empire. The inscription records that Duilius:

> was the first Roman to fight a naval battle. He was the first to equip and train crews and fleets of fighting ships, and with these ships he defeated in battle on the high seas the ships of Carthage and all their most formidable troops in the presence of Hannibal, their commander in chief. By his strength he captured one "seven" and thirty quinqueremes along with their crews, and he sank thirteen. He was the first to bring the people booty from a naval battle and the first to lead free-born Carthaginians in a triumph.

The joy of the Romans was so great that every kind of honour was showered on Caius Duilius, who contented himself with accepting two honours which permitted him to be distinguished from all other Romans as long as he lived. For the rest of his life he was permitted to have a torch-bearer walk before him, and when returning home from supper he was always to be preceded by a flute-player. The gift of a flute-player was not a barren honour, for the Romans attached great significance to their flute-players, who were present at all religious festivities.

The naval victory, however, was not followed by any immediate advantages to Rome. During the next twenty years the Romans suffered a long series of defeats, interrupted by rare victories. Atilius Regulus, a stern and capable commander, sailed for Africa with a great army, and lost his entire force, except for 500 men, in a battle on the shore of the Bagradus River west of Carthage. The Carthaginians celebrated their victory by leading Regulus in chains in their own triumphal procession.

Fleets sailed from Italy to devastate the coast of Africa: some that set out never returned. In 253 B.C. a great armada of 260 ships sailed for Africa and acquired vast amounts of booty, only to lose the greater part when the ships foundered off Cape Palinurus in Lucania. Three years later Lucius Caecilius Metellus fought a pitched battle with Hasdrubal at Panormus (Palermo). Metellus held the city, and when Hasdrubal drove his elephants against the walls he gave orders for a sudden shower of missiles; the elephants panicked and stumbled back through the lines, killing many of the Carthaginian infantry. Then Metellus ordered a sortie, and fell on the flank of the enemy. Twenty thousand Carthaginians fell; 26 elephants were killed, and 104 were captured. The elephants were led through Italy to grace the triumph of Metellus, and a commemorative coin shows the conqueror in a chariot drawn by elephants, while a winged victory hovers above his head bearing a laurel crown.

The triumph of Metellus was followed by a series of disastrous defeats in Sicily and the loss of a carefully assembled transport fleet intended for a massive raid on Carthaginian positions in Africa. Rome was exhausted by the long-drawn-out war. She lost Sicily; one-sixth of her population had perished in the war; the coinage was debased; taxation had increased. No longer able to meet the Carthaginians in the field, she was compelled to put all her hopes in a great naval victory, and by acquiring mastery of the seas prevent a Carthaginian invasion.

The decisive battle took place on March 10, 241, off the Aegates islands near the western tip of Sicily. Caius Lutatius Catulus was blockading the harbours of Lilybaeum and Drepana. He had 200 ships, and had sent parties ashore to besiege the towns when he heard that a Carthaginian fleet of 250 sail was fast approaching. He was in a quandary. If he gave battle, he risked losing his fleet; if he hesitated, the Carthaginian sailors would land, make common cause with the garrisons on shore, and sweep across Sicily. The wind was blowing half a gale. Everything seemed to be working in favour of the heavy Carthaginian ships, which were steadier in stormy weather. All night the opposing fleets confronted each other, so close that their anchor chains were almost intertwined. At last Catulus gave the signal for attack. It was a ferocious battle, with the Romans fighting with the utmost desperation, losing twelve ships; but their losses were small compared with the enemy losses. When the battle was over, Catulus claimed that he had sunk 125 Carthaginian ships, captured 63, killed 14,000 men and taken 32,000 prisoners of war. When the news of the blood-letting reached Carthage, it was decided to sue for peace.

Rome had won the first round of the war with Carthage, but she was too exhausted to follow up the victory. For twenty-three years huge armies had poured out of Rome, vast areas of forest-land had been despoiled to provide timber for ships, and no one was ever able to count the number of ships lost at sea. All available resources had gone into that last battle, and for a few years the Romans were content to enjoy a spiritless peace of exhaustion. So it happened that six years after the battle of the Aegates islands the gates of the temple of Janus were closed, as a sign that there was no war anywhere. It was the first time they had been closed since the reign of Numa.

In a characteristic passage the Christian historian Orosius pours scorn on the Romans for their incessant fighting and asks ironically how they came to enjoy that brief period of peace? Was it really peace, or only the shadow of peace? Had the oil fallen into the flames and extinguished the fire? The patient was suffering from a burning fever; he had taken a cupful of cold water; what then? Did the water restore the patient, or cause the fever to mount? For 440 years there had been uninterrupted war, and now at last there was a single year of peace, and the Romans were absurdly proud of having accomplished peace at last. With savage irony Orosius suggests that the Roman body politic resembled the body of a leper covered with so many sores that it is hardly possible to distinguish the small square inch of healthy skin, that almost insignificant year of peace. He asks pointedly: "Can one say of those who have enjoyed so little peace that they have ever lived?"

Writing in the fifth century A.D., when the Roman empire was already foundering, Orosius shared few of the traditions and beliefs of the Romans who fought in the Carthaginian wars seven hundred years before. Like St. Augustine he saw Roman history as a futile and endless succession of wars, massacres, pestilences, famines and rapes; and sometimes, overcome by weariness, he felt a great desire to consign it to oblivion. "Imagine," he says, "a man who has suffered overwhelming grief and misery through an entire year except for a single day. Will that one day give him consolation for his misfortunes?"

We have watched the gradual emergence of the *triumphator* as a man set apart, curiously remote from the people, enjoying many of the honours paid to the gods, attended by increasing ceremony, a stiff hieratic figure from whom nearly every vestige of ordinary humanity has been removed, so that he resembles Aristotle's *megalopsychos*, "who covets only the greatest honours and learns to disdain them." But if we try to draw his portrait from the scattered references in Polybius, Dion Cassius and Livy, we find ourselves in a quandary. There was, of course, no characteristic *triumphator*. There were men who lusted after triumphs, and others who simply performed their duty and had triumphs thrust upon them, and still others who took command of armies regretfully when they preferred to be living in their country farms. And just as there were many kinds of *triumphatores,* so there were many kinds of triumphs, depending upon the whim of the conquering general.

Yet it is possible to reconstruct the general type of a triumph as it was enjoyed in the time of the first Carthaginian wars. Our chief authorities are a small bronze cista dating from the third century B.C., found at Praeneste (Palestrina) and some lines from the comic poet Plautus. They say nothing about the great procession winding through the streets of Rome, but they tell us a good deal about the supreme moment of the sacrifice on the Capitoline hill.

At first sight the bronze cista with its delicately traced engraving is a puzzling document. It shows the *triumphator* standing with his legs apart, shoulders thrown back, with a look of purposeful decision on his heavy features. He wears a short tunic, an embroidered cloak, greaves, thigh-armour, a laurel crown, and holds in his right hand a long staff or sceptre surmounted by an eagle. The staff has a helical design like sugar-candy, and may be of ivory; and an eagle perches on it. To the *triumphator's* left is a god-like youth, bare to the waist, with long hair falling to his shoulders, one hand lifted towards the four horses of a triumphal chariot, in which Jupiter rides in sovereign ease, wearing a diadem and with a sceptre in his right hand. The wheel-spokes are curved like those of present-day Sicilian carts and the only decoration on the chariot is the characteristically Greek meander pattern on the chariot-wall. Bacchic rites were being introduced in Rome throughout the third century B.C.—they were to become widespread after the conclusion of the second Carthaginian war—and the god-like youth may well be Bacchus, crowned and garlanded. At his feet lies a vase with flowers.

All that belongs to the gods lies to the right of the *triumphator;* all that belongs to the sacrifice lies to his left. At once we are confronted by an unexpected difficulty. There are no white oxen, nothing to suggest a sacrifice, unless it is the man who stands to the left of the table, wearing the apron-like cloth worn by the *victimarius,* who kills the oxen. Beside him is a priest with a veil drawn over his head, and beside the *triumphator* stands a *camillus,* bearing a ladle and a wine-jar, and a flower which he lifts to his face. On the extreme right a laurelled attendant carries a curved Etruscan trumpet over his shoulder. Tiptilted below the wine-jar is a table where the sacrificial dishes (*paterae*) are displayed, and the priest holds two more in his hands in a gesture indicating that they are empty. There are cloud patterns behind the figures, suggesting that the scene takes place in the open air.

Clearly the artist has attempted to depict in the small space allotted to him the supreme moment of the triumph; and for him that supreme moment is not the sacrifice of the oxen, but the moment when the *triumphator* and Jupiter confront one another. The *victimarius* puts his finger to his lips in the familiar call for silence, the wine is offered to the *triumphator*, who pours a libation to the god, and at that moment the triumph is consummated.

We need not be surprised that Bacchus has entered the ceremony unannounced, for in fact he had been present from the beginning. The cult of Liber, which imperceptibly merged with the cult of Bacchus, was among the most ancient of all. Servius suggests he was the god who was worshipped at the Lupercalia, and Pliny says he invented the emblems of royalty, the crown and the triumphal procession. Lucretius gives him credit for the introduction of wine. He was the god of wild and happy license, and St. Augustine describes with horror how his emblem, the phallus, was carried through the market-place to be crowned by a chaste matron. Similar festivals took place in Greece. Athenaeus describes how the Ithyphalli, wearing wreaths and masks, entered the theatre and addressed the audience:

> Come, make way for the god,
> Erect and in full vigour,
> He will pass through our midst.

As we might expect, the supreme moment when the *triumphator* confronts Jupiter on the Capitol inevitably involves a host of contradictions. The presence of Bacchus can be explained, but if Bacchus is present, why not Mars, who was always invoked by the general before joining battle with the cry: *Mars, vigila!* (Mars, awake) and the clashing of a holy lance against a holy shield. What was the purpose of a libation—the pouring of the wine—as distinguished from the sacrificial killing of the oxen and the shedding of their blood? What precisely is the function of Bacchus, as he stands on the right hand of the *triumphator*? We can hazard the guess that the Romans were perfectly capable of taking these contradictions in their stride, and if an explanation were demanded, they would answer that the powers of Mars were included within the vaster powers of Jupiter, and Bacchus is present as the god of the earthly triumph, while Jupiter is the supreme guardian of the heavenly triumph.

German, and some English, commentators have gone to great lengths in suggesting that the *triumphator* was invested with the powers of Jupiter at the supreme moment of his triumph: he sometimes wore the robes of Jupiter provided from the temple treasury, and like the god appeared with his face painted with red paint. Was he then Jupiter incarnate? Mrs. Eugenie Strong, who wrote admirably about Roman sculpture, concluded that "during the pageant the general *was* Jupiter". Livy speaks of *Iovis optimi maximi ornatu decoratus*, and Servius much later refers to the *triumphantes, qui habent omnia Iovis insignia,* but neither speak of an act of incarnation, an idea foreign to the Romans. Nor does the Praeneste cista depict a god. The *triumphator* is all-too-human as he stands there with his feet apart, looking a little lost and puzzled among the gods. He no longer rides a triumphal chariot. Only his sons continue to ride in the divine procession, perhaps because the Romans regarded boys as peculiarly holy and undefiled.

Many ancient Roman prayers have been handed down, but we lack the authentic text of the prayers uttered by the *triumphator* in the presence of Jupiter. Livy has preserved in full the savage prayer uttered by a Roman soldier before deliberately sacrificing himself in battle, and Macrobius has recorded at length the still more terrible prayer in which the Roman general in the field called on the gods of the enemy to desert his city. *May they suffer flight, panic and terror, and may no light ever shine on them. . . .* But these were prayers before the battle. The comic poet Plautus, who lived at the time of the Carthaginian wars, puts in the mouth of a drunken slave a prayer which looks remarkably like the prayer uttered by a *triumphator*. The slave Toxilus is in fine fettle. All his nefarious plans are proving fruitful, and he is about to give a banquet to his fellow-slaves. Then he delivers a passionate speech to Jupiter:

Hostibus victis, civibus salvis, re placida, pacibus perfectis,
bello exstincto, re bene gesta, integro exercitu et praesidiis,
cum bene nos, Iuppiter, iuvisti, dique alii omnes caelipotentes,
eas vobis habeo grates atque ago, quia probe sum ultus meum
    inimicum.

The enemy defeated, the citizens safe, the state tranquil, peace
    assured,
War brought to an end, the affair successfully administered,
    army and garrisons intact,
Therefore, O Jupiter, I give thanks to thee and all the other
    powers of heaven
For the aid thou hast given me in taking vengeance on my
    enemy.
                       (*Persa*, 753–756)

Nearly everything about this prayer suggests authenticity. Livy records a tablet set up in a temple in honour of Tiberius Sempronius Gracchus's conquest of Sardinia, which speaks in much the same way: the state has been successfully administered, the army is safe, the revenues have been restored. *cum bene nos, Iuppiter, iuvisti* . . . is a typical introduction to the ancient Saturnian prayers. There is only one thing wrong with it: it is painfully tame.

Yet the more one studies these four astonishing lines from the *Persa*, the more it becomes possible to believe that these were the words spoken by the returning general to Jupiter. They echo the tone of the *devotio* consigning enemy cities to perdition; they are almost perfunctory, and yet they have an authentic ring. The Roman general cursing a foreign city struck the same personal note, calling upon the enemy gods to surrender "in my own name, and on behalf of the Roman people, the army and the legions". But it remains disturbing that the *triumphator* should have recourse to such mechanical prayers after so much excitement: so many murders and so many cities in flames.

4

THE TRIUMPH HUNTERS

In his great work, *The Muqadimmah*, the Arab philosopher Ibn Khaldun, after a lifetime of careful study, analysed the processes of corruption which attack nations. He showed that these processes were unchangeable, relentless, and fatal. Inevitably every nation must pass through these processes, and come to destruction in the same manner. He was saying, in effect, that every nation in time loses its primitive power (*asabiyya*) and acquires a dangerous sophistication which leads it inevitably to overreach itself; and no man can turn back the clock. The seeds of *hubris* are sown from the beginning. Only by means of a divine miracle can the original simplicity be restored to a nation, and such miracles are rare. Ibn Khaldun himself could not recollect a single occasion when power had been restored to a nation once it had begun its downward march.

At the end of the first Carthaginian war there could be observed all the symptoms of corruption which Ibn Khaldun had observed in his studies of Arab nations. Enormous power had fallen into the hands of a few families. There was the frenzied desire for excitement, the hankering after luxuries, the decay of belief in the gods. The close bonds which once united the people and the rulers had broken. Rome had never been so powerful in appearance, or so weak in reality as she was on the day when the gates of the temple of Janus were closed. On the evidence Ibn Khaldun would have concluded that the processes of corruption were hard at work, and Rome herself was on the eve of inevitable destruction.

She was in fact very close to destruction—much closer than any Roman thought. She was exhausted. She needed, as all nations do after lengthy wars, a period of relaxation to allow her wounds to heal. It was necessary to build up a civilization and put aside the temptations of war, the need to live perpetually on the edge of danger. Dedicated to violence, she needed to learn the blessings of peace.

Unlike the Arabs the Romans seem to have possessed hidden reserves of strength. Abominable crimes continued to be committed, the triumph-hunters continued to wage war against the

tribes on the frontiers, the princely families ruled mercilessly over
a debt-ridden people, but the Romans succeeded in retaining their
primitive power. They retained it even when the Gauls massed in
the north and threatened for the second time to march on Rome.
Then Rome panicked, and resorted first to witchcraft and then to
a *levée en masse* to conjure away the threat on the frontiers. The
witchcraft was particularly nauseating. At a great ceremony on
the Forum Boarium they buried alive two Gauls, a man and a
woman, and two Greeks, also a man and a woman; and then
stamped the earth flat. Nothing quite like this act of calculated
savagery had happened before, and it was never to happen again.

Panic-stricken, the Romans assembled the largest army ever
known, amounting to 700,000 men. Strong forces were put under
the command of the two consuls, Publius Furius and Caius
Flaminius, who immediately marched to the north. When unfavourable auspices were reported to the Senate—a river turned
to blood and three moons were seen in the sky—letters of recall
were despatched. The consuls decided to disobey the letters, continued their march and won a victory over the Gauls. The Romans,
terrified by the auguries, refused to go out to meet the returning
generals, and it was some time before they were permitted a
triumph. After their triumphs they were deprived of their consul-
ships by senatorial order for disobeying orders.

Two men dominated the period: the slow, cautious Fabius
Maximus, and the quick-tempered, fine-spun and studious
Marcellus. Fabius Maximus was the master of the delaying action,
Marcellus of the sudden attack. Marcellus entered the college of
augurs and acquired a taste for religious ceremonies, but he was
in his element in war, and happiest in the saddle. He was on the
march somewhere near Milan, the Gallic capital, when he learned
that Britomartus, the king of the Gauls, with ten thousand troops,
was in the neighbourhood. With a small detachment of cavalry and
some 600 infantry he decided to surprise Britomartus, who seems
to have been amused by the presence of the small Roman troop
near his camp and suggested, perhaps ironically, that the issue
should be decided by single combat.

Britomartus wore a suit of armour of many colours and he
towered over the Roman; but Marcellus had the gods on his side.
There was a short sharp engagement; Britomartus fell with a lance
piercing his breastplate, and then Marcellus jumped from his
horse and hacked the king to death. In his joy and excitement he
called out to Jupiter, exultantly reminding the most powerful of
the Roman gods that this was the third time that the commander

of a Roman army had fought in single combat against the commander of an enemy army and won. Before him only Romulus and Cossus had won the *spolia opima*. He was almost mad with joy when he returned to receive a triumph.

"Of all triumphs," says Plutarch, "it was the most remarkable for magnificence, opulence, spoils and the huge numbers of captives." Marcellus revived the rare and ancient practice of parading with a trophy bearing the armour of a dead king. The trophy, which consisted of an oak-tree hung with the king's armour "with all the pieces arranged in the proper places", was mounted in his chariot, and Marcellus rode with it. To celebrate the occasion the Romans sent a heavy gold cup to the temple of Apollo at Delphi, and distributed part of the spoil among friendly cities.

The defeat of the Gauls took place in 222 B.C. Four years later Hannibal marched over the Alps and began the long campaign against Rome which did not end until he had destroyed 400 towns and killed 300,000 men. Defeat after defeat met the Romans. Flaminius and his entire army perished in a battle on Lake Trasimene in Tuscany—a strange and fearful battle which took place simultaneously with an earthquake, which destroyed towns, changed the course of rivers and carried off huge cliffs. In the following year there was an even greater disaster at Cannae in Apulia. After the battle Hannibal was able to send to Carthage as proof of his victory three pecks of gold rings pulled from the fingers of Roman knights and senators. Hannibal went on to capture Tarentum in the heel of Italy's boot, and to lay siege to Capua. He marched right up to the walls of Rome and despoiled the surrounding countryside. The Roman allies defected. Philip V of Macedon prepared to form an alliance with the Carthaginians, and Syracuse went over to the enemy. The Romans survived, but only by a miracle, or perhaps Hannibal's hand was failing. The Christian historian Orosius wondered whether it was Roman courage or divine compassion which saved Rome, but it was more likely Hannibal's failure of nerve.

The Romans saw that they would have to break through the net or lose the war, and determined upon a large-scale attack on all fronts. It was decided to send Marcellus to Sicily to capture Syracuse, then in the hands of two Carthaginian generals. There was a prolonged siege, and the Romans amused themselves by harrying the neighbouring countryside to put the fear of the Roman name in the hearts of the Sicilians. They massacred all the inhabitants of the city of Enna, sacred to Ceres and Proserpina; and the Syracusans were more than ever inclined to fight to the uttermost. Marcellus was patient. He waited for the ripe fruit to fall, and one day when the Syracusans were celebrating the feast of Artemis some traitors allowed the Romans to enter the gates. The city, the greatest in Sicily, was given over to plunder. Among those who were killed when the Romans surged into the city was an elderly member of the Greek royal household who was pondering geometrical problems when he was accosted by a Roman soldier with a drawn sword. The scholar begged to be allowed to finish the problem, but the soldier cut him down without bothering to ask who he was. His name was Archimedes.

Marcellus returned to Rome and demanded a triumph. This was refused, apparently on the grounds that he had turned over his command to his successor on the field. He was permitted, however, to enjoy an *ovatio*, a much less important form of the triumph. He sacrificed on the Alban Mount and on the next day entered Rome. In the procession were a number of statues taken from the public buildings of Syracuse; a model, perhaps made of painted wood, of the captured city; much silver and bronze and costly fabrics. There were eight elephants to represent the triumph over the Carthaginian forces. There were engines of war—*catapults* and *ballistae*. Never before had so many rich prizes been taken from a Greek city, and Livy described the appearance of the spoils in one of those majestic phrases which from time to time illuminate his mechanical prose. They were, he said, the ornaments of a lengthy peace and of royal opulence—*pacis diuturnae regiaeque opulentiae ornamenta.*

All through their history the Romans had felt an instinctive distrust of opulence. Tarquinian extravagance and Samnite gold were mixed blessings, sapping at their strength; and they were aware of the penalties of wealth. Most of these statues, which went to grace two temples outside the Porta Capena, were originally set up by Hiero, tyrant of Syracuse, the devoted ally of the Romans. There were some who regarded the purloined statues with horror, speaking of a breach of faith. When Fabius Cunctator sacked Tarentum in 209 B.C., enslaving thirty thousand of the inhabitants and acquiring 3,080 pounds of pure gold and immense quantities of silver, he pointedly refused to have the statues carried to Rome, remarking: "We shall leave to the Tarentines their offended gods!" He did, however, remove one statue of Hercules which was set up in the Capitol, with a bronze equestrian statue of himself nearby, thus proclaiming his own vanity while avoiding the charge laid against Marcellus that he was not content with enslaving the conquered people, but must also enslave their gods.

Marcellus died the following year. Rashly, with a small company of guards, most of them Etruscans, he penetrated territory conquered by the Carthaginians, and was killed in an ambush. Plutarch says that Hannibal was informed and came to view the body, and for a long time gazed at it. Then he removed Marcellus's ring, ordered a funeral pyre to be lit, and placed the ashes in a silver urn with a crown of gold to cover it. Some said the silver urn was safely carried to Rome and given to Marcellus's son, others that it was stolen by Numidians on the way and the ashes scattered to the winds.

The days of the Carthaginians were numbered. A long series of minor defeats led them to embark on more and more audacious adventures. In the spring of 207 B.C. Hasdrubal, the brother of Hannibal, crossed the Alps at the head of a mixed force of 60,000 Carthaginians, Ligurians, Celtiberians and Gauls. That year the two consuls were Marcus Livius Salinator and Gaius Claudius Nero, two men who hated one another. The command of Gaius Claudius extended over southern Italy: his army was keeping watch on Hannibal. The command of Marcus Livius extended over northern Italy, and he was well-placed to prevent a meeting between Hasdrubal and Hannibal, but needed reinforcements. The Carthaginians had shown themselves masters of the sudden attack and the unexpected ruse: some new and powerful stratagem was needed to prevent the dreaded meeting of the Carthaginian armies. Gaius Claudius decided to sink his differences with Marcus Livius, disobey orders and march with 7,000 picked troops to the assistance of the Roman army in the north. These new troops saved the day. In a pitched battle near the banks of the Metaurus River in Umbria, Hasdrubal's army was destroyed, and Hasdrubal himself was killed. Except for some five thousand prisoners taken, there were almost no survivors of Hasdrubal's army. Six days later, after another forced march to the south, Gaius Claudius came in sight of Hannibal's camp. He had brought with him Hasdrubal's head. He gave orders that the bloody head should be lobbed into the enemy camp. When the head was taken to Hannibal, he is reported to have said: "Now Carthage herself is doomed."

According to Livy, the triumph following the battle of the Metaurus River was a true triumph, *verus triumphus*, distinguished by honour and great accomplishment.[1] A powerful and decisive blow had been struck at the enemy. No traitors had assisted the enemy. The battle was won largely because one of the

---

[1] It is just possible that Livy's judgement was affected by the fact that he bore the same name as one of the triumphing generals.

consuls had not hesitated to disobey his standing orders: and his dangerous journey was crowned with success.

Up to this time we have been able to watch the triumph only from a great distance. The machinery of the triumph: how it came about, what formulas were used, on what conditions it was granted —all these things have been largely hidden from us. Now at last Livy describes the making of a triumph at considerable length, writing as though the records lay before him, and we come to share his excitement, the sense of veils lifting, the machinery at last revealed.

As Livy tells the story, the two generals arranged by letter to meet at Praeneste, twenty miles south-east of Rome, and from there they issued an order (*edictum*), requiring the Senators to meet in three days at the Temple of Bellona, which lay below the Capitol. All Rome came out to greet the conquerors. There was much cheering, and everyone tried to shake the right hands of the generals. In the Temple of Bellona the serious business of the day began. The Senate was in session, and the two generals were called upon to review their own conduct in the war. They wore military uniform, their armour concealed under their scarlet cloaks. At the conclusion of their reports, they demanded that for their vigorous and successful war on behalf of the Republic there should be a special tribute to the immortal gods, and they them-selves should be permitted to enter the city in triumph—*postu-lassent ut pro re publica fortiter feliciterque administrata et deis immortalibus haberetur honos et ipsis triumphantibus urbem inire liceret*. Such was the formula, and Livy specifically states that it was used by all commanding generals seeking a triumph. The Senators answered by decreeing special honours to the gods, to be followed by special honours to the generals. A thanksgiving (*supplicatio*) in the names of both consuls was authorized, and since they had both taken part in a single war, it was decreed that they should enjoy a single triumph. There was some debate about how two generals could take part in a single triumph, and finally it was decided that since the battle had been fought in the territory of Marcus Livius, and the *imperium* and the auspices had on that day both belonged to him, and moreover Marcus Livius alone had returned to Rome at the head of his army, for the army of Gaius Claudius was still guarding the army of Hannibal, then Marcus Livius should be permitted to enter the city in a triumphal chariot drawn by four horses, and Gaius Claudius should be allowed to ride on horseback without his soldiers.

Such was the decision of the Senators, a decision imposed upon them by the logic of the occasion. Livy warmly applauds them. He says:

> This triumph celebrated by two men together increased the glory of both, but still further increased the glory of him who yielded to his colleague in honour while achieving far more. For this man, who rode on horseback, had in six days traversed the whole length of Italy and had fought, standards against standards, with Hasdrubal in Gaul on a day when Hannibal believed the consul was standing guard over his own camp in Apulia. Thus it happened that a single consul had opposed two armies and two generals in two widely different fronts, fighting one battle by stratagems, the other in person. His name, people said, had been enough to contain Hannibal within his camp. Only by his arrival on the battlefield was it possible to overwhelm and completely destroy the forces of Hasdrubal. Then let the other consul, if he wished, drive in a chariot with many yokes and many horses, standing erect. But the true triumph was enjoyed by him who rode on horseback, and even if he triumphed on foot, he would be memorable for the glory he had won in the war, or for his contempt for glory in that triumph. Such were the comments of the spectators as they followed him to the Capitol.   (Livy, *Ab Urbe Condita*, XXVIII, ix.)

Over the years we have watched the slow emergence of the *triumphator* as a man existing in his own right, standing a little apart from the sacrifices, the prisoners and the soldiers. We have seen him offering paintings of himself robed in the garments of his triumph to the temples. Now for the first time we see him riding alone, enjoying the supreme honour formerly given only to kings. It is a dangerous moment, not to be repeated until Julius Caesar entered the city alone on the occasion of his last triumph. For the first time, too, we are aware of the intruding element of doubt and self-consciousness. Only of Gaius Claudius does Livy speak of a conqueror's contempt for glory in his triumph: that contempt of glory which is perhaps the highest form of glory. At this moment something of quite remarkable importance is taking place: the conqueror, followed by multitudes, enters Rome like a king.

During the closing years of the second Carthaginian war, a vast change was taking place in the Roman *ethos*. In a hundred subtle ways they were showing themselves immune from the fears which had weighed down upon them in the past. More and more they were becoming aware of their uneasy destiny as builders of an empire which would one day include the whole of the known world. But while one kind of fear was lifted from them, another came to take its place. In the past they feared for their safety, the mere survival of the state. Now they were afraid of the responsibility they had assumed in the face of the gods.

So it happened that in 212 B.C. there was inaugurated for the first time the public worship of Apollo, who had assumed by virtue of his prophetic role at Delphi almost the aspect of a god of destiny. His worship was associated with that of Juno the Queen, who had her temple on the Aventine. In 207 B.C. for the first time the appropriate sacrifices were performed. From the temple of Apollo in the Campus Martius two white cows were led through the Porta Carmentalis, and behind them two statues of Juno in cypress wood were carried by the worshippers. The procession entered the Forum and then halted, while twenty-seven maidens in long robes sang archaic songs while passing a rope between their hands, and stamping with their feet. Then, winding past the Temple of Castor and Pollux and skirting the Palatine, they made their way to the temple of Juno the Queen, where the cows were solemnly sacrificed and the cypress-wood statues were borne into the temple.

There was something very odd about this procession. It was as though very quietly and hesitantly Apollo was being introduced into the Roman pantheon, a foreign god in association with a foreign goddess: for Juno the Queen was an Etruscan goddess, captured long before by Camillus when he destroyed the city of Veii. Apollo was in the ascendant. In 216 B.C. the Roman ambassador had inquired about the fortunes of the Republic from the oracle at Delphi; he had received a hopeful reply, and Apollo bade them send a gift when they had preserved the state. After the battle of Metaurus the preservation of the state seemed to be assured, and two years later a golden wreath weighing two hundred pounds and silver trophies weighing a thousand pounds, all taken from the spoils of Hasdrubal, were carried to Delphi.

Apollo, however, was only one of the great gods to be propitiated. Another embassy was sent to Delphi to ask what should be done to preserve the state, and received the reply that they should go in search of the stone sacred to Cybele, *Magna Mater,* the Mother of the Gods, who was worshipped with great solemnity at Pessinus in Phrygia, then under the control of the aged and very learned King Attalus of Phrygia. The Oracle also ordered them to seek out the best man in Rome who alone should be allowed to receive the stone.

King Attalus seems to have been delighted to present the Roman

with the stone, and in April, 204 B.C., they returned
a, bearing the stone with them. The best man had
hosen. He was the thirty-year-old Publius Scipio,
overed himself with glory as commander of the Roman
es in Spain, driving the Carthaginians before him, burning
their towns and ruthlessly depriving them of every last vestige of
power. Returning to Rome, he demanded the triumph which was
his due, but did not insist when it was pointed out that no triumph
had ever been awarded to a man who was not of consular or praetorian rank. Instead he celebrated a private triumph, displaying
six tons of captured silver and sacrificing 100 oxen at the Temple
of Jupiter Capitolinus. Brilliant, handsome and graceful, the
possessor of great administrative talents, contemptuous of power
and at the same time consumed with a blinding adoration of
power, he was already being regarded as the destined saviour of
Rome: the man who would put an end once and for all to the
Carthaginians. He wore his hair long and liked to dress in the
Greek mantle, but these intimations of effeminacy were not
counted against him.

When the ship bearing the stone anchored at the mouth of the
Tiber, Scipio sailed out to meet it, and carried it to land. The
entire city poured out to watch the stone as it was borne to the
Temple of Victory on the Palatine. Censers were placed before
the doors along the route, and prayers were offered to the goddess
of the stone, which was black and quite small. Not long afterwards
Scipio set sail for Africa with a vast fleet to conquer Hannibal,
who had abandoned Italy forever.

No one knows how many ships or how many men accompanied
him to Africa. The historian Coelius said there were so many men
that when they shouted, the birds in the air fell dead at the sound.
At last in the spring or early summer of 202 B.C., at Zama, five days
march from Carthage, the Roman and Carthaginian armies met.
According to Appian, the two commanders engaged in single
combat before the battle. They were on horseback. Scipio pierced
Hannibal's shield, and Hannibal hit Scipio's horse, but the combat
was resumed when Scipio acquired another horse. Yet nothing
came of the brief engagement between them, to the bitter regret
of Scipio, whose greatest ambition was to be the fourth, and the
first after Marcellus, to win the *opima*. The hard-fought battle
ended with a complete Roman victory, with 20,000 Carthaginian
dead, nearly as many prisoners, and Hannibal in flight. Carthage,
the impregnable city, remained unharmed, but her claws had
been torn from her.

The next year the conqueror of Spain and Africa, still in the freshness of his dazzling youth, returned to enjoy a triumph which could no longer be forbidden to him. Livy calls it *triumphus omnium clarissimus*, the most distinguished of all, though for some reason he makes no effort to describe it, contenting himself with the statement that 123,000 pounds of silver were carried in the procession and a certain Senator, freed from his Carthaginian captivity, wore a liberty cap as he followed the triumphal chariot. We do not know whether any captured African kings or princes were led in the procession. The poet Silius Italicus, writing his long epic poem *Punica* some three hundred years after the event, draws a picture of the Numidian King Siphax borne on a litter with chains of gold round his neck; Livy says the king was dead before the triumph took place. The historian Appian, writing about A.D. 105, gives the most complete description of the triumph, but unfortunately it is not entirely trustworthy. He writes:

This is the form of the triumph, which the Romans continue to follow. All who took part in the procession wore crowns. Trumpeters led the advance, and were followed by carts laden with spoils. Then came towers representing the conquered cities, and pictures of the principal episodes of the war. Then came gold and silver and bullion, and whatever else of this sort had been captured, and then the crowns offered to the general as a reward for his courage by cities, by allies and by the army itself. Afterwards came the white oxen, the elephants and the important Carthaginian and Numidian chiefs.

Lictors dressed in purple tunics went before the general; there was also a chorus of harpists and flute-players, wearing belts and gold crowns, and they advanced in regular order, keeping step with their dances and songs in imitation of the Etruscan procession. They are called Lydi, and I believe they derive their name from the fact that the Etruscans once formed a Lydian colony.

In the midst of this procession appeared one in a purple cloak reaching to his feet, wearing golden bracelets and a necklace, and his task was to cause laughter, accomplishing this purpose by the gesticulations of a man dancing in triumph over an enemy. Afterwards came a group of incense bearers. Then came the general in a chariot embellished with various figures. He wore a crown of gold and precious stones, and according to the Roman custom he was robed in a purple toga embroidered with gold stars. He carried a sceptre of ivory and a laurel branch, always the Roman symbol of victory.

Riding in the chariot with him were boys and girls, and on the trace-horses on either side of him were young men, all related to him. Behind came those who had served him in the war as secretaries, personal aides and armour-bearers. Lastly came the army arranged in squadrons and cohorts, all of them crowned and carrying branches of laurel, the most courageous of them carrying their prizes of war. They praised some of their officers, and derided or reproached others, for in a triumph everyone is free and allowed to say what he pleases.

When at last Scipio came to the Capitol, the procession ended, and the general entertained his friends at a banquet in the Temple, according to the custom.

(Appian, *Punic Wars*, 66.)

Appian's account has a sweet reasonableness. Everything is in its proper order, neatly arranged by categories, with curious omissions. Nothing is said about the priests or the butchers who sacrificed the oxen. He says nothing about the garlanded temples. It is the description of a triumph completely without religious significance, saved from being a mere catalogue by the unforgettable picture of the single gesticulator, robed in purple, with gold bracelets and a necklace, who mimics the triumphant general in front of the chariot. It is a good description of a *generalized* triumph, and adds very little that is new except the ivory sceptre, which may well have been introduced by Scipio, who sent to Rome in advance of his triumph a large quantity of carved ivory.

Only two generalized descriptions of a triumph have survived, and we may compare Appian's with a longer and more detailed account written by the twelfth-century Byzantine historian, Zonaras, who wrote when all human memory of the triumph had vanished from the earth. Yet his detailed description is not to be dismissed lightly. Zonaras wrote with care and considerable art; available to him were many books on history and state festivals which are no longer available to us; and he is the first to admit that the triumph changed with the changing times:

Arrayed in the triumphal garments and wearing armlets, a laurel crown on his head and a laurel branch in his right hand, the *triumphator* summoned the people. First he praised the troops who had served with him, addressing them all collectively, mentioning some by name; and he presented them with money and honoured them with decorations. Some received armlets, others untipped spears; and to some were given crowns, either of gold or of silver, bearing the name of the man and a representation of his brave exploit.

As soon as these ceremonies were over, the *triumphator* mounted his chariot. It was not at all like the chariots used in games or in war, but was fashioned in the shape of a round tower. He did not stand alone in the chariot, but if he had children or young relatives he would make the girls and boys get up beside him, and he would put the older ones on the horses—out-riggers as it were to the yoke-horses. If there were many of them, they would accompany the procession on chargers, riding beside the *triumphator*. None of the others rode, but all went on foot, wearing laurel wreaths.

In the chariot there rode with the *triumphator* a public slave, who held over his head a crown of gold set with precious stones, who kept saying: "Look behind!" meaning: "Look to the aftermath—look to all the years that remain. Do not be puffed up or elated at your present good-fortune." A bell and a whip were fastened to the chariot, and these signified that it was possible for him to meet misfortune even to the extent of being scourged or condemned to death. For it was customary for those who were condemned to death for their crimes to wear a bell, and this was done as a warning to those who might come near them, lest they be contaminated.

In such wise did the *triumphator* enter the city, with the spoils and trophies and representations of captured fortresses, cities, mountains, rivers, lakes and seas leading the way. If one day did not suffice for the exhibition of these things in the procession, the celebration was held during a second and a third day. When all these prizes of war had passed in procession, the *triumphator* arrived at the Roman Forum, and after commanding that some of the captives be led to prison and put to death, he rode up to the Capitol. There he performed certain rites and made offerings and dined in the porticos up there, and towards evening he departed homeward, accompanied by flutes and pipes.

Such were the triumphs of ancient times, but factions and powerful cliques effected many changes in them.

(Zonaras, VII, 21)

The particular merit of Zonaras is that he filled in many of the details of the triumph, which escaped the attention of Plutarch and others who have written about it. He wrote with apparent authenticity. The summons to the people, the placing of the younger children in the chariot and the older ones on the horses, the bell and the whip, the pause in the Forum, all these details possess a proper logic, but they belong to the time of the Emperors. The historian Tzetzes, writing about the same time, adds a curious note about the pause in the Forum. He says: "The *triumphator* runs thrice about the place in a circle, mounts the stairs on his knees, and then lays his garlands aside. After this he departs home, accompanied by the musicians." (*Epistolae*, CVII.) Once again we are made aware of an imperial procession: only Julius Caesar and Claudius went up the Clivus Capitolinus on their knees. We search in vain among the historians for any other reference to the *triumphator* running thrice around the Forum; and, however much we would like to believe he did so, we must defer judgment. It may have happened under the Republic, but it is unlikely.

With the victory at Zama the second Carthaginian war came to an end, and the Romans, free of their fears, were able to stretch their young muscles and conquer where they pleased. "For the Carthaginians," says Polybius, "it had been a struggle for their own lives and for the sovereignty of Libya, while for the Romans it was a struggle for universal dominion and supremacy." The time for universal dominion and supremacy had come, and in one savage attack after another the Romans destroyed their enemies and most of their friends.

5

THE BURDEN OF GUILT

In the lives of all great nations there are periods of conquest, but only the Romans were compelled to conquer the same nations again and again. By the very nature of their warfare they compelled the defeated to rise against them. Revolt after revolt was put down, until it seemed that with so much casual bloodshed there could hardly be anyone left to kill. The wars went on in interrupted sequence, as regular as clockwork, and in the ninety-eight years between the battle of Zama and the destruction of the army of King Jugurtha, altogether sixty-eight triumphs were held. In every three years there were at least two triumphs.

Carthage was stunned and bleeding from her wounds, and in no position to deal effective blows against Rome. For a few more years the great city was permitted to exist, but she was not allowed to move a single soldier without the permission of the Romans, her trading fleets were confiscated, and her colonies were reduced to insignificance. She was dead long before the Romans destroyed her completely.

Meanwhile the Romans were free to roam the world like free-booters. From their enemies they had learned new techniques of destruction. They possessed elephants and used them in battle; the cavalry was equipped with the long slashing sword borrowed from Spain; their ships were the best of the time. So in this breathing-space, before they threw themselves once more and for the last time against Carthage, they fought on all fronts—against the Gauls, the Greeks, the Spaniards, the Dalmatians, Istrians, Ligurians and Illyrians. There was no tribe on their borders which did not feel the weight of their power.

Triumph-hunting became a major occupation of Roman generals; and the records of those years are filled with the disputes of conquerors as they jockey for positions in the *acta triumphorum*. There was a bitter quarrel in 200 B.C. when Lucius Furius Purpureus returned after a victory over the Gauls to claim a triumph. He had won an immense victory, plundered the enemy camp, captured a hundred thousand pieces of silver and put the Gauls to flight, but he did all this without consulting the consul, who was his superior and therefore perhaps entitled to the triumph. It was argued that he should have summoned the consul before joining battle: others said the consul was at fault for not moving up his army in time. In the end Lucius Furius received his desired triumph, but no prisoners were led before his chariot, no spoils were displayed, and there were no soldiers in the train. Of that bleak triumph Livy comments that the consul gained everything except the victory.

In the Senate there were hot-tempered debates about the worthiness of commanders to enjoy triumphs. When Quintus Minucius Rufus demanded a triumph over the Ligurians, the tribunes claimed he had won no real victories, had lost too many men, and many of his reported victories over small towns and villages were figments of his imagination. He therefore celebrated a triumph on the Alban Mount, but he was so popular that immense crowds followed him.

Sometimes the Senate became a criminal court, presiding over the fate of conquerors. Cato, the censor, was particularly efficient in examining the evidence, and when Quintus Minucius Thermus sought a triumph, claiming that he had killed 9,000 of the enemy, Cato branded him as a liar and went on to charge him with *nefarium facinus,* perhaps extortion, and added a long list of other crimes. Minucius had killed ten men "and cut them up like bacon". He had ten other men scourged, though they belonged to allied tribes. He was guilty of unnatural vice. He was a man who knew nothing of "trust or the laws or shame". The surviving fragments of Cato's attack on him suggest a man thundering in outraged horror against the crimes committed by commanders in the field, sullying the Roman name. Quintus Minucius Thermus was refused a triumph. Marcus Fulvius Nobilior had better luck. Cato accused him of awarding crowns to soldiers for the most trifling reasons, to increase his popularity. According to Cato, they received crowns for building ramparts or digging wells. Nevertheless a triumph was awarded him, and there was a memorable parade of statues and bullion captured in the Greek wars. Livy says there were 230 marble statues, 243 crowns of gold, 83,000 pounds of silver and 118,000 Attic four-drachma pieces. Greece was being looted to provide a Roman holiday.

The first of the great looters (for there were many) was the vain, energetic and unscrupulous Titus Quinctius Flamininus, who defeated Philip V of Macedon at the battle of Cynoscephalae, fought in mists and pouring rain, so destroying the Macedonian hegemony over the Greek states. To curry favour with the Greeks, he proclaimed at the Isthmian Games that the Greek states were free. A herald announced the news from the arena. "The Roman Senate and Titus Quinctius, *imperator,* have conquered King Philip and the Macedonians, and now declare the Corinthians, the Phocians, all the Locrians, the island of Euboea, the Magnesians, the Thessalians, the Perrhaebians and Phthiotic Achaeans to be free, independent and subject only to their own laws." No one had ever made such a proclamation before, and the Romans had very little intention of carrying it out.

The Greeks were delirious with joy. Valerius Maximus says there was such a tumult of applause that birds flying over the arena fell into air-pockets brought about by the shouting. Livy says the games came to an abrupt end, because the Greeks were too happy to watch them. Joy rode them like a tempest, and there was a vast outpouring of affection for the thirty-three year old *imperator,* who was hailed as a saviour and received the homage usually reserved for the gods. He shared dedications with Hercules and Apollo, and solemnly placed his own shield within the temple of Apollo at Delphi. He ordered the issue of gold coins bearing his portrait and on the reverse a Victory: it was the first portrait of a living Roman ever to appear on a coin, though such coins had been frequently produced in Greece since the time of Alexander the Great; and not for a hundred and fifty years was there to be another Roman face on a coin. With this coin we see the emergence of the self-awareness of the *triumphator*; and perhaps it was inevitable that at this very moment the *triumphator,* having become a man to be distinguished from all other men, should also become a god. For in this year hymns were sung, celebrating the conqueror together with Zeus and Roma and Roman Faith: "Hail, Paean Apollo, hail, Titus our Saviour."

Flamininus received a triumph such as no one had received up to this time. It lasted for three days. The first and second days were occupied with displays of captured weapons and a great treasure of bronze and marble statues, vases, silver shields and bullion. There were 43,000 pounds of unwrought silver and 3,714 pounds of gold. Philip's treasury had been seized, with 14,514 gold coins bearing the head of Philip on them. On the third day came the prisoners, including Prince Demetrius, Philip's son, and 114 golden crowns presented by Greek and Roman cities were carried in the procession. There were also contingents of prisoners released from Greek slavery. The whole army returned to Rome, and followed the triumphal chariot.

The Romans had defeated Philip, given freedom to the Greek

states, and then departed, leaving a vacuum. Into this vacuum stepped Antiochus III of Syria, known as Antiochus the Great after his early conquests in Asia Minor, Palestine and Egypt. As he grew older, Antiochus became a happy voluptuary, and he seems to have embarked on his Greek invasion half-heartedly. For long months he remained on the island of Euboea, dallying with a beautiful Greek mistress; he summoned ambassadors, sent messengers to Rome proclaiming his undying loyalty, and prepared in a desultory fashion to assume the hegemony of Greece. Finally, he was defeated at the Pass of Thermopylae by Manius Acilius Glabrio, a member of one of the most ancient and noble families of Rome. Glabrio enjoyed a triumph, remarkable for a display of 230 military standards, the furniture and royal garments of the King. There were thirty-six noble prisoners, but no Roman soldiers accompanied the triumph: the legions of Glabrio were incorporated in the new army despatched to Greece under the command of Lucius Scipio, the brother of the conqueror of Africa. Then for the first time a Roman army crossed into Asia.

The great battle which put an end to the army of Antiochus the Great was fought at Magnesia in the autumn of 190 B.C., a thick mist flooding the plain as the armies of east and west faced each other. Antiochus himself commanded the right wing, and very nearly captured the Roman camp. The Romans had sixteen elephants; Antiochus had fifty-four. Following the usual oriental pattern Antiochus had impressed a large number of foreign tribesmen into his army; and while he was able to command the right wing brilliantly, he was unable to dominate his auxiliaries, who became terrified by the steady advance of the heavy Roman infantry through the mist. All the advantages were on the side of the Romans: the mist, the terrain, the homogeneity of the Roman forces contrasting with the singular variety of the forces of Antiochus, which included scythe-bearing chariots and Arab archers mounted on dromedaries. The Romans carried the day, and the triumph of Lucius Scipio was even more dazzling than his brother's. There were 224 military standards, 1,232 ivory tusks and 37,420 pounds of silver, together with an immense quantity of gold coins and vases. Thirty-two royal generals were led in the triumph. For the first time the donative to the soldiers was paid in silver. Scipio received the title of Asiaticus.

Zama and Magnesia were great victories, but the Romans were soon to learn that a terrible price had to be paid for them. After Zama the Romans became aware for the first time of the immensity of power. After Magnesia they became increasingly aware of the luxury and corruption which would sap at their strength for all the remaining years of the empire. "The conquest of Asia," wrote Pliny, "first introduced luxury to Italy." The Romans had already acquired a taste for luxury from the Tarquins, from the Samnites and from the Greek cities of southern Italy. Now the flood-gates were opened wide.

An odour of corruption hovers over those victories won from Antiochus. Cato the censor accused Glabrio of keeping some of the golden vessels of King Antiochus for himself. Graver accusations were made against Lucius Scipio. It was said that he received 6,000 pounds of gold and 480 pounds of silver from the hands of Antiochus to induce him to make a favourable peace. These rumours led to the trial of the two conquerors; and when Lucius Scipio was ordered to produce his account books he did so, giving them to his brother, who spoke in his defence, reminding the senators of the vast treasure which had come to Rome from the treasury of Antiochus; then he disdainfully tore the account books to pieces, suggesting that the accusers might amuse themselves by examining the scraps. On that day, or on another day during the course of the trial, Africanus reminded his listeners that it was the anniversary of the battle of Zama and he proposed therefore to offer homage to Jupiter, Juno and Minerva on the Capitol, "for having allowed me to render great services to the state, and to pray that they will grant the Roman state other citizens like myself". The whole court flocked after him; and he went on from the Capitol to visit all the temples in turn, followed by the adoring Romans. Livy comments that he enjoyed that day a greater triumph than the one he enjoyed after defeating Hannibal, but it was a triumph over the Roman people—he had simply refused to submit himself to the law, and holding himself above the law, he had shown himself contemptuous of the Roman state.

Soon Africanus disappeared into obscurity, to spend the few remaining years of his life on his country estate, but his brother was less fortunate. There were renewed attempts to impeach Lucius Scipio; and the death penalty was demanded. Finally he was released on payment of a fine, and a search was made for the gold and silver said to have been concealed. None was ever found.

Now, increasingly, the Romans were confronted with the problem of corruption. The wars in Asia tended to make armies richer rather than braver; and commanders tended to make private agreements with the enemy. We can almost watch the processes of corruption at work on the great general Aemilius Paulus, who led the next great expedition against the Macedonians.

At the beginning of his career Aemilius Paulus was the stern unyielding soldier, dedicated to *gravitas*. His father had fallen at the battle of Cannae. He was a humourless man with deep religious f elings, who delighted in nothing so much as enduring the hardships of his soldiers. As a young man he entered the college of augurs, and Plutarch says that when he was instructing his soldiers "he was like a priest teaching them ceremonies and dreadful mysteries". He was about forty when he was sent to Spain to put down a rebellion, and was granted a triumph. It was a very modest triumph, and took place in 189 B.C., the year following the great triumph of Lucius Scipio over Antiochus.

Aemilius Paulus took no part in the eastern campaigns. He had married the daughter of a consul, and she had given him two children before he divorced her. After his remarriage he gave out his children for adoption: the elder child was adopted by Fabius Maximus, the younger by Publius Scipio, the son of Africanus. He was given important commands in Italy, but it was not until 182 B.C., when he became consul, that he was given command of an army in the field. He fought the Ligurians in the Alpine foothills. He had 8,000 troops; the Ligurians had 40,000. He gained his second modest triumph after a savage engagement, with 15,000 of the enemy left on the battlefield. Twenty-five crowns were displayed in the procession. It was a real battle, unlike the battles fought by Gnaeus Manlius Vulso against the Gauls in Asia, which seem to have been carefully staged by the Roman commander; and Aemilius Paulus was beginning to be regarded as a man capable of greater victories. Liguria was pacified. It was however only a temporary pacification, for in the course of the next twenty-five years ten Roman generals enjoyed triumphs over these indestructible mountaineers.

After his second triumph Aemilius Paulus remained in Rome. He had once before been consul, and hoped to receive the consulship again, but his qualities were those of an earlier age, and he made too many enemies by his devotion to duty, and all his efforts to acquire the supreme position in the state failed. He retired from the army and took up his old position in the college of augurs. It was a time when the Republic was being shaken to its foundations by the new vices and strange religions imported from Asia and Greece in the wake of victory. An unknown Greek had introduced Bacchanalian rites into Etruria and from there they had spread all over Italy. This "fortune-teller and dabbler in sacrifices", according to Livy, brought about a reign of terror among his enthusiastic followers, who obeyed his least whims and murdered at his bidding. Accordingly all forms of Bacchic worship were outlawed by order of the consuls "except where an ancient altar or an image had been consecrated". Worse than the Bacchanalia was the steady stream of luxuries imported from the east, affecting the entire economy of Rome and subverting the strict morality of the Romans. The fashionable took to wearing silken robes; they hung expensive tapestries on their walls and reclined on couches of bronze. Female lute-players began to appear at banquets, and the banquets themselves began to assume proportions hitherto unheard of, with complicated and delicate meals served by cooks, who were beginning to regard themselves as culinary artists and demanding high fees. And all these things, regarded as remarkable at the time, were no more, says Livy, than the seeds of the luxuries to come—*semina futurae luxuriae*.

From his seat in the college of augurs Aemilius Paulus could see the ruin of luxury and corruption falling over his country. There were ominous portents—lightning struck the temple of Ops on the Capitoline hill, and about the same time a twelve-year-old hermaphrodite was discovered in Umbria, while showers of stones fell on Picenum and in various places in Italy it was observed that the sky was in flames. There were uprisings in Thessaly, the Transalpine Gauls came over the mountains to settle in Venetia, and the Romans were being met with continual threats of war from King Perseus of Macedonia. Aemilius Paulus continued his study of Greek, presided at the auguries, spoke longingly of the days when the ancient Roman virtues were celebrated, and retired more and more into the background. He had joined the ranks of those elder statesmen who withdraw from the political scene only in order to train themselves for office at a time of crisis.

Meanwhile the wars continued, with triumph following triumph. Quintus Fulvius Flaccus, who became consul following the mysterious death of his stepfather, enjoyed a triumph over Celtiberi in 180 B.C., and in the following year he enjoyed another over the Ligurians.[1] The elder Gracchus attacked Sardinia, and he too enjoyed a triumph. There were altogether three triumphs in 175 B.C. Not one of these triumphs, according to Livy, reflected any

---

[1] Quintus Fulvius Flaccus met a fate unusual for *triumphatores*. Eight years after his second triumph, when he was *pontifex maximus*, he learned that of his two sons serving with the army in Illyria, one had been killed in battle and the other was dying of a mortal disease. Slaves entering his bedroom the next morning found him hanging by a noose. *Hic foeda morte perit*, says Livy. "He perished disgracefully." It was perhaps a fitting end to a man who came to power by murder, desecrated a temple by removing its tiles so that he could use them for a larger temple he was building in his own honour, and who achieved his two triumphs by easy massacres.

credit on the *triumphatores*. In 172 B.C. Caius Cicereius, fresh from
a murderous war in Corsica in which he had lost 3,000 of his own
men, demanded a triumph and was refused. He had to content
himself with an *ovatio* on the Alban Mount. After the Corsican
war, he had sailed to Italy with his army and attacked a peaceful
tribe of Ligurians, promising them their freedom if they surrendered and then breaking his promise by selling them into
slavery. The Senate, outraged by his actions which seemed to be
designed to dishonour Rome, took the unusual recourse of buying
back the slaves and setting them free, and ordered Cicereius to
remain in the province until every one of the captured Ligurians
had safely returned to his own home. Cicereius defied the Senate,
hurried to Rome, demanded a triumph, and when rebuffed for the
second time he returned to Liguria and continued to carry out his
own plans without paying the least attention to the senators, who
attacked him bitterly and helplessly because he was out of their
reach. A shocked Senate issued a proclamation, reminding the
Roman generals that "brilliant victories come from defeating men
in battle, not from torturing the distressed".

The warning came none too soon: too many triumph-hunting
generals had massacred innocent tribesmen and claimed resounding victories. The time had come for the Roman army to retrieve
its honour. What was needed was a brilliant victory over an opponent worthy of their steel, not a series of bloody skirmishes with
tribesmen.

For three years King Perseus had been defying the Romans. He
had amassed a large army and a huge quantity of treasure, and
hoped in time to regain all the lost provinces of the Macedonian
empire. Singularly handsome, a talented and fearless strategist,
beloved by his troops and revered throughout Greece and Asia,
he had hurled back three successive Roman invasions and was
openly threatening to march against Italy. The Romans were
determined to put an end to his growing power in northern
Greece, and in the early spring of 168 B.C command of the army in
Greece was placed in the hands of Aemilius Paulus, the only
general whose reputation remained untarnished.

Aemilius Paulus accepted his new command with the air of a
man embarking upon a campaign which would lead to certain
victory. He had a dry wit, and it amused him just before sailing
across the Adriatic to address the Roman people in the Forum and
warn them against armchair strategists. Everyone, he said, counted
himself an authority on the war. There were people who would
tell you where the camp should be placed, and through what pass

Macedonia should be entered, and the proper moment to engage the enemy, and the proper moment to lie low. There were too many of these strategists, and the more powerful ones were inclined to place the consul on trial if he so much as disputed the least of their suggestions. Then he went on to suggest how the advice of these armchair strategists could be put to better use:

If any of you thinks himself qualified to give me advice respecting the war which I am about to conduct, which may prove advantageous to the public, let him not refuse his assistance to the state, but rather let him come with me to Macedonia. He shall be furnished by me with a ship, a horse, a tent; and I shall even pay his travelling expenses. But if he thinks this too much trouble, and prefers the repose of city life to the toils of war, let him not on land assume the office of a pilot. The city in itself furnishes an abundance of topics for conversation; let it confine its passion for talking, and rest assured that we shall be content with such councils as shall be framed within our camp.

(*Livy*, XLIV, 22.)

In this mood of cautious determination to carry on the war by his own lights, Aemilius Paulus set sail for Greece. He sailed from Brundisium, and five days later he was in Delphi, where he offered sacrifices. It was an unusually quick journey, offering excellent auguries for the future. Four days later he was with his army on the Enipeus. Fifteen days later the Macedonian army had been destroyed, and the Hellenistic world lay in scattered pieces at his feet. For nearly a hundred and fifty years the Companions of Alexander the Great had continued to rule over his empire, and now the most powerful of them was a fugitive wandering along the seashore near Samothrace.

Aemilius Paulus had fought the Macedonians on his own terms, aided by his knowledge of celestial auguries. On the night before the battle of Pydna there occurred an eclipse of the moon, which terrified the Macedonians, but left the Romans who had been forewarned by their general undisturbed. On the next evening, when it was growing dark, he attacked. Afterwards he admitted to having been terrified by the sudden appearance of the Thracians, "tall men with bright and glittering shields over their black tunics". They were followed by a phalanx of Brazen Shields and by Macedonians wearing gilded armour and scarlet cloaks. But after that first moment of panic, the general remained calm. Had he not sacrificed twenty heifers to Hercules during the eclipse of the moon, receiving no sign from heaven? But upon the sacrifice of the twenty first heifer he had received incontrovertible proof of heaven's blessing. So he fought calmly, and soon he was privileged to observe by the light of the full moon that the Macedonians were breaking into small groups, and there were twenty different battles being fought across the plain. By midnight the enemy was in flight. The slaughter was appalling. According to Livy, the Macedonians lost 20,000 killed and 6,000 captured, and another 5,000 were taken during the pursuit, which was pushed for fourteen miles. Perseus himself with a small escort escaped to his ancestral home at Pella, the birthplace of Alexander the Great. The Romans claimed that they lost only eighty men. Only one thing disturbed Aemilius Paulus: his young son Scipio, who had accompanied him from Rome, had vanished during the course of the battle. Scouts were sent to search for the boy, and the whole camp was plunged in grief because he was believed killed. But the boy turned up later, covered with blood, having taken part in the pursuit. It was this same Scipio who was later to destroy the Carthaginian empire.

With the battle won, a strange change came over the general. The dour old man, who loved nothing better than examining the entrails of bulls and sheep to determine the auspices, consciously modelling himself on the heroes of ancient Rome, gave way to weeping fits in his excitement and surrounded himself with all the luxuries which a prostrate Greece could offer him. When Perseus was captured and brought to his tent, he burst into tears and delivered a speech on the brevity of life and the impermanence of glory; and when Perseus asked for pity for the defeated Mace-donians, he gave them their freedom: they could keep their own laws, elect their own magistrates and live undisturbed in their own cities, paying to Rome only one half of the tax they had previously paid to their King. He had always been a philhellene, and it pleased him to make a triumphal progress through Greece, visiting Delphi, Lebadea, Athens, Corinth, Sicyon, Argos, Epidaurus, and Olympia, following almost exactly the path taken by the modern tourist. At Amphipolis he celebrated a festival of triumph with great pomp, presiding at the altar when a miraculous thunderbolt set the wood on fire and completed the immolation of the sacrifice. When asked how he proposed to organize the festival he answered: "A man who can conquer in war should know how to arrange banquets and games."

His triumphal procession in Amphipolis had an extraordinary effect on the half-mad Antiochus IV Epiphanes, King of Syria and conqueror of Egypt, long a hostage at Rome, who succeeded his brother on the throne of their father, Antiochus the Great. The

young king loved glory to the edge of madness, and there was a
strangeness about him that puzzled everyone he met. Livy said of
him that "he never spoke to his friends, smiled in a most friendly
way at mere acquaintances, and with an inconsistent generosity
delighted in making a laughing-stock of himself and others".
Polybius tells a strange story of how he once ushered in his guests
to a banquet, drank toasts to them, sat beside them, and spoke
charmingly and wittily to all of them. Suddenly he disappeared,
and he was next seen when a troupe of performers carried him
into the banqueting hall wrapped in a sheet, from which he
emerged stark naked, to join the performers in their performances.
The guests were shocked, and one by one they left the palace.
Antiochus was still dancing when the last guests left.

The greatest desire of Antiochus was to celebrate a triumph as
great as the triumph of Aemilius Paulus. The triumph took place
at Daphne, a suburb of Antioch:

The festival was opened with a procession as splendid as any
there has ever been.

It was led by 5,000 men in the prime of life armed after the
Roman fashion and wearing breast-plates of chain armour. They
were followed by 5,000 Mysians and 3,000 Cilicians armed in the
manner of light infantry, wearing gold crowns. Next came 3,000
Thracians and 5,000 Gauls followed by 20,000 Macedonians of
whom 10,000 bore gold shields, 5,000 brazen shields and the rest
silver shields. Next there marched 250 pairs of gladiators, and
behind them 1,000 horsemen from Nyssa and 3,000 from Antioch,
most of them wearing crowns and trappings of gold and the rest
trappings of silver. Then came the royal guards and the mailed
horsemen wearing purple surcoats embroidered with gold and
heraldic designs, and these were followed by a hundred chariots
each drawn by six horses and there were forty more drawn by
four horses and then a chariot drawn by four elephants and
another drawn by a pair of elephants, and finally thirty-six
elephants in single file with all their housings.

This was by no means the end of the procession. After this
came 800 young men wearing crowns, 300 sacred cows and 800
ivory tusks, and then a whole medley of images of gods and
guardian-spirits and heroes, some gilded, others draped in gold-
embroidered tissues. There were images of Night and Day,
Earth and Heaven, Noon and Dawn. Finally came a procession
of slaves carrying gold and silver plate, and 200 women sprinkl-
ing the crowd with perfumes, and behind these came eighty

women in litters of gold and some 500 in litters with silver feet.

The King himself rode in the procession, ordering it to advance and halt according to his whim; and he quite deliberately rode the most sorry nag he could find.

(Polybius, XXX, 25; from Athenaeus, V, 194, and X, 439.)

The most revealing part of the account of the Syrian King's triumph lies in the last paragraph with the disturbing suggestion that he was simply amusing himself at the expense of the crowds. But if the King annoyed them by his conduct, he went on to reward them amply with feasts and spectacles, and he was especially generous in providing expensive perfumes for his guests. Polybius continues his description of the triumph over Egypt:

When at last the games, gladiatorial shows and beast fights were over thirty days later, for the first five succeeding days everyone who chose anointed himself in the gymnasium with saffron ointment out of gold jars. Of these there were fifteen, and there were the same number of jars with ointment of cinnamon and spikenard. . . . For the banquets there were sometimes 1,000 and sometimes 1,500 tables set out for his guests, and these were furnished with the most expensive dishes.

(Polybius, XXX, 26.)

Later generations were inclined to view Antiochus IV Epiphanes with less compassion than many of his contemporaries. The Jews remembered him bitterly because he converted the Temple of Solomon into a temple in honour of Zeus Olympius, and the revolt of the Maccabees started during his reign. In time he became the "Little Horn" of *Daniel*, and the prototype of Antichrist. An inscription in Babylon calls him the founder of the city and Saviour of Asia. He died falling from his chariot on his return from an expedition to Persepolis in search of treasure, and some said he was completely mad before he died, having been punished by the gods for despoiling so many shrines. It is just possible that he was a gay and witty prince who regarded kingship as a ridiculous joke.

While Antiochus was superintending his triumph over the Egyptians in Antioch, Aemilius Paulus was busy collecting from all the cities of Greece the greatest collection of Greek statues in marble and bronze ever assembled together. Wearing the guise of a civilized conqueror, promising all things to all men, he was perhaps the greatest of all vandals. Not content with despoiling the cities, he despoiled the homes of the people. When his soldiers demand a donation, he ordered the citizens of Epirus to carry their gold and silver vessels out of their houses, and permitted his soldiers to plunder unmercifully. Epirus, a rich and large province, was sold into slavery, and in a single hour, according to Plutarch, seventy cities were sacked. But when the distribution of booty was made, the soldiers discovered to their horror that each one was awarded no more than eleven drachmas, and they accused Aemilius Paulus of retaining for his own profit the great bulk of the treasure.

The soldiers were still complaining when Aemilius Paulus sailed up the Tiber in the royal galley of King Perseus, the deck piled high with bolts of purple and scarlet cloth and the captured weapons of the enemy. The crowds lined the banks, stunned by the appearance of the great ship with its sixteen banks of oars; and some complained, as the ship rode slowly against the stream, that he was celebrating his triumph too early. He had enemies in the Senate who demanded that a triumph should be refused to him, but he also had loyal defenders, among them a certain Marcus Servilius, a former consul, famous for having killed twenty-three of the enemy in single combat. Servilius protested against the calumnies heaped on the victorious general, who surely deserved the highest honours for having fought with an army composed of seditious soldiers. As he spoke, Servilius threw off his toga and exposed his wounds, especially a swelling in the groin due to un-counted days of riding horseback in the service of the Roman state; and when the senators laughed, he added quietly that he would follow them when the votes were counted and he would take note of those who were so ungrateful as to vote against Aemilius Paulus. His speech was credited with having produced an overwhelming vote in favour of granting him a triumph.

Five days before the triumph Aemilius Paulus lost one of his young sons by his second wife. Utterly grief-stricken, he prayed to the gods that if anyone envied him his good fortune, he would be happier if they vented their wrath upon him than upon the state. He was to lose another son a few days later.

There had been many triumphs, but none that blazed with so much colour as this. In honour of the occasion the Romans decked themselves out in white. Tiers of seats were erected in the Forum; the temple gates were thrown open, and the temples themselves were hung with garlands. Police officers patrolled the route of the procession to prevent anyone from crossing the conqueror's path.

The spectacle occupied three days. On the first day 250 chariots loaded with sculptures, bronzes, marbles and paintings passed along the Via Sacra; among the paintings was a series of immense representations of the battle of Pydna painted by the Athenian

poet-painter Metrodorus. On the second day the captured weapons
and all the silver treasure passed in review: there were 750 bowls
filled with silver coins carried by 3,000 men, and there were more
men carrying silver goblets and cups. The weapons were heaped
up in carts, carefully arranged to give an impression of disorder;
and the carts made such a clanging noise as they passed that it
sounded like the passing of great armies. On the third day came the
gold treasure and the captives, while the *triumphator* rode in his
chariot in all his glory. Plutarch describes the scene vividly:

> The trumpeters, who appeared early in the morning, did not
> sound processional music, but instead they sounded the charge.
> After the trumpeters came youths wearing tunics with orna-
> mental borders, leading 120 stalled oxen to the sacrifice: the
> horns of the oxen were gilded, and their heads were adorned
> with ribbons and garlands: and with the youths came boys
> carrying the silver and gold basins for libation. After these came
> those who carried the gold coins in vessels that weighed three
> talents like those that contained the silver: there were altogether
> seventy-seven vessels heaped with gold coin. After this came the
> consecrated bowl weighing ten talents and studded with precious
> stones, which Aemilius had ordered to be made, and there were
> the goblets of Antigonus and Seleucus and those of Thericlean
> make, and all the gold plate which graced the table of Perseus.
> Then came Perseus's chariot in which his armour was placed,
> and on that his diadem.
>
> A little way behind came the captives, the king's children with
> their servants, masters and teachers, all of them shedding tears
> and stretching out their hands to the spectators, and making the
> children beg for mercy. There were two sons and a daughter, too
> young to realize the gravity of the occasion, and their very insen-
> sibility of their condition rendered it all the more deplorable,
> so much so that hardly anyone paid any attention to Perseus, and
> the pity of the Romans was concentrated upon the children.
> Many of the Romans wept, and they watched in mingled sorrow
> and happiness, until the children passed.
>
> *(Aemilius Paulus, XXXIII.)*

Plutarch goes on to tell how King Perseus followed his children,
dressed in black, looking like a man dazed and stupefied by the
suddenness of the disaster. He had previously begged to be allowed
not to march in the procession; he had not been captured, but
had surrendered, and was therefore not in the strict sense a
proper candidate for a triumph. As usual, Aemilius Paulus dealt

with the matter bluntly, reminding Perseus that he could avoid taking part in the triumph quite easily by killing himself. Immediately behind Perseus rode the *triumphator* in his chariot, wearing a robe of purple interwoven with gold, with a laurel branch in his right hand. He had hoped the remaining son by his second wife would accompany him, but the boy was ill, and he rode alone. Behind him came the army, singing the usual verses of praise and raillery, waving laurel boughs. Soon they would receive their donations, amounting to 100 denarii for every foot-soldier, 200 for every centurion, and 300 for every cavalryman. He could well afford these donations; for the captured silver alone amounted to 120,000,000 sesterces and never before had such a phenomenal amount of wealth appeared in a triumphal procession. So much treasure had been acquired that no taxes were needed until the time of Julius Caesar.

More than anyone else Aemilius Paulus, the strict votary of the ancient Roman virtues, was responsible for the invasion of luxury into the Roman state. In a hundred different ways his victory over Macedonia contributed to the gradual weakening of the Roman fibre. Pliny says there were no bakers in Rome until the war with Perseus, for previously every Roman baked his own bread.

Three days after the triumph Aemilius Paulus lost his fourteen-year-old son, and was so overcome with grief that he addressed the people from the rostrum, begging for their pity. He spoke of how in the space of fifteen days he had landed on Greek soil, performed the sacrifices and defeated the enemy, and now the people were shouting in their delirious triumph, while the conqueror himself was deprived of any reason for living. As a good augur, knowing the purposes of the gods, he believed that his own griefs only pointed to greater blessings for the Roman people: the jealous gods had wreaked all their vengeance on him, leaving none to be wreaked on Rome. As for Perseus—"He, though conquered, can still enjoy his children, while I, the conqueror, have none!"

Perseus however did not enjoy his children for long, and they were soon separated from him. For a while the king was kept in prison, later he was allowed to live under house arrest. Plutarch mentions the rumour that the guards detested him and deliberately kept him from sleep, so that eventually he died from exhaustion. Two of his children died soon afterwards, while a third, his youngest son Alexander, fell into poverty and to earn a livelihood learned the art of working brass and proved to be "an exquisite artist in turning and graving small figures". Afterwards Alexander learned to speak Latin so well that he was offered a post as clerk to the Roman magistrates. He died in Rome in great obscurity many years later.

The triumph of Aemilius Paulus was not the only one presented to the Roman people that year. In December one of the rare naval triumphs was enjoyed by Gnaeus Octavius, the commander of the Roman fleet in Greek waters, who had accepted the surrender of Perseus in Samothrace. This triumph was granted readily by the Senate, but seems to have been an afterthought. There were no prisoners and no spoils. In February a triumph was celebrated for the victory over King Genthius and the Illyrians. It was not, of course, as glorious as Aemilius Paulus's triumph, but it pleased the Romans, who had long feared the Illyrians. The soldiers in the triumph were in high spirits, many military standards were displayed, and King Genthius, his brother, wife and children were led in the procession. No harm came to the king, who was permitted to live quietly in Spoletum. The triumph took place without incident, but there were extraordinary scenes at the triumphal games which took place immediately afterwards.

According to Athenaeus, the *triumphator* Lucius Anicius Gallus constructed a huge stage and commanded the most famous Greek actors of his time to perform for him. On the stage were the performers, some flute-players and a chorus. The *triumphator* took his seat on the special throne provided for him, but soon became bored by the play and ordered them to show more competitive spirit. How? they asked. They were told to show more fighting spirit, more license, more courage. So the actors began shouting and the flute-players played unintelligible discords and the dancers wheeled round and confronted one another, and then one of the dancers assumed the posture of a boxer against the advancing hordes of flute-players and a pitched battle ensued, with four prize-fighters mounting the stage accompanied by buglers and trumpeters. It was like the last scene of Trimalchio's banquet; and everyone cheered.

Behind this strange and unexplained incident there may have been a deliberate protest by the new *triumphator* against the excesses and luxuries introduced from Greece. Greek performers were noted for their effeminacy and delicacy; and the Romans, mistaking their high fluted voices for weakness, may have decided to put an end to an un-Roman display. In time they would come to know and value the Greek players better.

About this time a speaker in the Senate, passing in review all the recent wars fought successfully against powerful rulers, spoke of the vast good fortune which had come to the Roman people, and the terror of their name. *Magna fortuna populi Romani est, magnum et terribile nomen.* It was a simple phrase, which concealed many complexities; for terror breeds many kinds of terror, and too much good fortune is not always fortunate. Soon the Roman terror was to turn inward, and a long series of terrifying civil wars was to plague the people who had brought terror to the world.

The climax came in 146 B.C. when two of the greatest cities in the world were completely destroyed. Corinth fell to Lucius Mummius, a good-natured ignoramus of little wealth or personal distinction, who was so overwhelmed by his easy victory that he put the city to the flames, killed the men and sold the women and children into slavery. Velleius Paterculus tells the story that when he was arranging for the marbles and statues to be shipped to Rome, he warned the shippers not to lose them, otherwise they would have to replace them with new ones.

Scipio Aemilianus, the son of Aemilius Paulus, was far from being an ignoramus. He possessed wealth and personal distinction, and employed the historian Polybius as his secretary. He was even more ruthless than Mummius. He calmly gave orders for the complete obliteration of the city of Carthage, which had withstood a three-year siege. For six days the Roman soldiers were permitted to burn and tear down the buildings, to trample the survivors to death, to murder and rape as they pleased. The thirty-eight-year-old commander watched the destruction impassively, and there came a moment when he turned to his secretary and said: "It is all so beautiful, and yet I have a foreboding that the same fate is reserved for my own country." In the manner of a well-bred Roman he recited some appropriate lines from Homer, and wept a little.

Carthage was razed to the ground until no stone stood upon another; and then the rubble was solemnly cursed, and sown with salt. Scipio returned to Rome to enjoy a triumph, the most glorious, according to Appian, that had ever been seen. Great quantities of gold and ivory passed in procession, and all the great statues and votive offerings which the Carthaginians had gathered from the ends of the world. Scipio assumed the title of Africanus, and Africa became a Roman province.

Thirteen years later he repeated the crime. A rebellion had taken place in the Spanish city of Numantia, and Scipio was sent to squash it. He had become by this time a strangely reserved and disquieting figure, given to frequent visits to the Capitol, where after closing the doors he enjoyed a prolonged communion with the gods. His temper was aristocratic and unforgiving. He built a great wall round the Spanish city and starved out the inhabitants, who set fire to it so that nothing of value should fall into the hands of the conqueror. Some took poison, others killed themselves, or perished in the flames. A few survivors surrendered and were brought to Scipio who received them coldly. They smelt horribly, their bodies were foul, and their long hair hung down to their shoulders. They wore on their faces expressions of hate, pain and weariness; and they had the look of guilt which comes from the knowledge of having eaten human flesh. Scipio reserved fifty of them for his triumph, and sold the rest. The historian Orosius wrote that the Romans did not consider they had defeated the people of Numantia: they felt instead a great feeling of relief in having escaped their fate. He says, too, that no Numantines appeared in Rome in chains, and that the Senate saw no reason to reward him with a triumph. Unfortunately Orosius was wrong, for the triumph appears in the *acta triumphorum* and Scipio was not the kind of man to permit an honour to escape him.

One night three years later he returned to his house in the evening from the Senate, and he was seen working on some papers. In the morning he was found dead in bed with marks of strangulation round his neck. His slaves, under torture, spoke of some mysterious visitors who had entered the house during the night. He may have been murdered by political enemies, or by his wife, or by his mother-in-law. No inquest was held. The conqueror of Africa and Numantia was buried privately. It was as though very quietly, in secret, the Romans were burying with him the terrible load of guilt which had accumulated through the years.

6

TRIUMPH AND DEFEAT

ROME had no enemies she could not destroy, but she was well on the way to destroying herself. She had survived, as perhaps all nations survive, by a series of unlooked-for events that fell to her advantage. There were times when only a hair-breadth separated her from defeat at the hands of the Carthaginians. She had held her breath when Hannibal stood outside the gates, and she held it again when Hasdrubal appeared out of the north, only to lose his way during a night march and fall prey to a Roman army commanded by two consuls. Rome knew, as we know, that civilizations can perish.

There was no lack of warnings. Cato, implacable against the Carthaginians, could be equally implacable against the Romans. He once suggested that if the Romans had grown great by folly, then it was time they changed; for folly had made them great enough in all conscience. Sometimes, thinking aloud, he would ask whether the gods would deem it worth their while to preserve a city where a fish on an epicure's table cost the price of a whole ox. He reserved his most bitter attacks for those who despised the ancient Roman virtues, but it was left to Sallust to describe the tragedy which was fast overtaking the Roman state. He wrote:

A handful of men control policy at home and in the field. The treasury, the provinces, the magistrature, the glories and the triumphs—all these are in their power, and at their disposal. The people are burdened with military service and poverty; and the generals divide the spoils of war among the few. Meanwhile we see the fathers and mothers of soldiers, and their little children, thrown from their homes; and those who have powerful neighbours leave their homes earliest. And together with power there comes the invasion of greed, measureless and ruthless, tainting and spoiling everything, without scruple or reverence, until it hastens its own downfall. And then it happens that as soon as nobles are found who prefer true glory to lawless power, the state is shaken at the roots and civil wars arise with the effect of earthquakes.

(Sallust, *Jugurtha*, 41.)

Sallust, of course, had the advantages of hind-sight. Those nobles who "prefer true glory to lawless power" were the Gracchi, the two grandsons of Africanus, who hoped to save the nobility by curbing its power. Tiberius Gracchus, passing through Tuscany on his way to Spain, had seen the misery caused by the wars, the great estates in the hands of the wealthy, the returning soldiers without any land they could call their own. He taunted the Roman generals who exhorted the soldiers to fight for the hearths of their ancestors and the sacred altars—they had no altars, no hearths of their own. In a series of extraordinary speeches, he denounced their poverty. "They fought and died," he declared, "but it was only to maintain the luxury and wealth of others. They are called the masters of the earth, but they have no foot of ground they can call their own."

Tiberius and Caius Gracchus failed to bring about the much-needed revolution; and the entrenched nobility had no compunction in destroying them by setting armed thugs against them. The revolution died, but the venality and incompetence of the military commanders in the field, and of the senators, continued. Again and again we come upon generals celebrating triumphs against all evidence, for no reason except personal aggrandisement. We hear of Appius Claudius Pulcher celebrating a triumph after instigating a war against some Gallic tribes, and Dion Cassius comments acidly: "He knew perfectly well he had won no victories. He was so arrogant that he never brought up the matter in the Senate or the Assembly, but simply acted as though he had a right to a triumph, whether or not anyone voted for him, and therefore he demanded the necessary funds" (Dio, XXII, 74). Such triumphs, of course, were bought at the price of innumerable dead Romans and innumerable towns and villages put to the flames.

We hear of other and even more frightening triumphs. There was, for example, Lucius Caecilius Metellus, who marched into Dalmatia, wintered pleasantly with the people of Salona, and suddenly announced that the treasure of the city and all her most important citizens would be seized to decorate his triumph. It was the triumph of treachery over the ancient Roman virtues; and there were to be many such triumphs in the future.

Jugurtha, the able and handsome king of Numidia, raised the standard of revolt. He possessed to an extraordinary degree the virtues which the Romans once cherished. He rode well, hurled the javelin and ran foot-races with his subjects, who idolized him. He despised the Romans, and said of Rome that it was "a city for sale, and doomed to perish if it finds a purchaser". He was able to bribe senators, and he possessed his own agents in the Roman army. He fought magnificently, and at one period during the campaign he captured an entire Roman army and passed it under the yoke. The Senate sent a new army to Africa under Quintus Caecilius Metellus, a dry formal man of an ancient and illustrious plebeian family, but with aristocratic sympathies. He was almost the caricature of the Roman general of his time, stiff-necked, unapproachable, growing increasingly cautious as he grew more famous. Under him, serving as his legate, was the supremely incautious Caius Marius, born in the little town of Arpinum in the rugged Volscian mountains, his father a common labourer. He drew his own remarkable portrait when he defended himself in the Comitia—harsh, brutal, self-made, despising all frivolities and the imbecilities of the aristo-crats. Under shaggy eyebrows, he looked out at a world he increasingly distrusted. He was fifty, and grown fat, when he was appointed consul, with orders to destroy Jugurtha. He raised an army of slaves and poor people, and appointed as his quaestor Lucius Sulla, a thirty-year-old aristocrat of a family reduced to obscurity. It was Sulla, the *bon vivant* devoted to glory, who pre-pared the trap into which Jugurtha fell. It was a very simple trap. Sulla knew about the hatred existing between Jugurtha and his father-in-law, King Bocchus of Mauretania. Jugurtha was at the court of the Mauretanian king when he was betrayed, bound and delivered over to Sulla, who gave him to Marius. The war came to an end, for the Numidians had no more heart to fight, and Marius celebrated a triumph that rivalled the triumph of Scipio Africanus.

Great treasures of bullion fell into the hands of the Romans. Plutarch says there were 287,000 drachmas in gold and silver, 3,007 pounds of gold, 5,775 pounds of silver: all of these were displayed in the triumph. Jugurtha himself, with his two sons, all wearing their royal robes, walked before Marius's chariot. Jugurtha was a strange figure, tall and commanding, and the Romans who had fought him for fourteen long years were overjoyed to see him at their mercy, and puzzled because he behaved in his chains like a madman. He was not feigning madness. Marius, always unscrupu-lous, had seen to it that the king should be tortured within an inch of his life in prison.

At the end of the day's festivities, when Marius was about to climb to the Capitol, the king's guards amused themselves by tear-ing the royal robes off his back, and his ear was split as they struggled to obtain possession of the single gold ring he wore in one of his ears, in the African fashion. He was then lowered, naked and bleeding, into the Tullian dungeon beneath the Capitol, and as he fell in the damp slime at the bottom of the pit, the guards heard his blood-curdling laugh and his bitter cry: "O God, how cold your bath is!" Plutarch says he was starved to death and died after six days, but he was not the kind of man to die so soon; and he seems to have been strangled by one of the jailers, who was let down into the pit by a rope.

Three men had contrived to bring that desolate triumph to birth. There was Metellus, the ageing aristocrat, who secured for himself the title of Numidicus; there was the young Sulla, who was responsible for the king's capture and who was himself to become a king unlike any that Rome had ever seen; there was Caius Marius, the consul and *triumphator*, who summoned the Senate to the Capitol and appeared before them in his triumphal robes, either because he was so delighted with his good fortune or because he had forgotten to change into his ordinary purple-bordered robe; and the senators wondered whether it was the ignorant blunder of a low-bred clown or the distasteful pride of an ambitious upstart. Later years were to prove abundantly that Marius suffered from a fierce and consuming pride, which became more terrible as he grew older: his white-hot pride fed itself on massacre.

In those early days after the capture of Jugurtha, Rome had need of a rough-hewn and tireless soldier, with no nonsense about him. Two German tribes, the Cimbri and Teutones, had moved from their original home in Jutland against the Roman frontiers, seeking lands to cultivate. They numbered perhaps half a million. In the course of their immense journey to the south, they had brought humiliation to several amateur generals. Among them was a certain Quintus Servilius Caepio, who had been awarded a triumph in 107 B.C. for his victories in Spain. Two years later he was in command of an army on the right bank of the Rhône, near Arausio (Orange), confronted by the massed army of the Cimbri and Teutones, and there he suffered the most spectacular defeat in the whole course of Roman history. It was worse than Cannae, which took place more than a hundred years before.

Caepio was already under a cloud when he engaged in the battle. While fighting the Cimbri he had sacked a temple in Tolosa (Toulouse) reputed to contain treasure which Brennus had captured from Delphi. The treasure disappeared. Some said Ligurian pirates had stolen it, others that it had passed secretly into the hands of the commanding general. There were inquiries, but the matter was hushed up, and his *imperium* was prolonged, not without misgivings. The "lost gold of Tolosa", had already become proverbial when Caepio on the morning of October 6, 105 B.C. quarrelled bitterly with the consul Gnaeus Mallius who was in overall command of the Roman forces. Caepio refused to attack when ordered. He seems to have hoped that the consul's forces would exhaust themselves, permitting him to retrieve the victory at the last moment. But the enemy came with surprising suddenness and overwhelmed the Romans, who were compelled to fight with the river at their backs, with no room for retreat. The entire Roman army was wiped out, with only a handful of survivors. 80,000 men were reported dead, together with 40,000 camp-followers. The enemy gleefully presided over the holocaust, destroying everything in sight, smashing the armour, burning the booty, ripping to ribbons every bale of cloth which fell into their hands, and pitching horses and treasure into the river. Caepio was one of the few who succeeded in escaping. Ten years later he was put on trial: his property was confiscated, he was solemnly expelled from the Senate, and thrown into prison. He escaped, and spent his last years an unhappy exile in Smyrna.

The way was now open for the Germans to attack Italy. If they had marched against Rome at once, they would have carried everything before them. They delayed for three years, giving Marius time to organize a powerful army. At last the Teutones made for Italy along the coast-road and the Cimbri came over the Brenner Pass. Marius annihilated them both in turn, at Aquae Sextiae (Aix) in 102 B.C., and near Vercellae in northern Italy in 101 B.C. He was refused a formal triumph for the first victory, but could not be prevented from celebrating a triumph for the second, if only because of the magnitude of the defeat inflicted on the enemy. 140,000 of the enemy fell, and some 60,000 were captured. It was a holocaust as dreadful as that at Arausio. The Roman soldiers amused themselves by scalping the women. Hundreds and perhaps thousands of women killed each other in a terrifying orgy of self-destruction. The triumph was complete, and in Rome there was a vast outpouring of joy when the news became known, with whole families making offerings and libations to "The Gods and Marius". No one could remember such a coupling of the name of a commander with the gods. The relief and joy of the Romans was completely genuine. Marius in their eyes was the supreme hero, the saviour of his country.

The victory was not Marius's alone; and Sulla, who was present at the battle, spoke of his conniving on the battlefield, his determination to overshadow the commander of the army which occupied the centre, and his rage when this commander was able to prove his own effectiveness in the battle by displaying the spears and arrows on which his name was carved. Marius had 32,000 troops, and these were arranged on the two rings. The centre was commanded by Marius who hoped to carry the battle with no help from his aristocratic fellow-consul Quintus Lutatius Catulus—the most elegant of men, a gifted orator, autobiographer, and Hellenized man of letters. Plutarch calls him mild, but it was a deceptive mildness; and to Marius's annoyance Catulus shared in the triumph. There were very good reasons for permitting Catulus to ride in triumph—his soldiers had threatened violence if their commander was not allowed to partake in the triumph. Also, the best spoils including the standards and trumpets of the enemy were in the hands of his army.

The triumph took place in an atmosphere of gloom. It so happened that a few days previously a certain Publicius Malleolus had killed his own mother. In the law-books there was no punishment for so heinous a crime, because it occurred so rarely. It was some time before a suitable punishment could be devised. Finally it was decided to sew him up in a sack and throw him into the sea. Grief and horror over the crime cast a pall over the whole city; and the two *triumphatores* were cheered by people terrified with a sense of doom. After the triumph Marius disbanded his army, and the fears of the Romans were increased by the spectacle of the veterans roaming the streets.

It was an evil triumph, and was to have evil effects. Between Marius, the ageing commoner, and Sulla, the young aristocrat, there was no love lost. King Bocchus, ruling over the Roman protectorate of Numidia, decided with Sulla's connivance to set up on the Capitol statues of Victory, with reliefs on the base showing him delivering Jugurtha to Sulla. Marius was infuriated and tried to destroy the statues, but Sulla sent his own private guards to prevent him. There might have been war between them if another war had not broken out.

This war went under many names—the Social War, the Marsian War, the Italian War. The origins of the war are obscure. It seems to have been precipitated by a rich aristocrat, Marcus Livius Drusus, a man of almost insolent courage, who took it upon himself to lead the Italian and Latin allies to believe they would be granted citizenship. He liked to speak of "our commonwealth", meaning the commonwealth of all Italy, and he suggested a number of reforms, among them the enlargement of the Senate to make it more representative. When he was struck down by an assassin— the assassin escaped and the crime was not investigated too closely —hopes of reform died with him; and the disappointed Marsians and Samnites rose in open revolt. The Marsians were mountaineers who delighted in leading Roman armies into the defiles and then ambushing them. The Samnites, never completely suppressed, showed so much unexpected resistance that the Romans found themselves fighting a war they thought they had won two hundred years before. Marius was sixty-six; he had many friends among the Italians; he was unwell; and he saw no prospect of adding to his fame by taking part in the war. At last, at the end of a year of desultory campaigning, he laid down his command and retired to his country estate.

Sulla brought the war to a conclusion: an unnecessary war, for the Italians were immediately offered the privilege of citizenship. In 88 B.C., when the war ended, Sulla was awarded the consulship and the eastern command was given to him in lieu of a triumph. Such commands provided spectacular opportunities for enrichment, and Sulla was eager to go, but Marius was still a power to be reckoned with in Rome with vast influence among the lawmakers he despised. A law was passed transferring the eastern command to Marius. Incensed, Sulla marched on Rome at the head of six legions, while Marius proclaimed a *levée-en-masse* and freed the slaves to fight against the consul, but the slaves were ineffective against the armed legions, and Marius escaped from Rome with a price on his head. Once at Minturnae when he was asleep a Gallic slave was sent to murder him. Marius was alone in a dark room, but the Gaul thought he saw the flash of fire in Marius's eyes, and his heart failed him; and when Marius roared: "Dare you kill Caius Marius?" the Gaul fled, dashing out of the doors like a man possessed. Marius escaped to the coast, hiding in a hut where he covered himself with leaves, and soon afterwards, finding a fisherman's boat, he set sail in a storm. The winds brought him to Carthage; and there the man who had triumphed over Africa lived alone amid the ruins. Velleius Paterculus was amused by the spectacle of the former *triumphator* reduced to poverty and misery. He wrote: "So Marius gazed upon Carthage, and Carthage gazed upon Marius, and they may have consoled one another."

Supreme power was now in the hands of Sulla, who saw no reason to delay the conquest of the east. He was powerfully built, with startling blue eyes, purple and white complexion, and a shock of golden hair. He was rich, generous and scholarly; he wrote comedies, and was friendly to actors; and his greatest gift was a kind of dry lucidity, which enabled him to weigh the forces working on any given problem with remarkable accuracy. Yet he remained a man of opposites: vengeful, forgiving, loving action, but happiest when he had put action behind him and rested quietly on his estates.

Sulla had good reason to invade the east, for Mithridates IV Eupator of Pontus, on the southern shores of the Black Sea, had massacred Italian colonists at his leisure—some 80,000 were killed in 88 B.C. Sulla marched across Greece, raising money as he went, demanding and receiving the gold offerings in the temples of Olympia, Epidaurus and Delphi, repaying the gods with half the territory of Thebes. Unlike Flamininus and Aemilius Paulus, he did not present himself as a saviour, but as a conqueror, the most ruthless who ever besieged Athens. The Athenian wits laughed at the sight of his strange mottled face, which was, they said, "like a mulberry sprinkled with meal". But they did not laugh for long. When the Athenians refused to submit, he sent his legions against the walls, and the blood shed in the market-place is said to have flowed down through the Ceramicus, past the gate, till it entered the suburbs beyond the wall. When he had occupied Athens, he went down to Piraeus and put it to the flames.

He was equally ruthless in his wars against Mithridates. Within less than three years he killed 160,000 men, recovered Greece, Macedonia, Ionia and Asia, and captured the fleet of Mithridates. But in the interval Marius had returned from exile to lead an army of slaves against Rome and to launch an unparalleled orgy of revenge and massacre. For five days and nights the blood ran. His pent-up hatred of the aristocracy resulted in a reign of terror: all the aristocrats who had ever stood in Marius's path were butchered, or committed suicide. Sulla was outlawed, his house was pulled down, his property was confiscated, and his relatives forced to flee to Greece. Sated with blood and more than half-mad, sleepless, drunk, frightened and delirious, Marius died a few days after entering his seventh consulship. In his last hours he was a raving maniac, fighting his battles over again.

No one like Marius ever ruled over the Romans again. He was like a throwback to some primitive tribe, ruthless and terrible. It was said of him that he was "rough and uncouth and austere in his life"—*hirtus atque horridus vitaque sanctus*—and that strange mingling of great vices and great virtues, of primitive force and unexampled austerity, gives him a place of his own in the long list of conquerors who stamped their impress on Rome.

Marius and Sulla were well-matched in their rages. When Sulla returned to Italy in 83 B.C., he found the Marians in control and had to fight every inch of his way to Rome. When he reached Rome there was another blood-bath even more terrible than the first, so that the son of the dead Catulus cried out: "If we kill armed men in time of war and unarmed men in time of peace, who will be left to win the victory?" It is a cry that can be heard whenever revolutions are followed by counter-revolutions.

When Sulla had exacted full vengeance—among other acts of vengeance he dug up the ashes of Marius and scattered them on the River Arno—he celebrated a triumph over King Mithridates. The triumph, says Plutarch, was distinguished by "the rarity and magnificence" of the royal spoils, but the Romans watching the great procession were more interested in the return of the exiles, who had fled to Greece to escape the Marian massacres. Crowned with garlands, shouting the praises of the *triumphator*, they followed his chariot: a visible and potent sign that the aristocracy had returned to occupy its traditional place. Sulla addressed the citizens. He was perfectly frank. He attributed his good fortune to luck, consecrated a tenth of the spoils to Hercules and offered banquets to the people. There was such an abundance of meat that some of it had to be thrown into the river. The oldest and rarest wines were drunk by the banqueters.

There was in Sulla a strange magnificence, and contempt for magnificence. For his triumph he brought the entire body of athletes from the Olympic Games: that year, for the first and last time until 1960, the games were held in Rome, but no record of the individual athletic feats has survived—the Greeks, detesting Sulla, simply expunged this particular year from their list of Olympic Games. Sulla gloried in the visible signs of his power, yet he was sometimes curiously ironical. At his orders a gilded equestrian statue was set up before the rostra, with the inscription: "Lucius Sulla, the ever fortunate." He assumed all the prerogatives of a monarch. Twenty-four axes were borne in front of him, the same number which were borne before the ancient kings. He permitted the Senate to grant him full powers to restore the Republic, which he had destroyed so completely that it never rose again. Even in the days when he was counting the heads displayed on the Forum— altogether 4,700 people were killed during the proscriptions following the capture of Rome—he showed by his behaviour that he was faintly amused by his own fortune, and he could recognize the good fortune of others.

Pompey (Gnaeus Pompeius), a brilliant cavalry officer, had joined forces with Sulla after his return from Greece. He was only twenty-two years old, as charming and popular as his father had been hateful and hated. He had great physical beauty, soft languid eyes, an athletic body skilled at running, leaping, riding and fencing. Sulla marked him out as a man to be watched, and always rose in his presence, though he rose to no one else. To Pompey went the African command, and at the end of a forty-day war against the Marians in Numidia, he amused himself by going on a big-game hunt after elephants. Then he sailed for Rome, and immediately demanded a triumph. Sulla pointed out reasonably that triumphs were awarded only to consuls and praetors—even the elder Scipio had not demanded a triumph after destroying the Carthaginians in Spain. As for Pompey, still a beardless youth, too young to be a senator, how could he demand a triumph? So Sulla argued with him gently, pointing out the error of his ways, until Pompey exclaimed: "More people worship the rising than the setting sun!" Sulla either did not hear, or pretended not to hear, yet he observed the amazement on the faces of those who were gathered around, and asked for the words to be repeated. He was astounded when Pompey repeated the insolent boast, but he had already granted to Pompey a title granted to no Roman before —he was Pompey the Great—and he could not refuse a man who was so obviously fated to accomplish great deeds. So he said twice: "Let him triumph!" and he seems to have spent the next few minutes discussing with Pompey the advisability of having the triumphal chariot yoked to elephants.

Pompey, with the brashness of youth, was determined to enjoy such a triumph as had never been seen before. He was the youngest of *triumphatores*, and he saw himself as the destined successor of Sulla. These were reasons enough for abandoning the ancient traditions. Unfortunately the gates of the city were too narrow to allow the elephants to pass, and he was forced to content himself with the customary four horses. At the last moment his soldiers complained that he had not given them a sufficiently large donation. He answered that he had not the least intention of flattering them, and if they insisted upon their absurd demand he would cheerfully surrender the honour of a triumph.

Pompey was a man without complexities, simple, lucid, with a talent for winning victories on the field and no particular talent for statesmanship; and Sulla came to regret the impulsive homage he paid to the young general, for Pompey's name was omitted from his will. But Sulla was rapidly ageing and growing increasingly indifferent to affairs of state. He was, says Appian, "weary of war, weary of power, weary of Rome". Suddenly at the beginning of 79 B.C., to the consternation of everyone, he abdicated and became a common citizen, dismissing his bodyguard and the lictors who had borne twenty-four axes in front of him since he became dictator. He retired to the quiet of his estate at Cumae, spending his days fishing, hunting, talking with friends and writing his memoirs. He died in the following year, apparently of cancer of the bowels brought on by his vices. Almost to the very last he was the aristocratic voluptuary.

When he died, his sins were forgiven, and his body was borne through Italy with royal splendour. He was carried on a golden bier, preceded by horsemen and trumpeters, with his battle-flags and the twenty-four axes going before him. The senators themselves lifted the bier and carried it to the Campus Martius. The knights carried golden standards and silver shields, and the trumpeters played dirges, and then there was a solemn leave-taking. To keep the body fresh the women of Rome provided immense quantities of spices: there was enough left over to make a large statue of the dictator in frankincense and cinnamon. Then, though he had given instructions that his body should be buried, he was burned, while the army marched past in the light of the flames.

Long ago Sulla had explained his system of government in a parable. "A husbandman," he said, "was bitten by fleas when he was ploughing. Twice he stopped ploughing to shake them out of his shirt. When they bit him again he burned the shirt, to prevent them from interrupting his work. You, who have felt my hand twice, take warning lest the third time you feel the fire!" It was a savage philosophy, with nothing to commend it except its simplicity, but it showed the way the wind was blowing. If Marius resembled Romulus, Sulla resembled the Tarquins; and soon the Republic would die and give place to a long succession of kings.

Anyone who lived through those years could compliment himself on his powers of survival. They were evil times, attended by evil omens. A mule foaled. A woman gave birth to a snake. There was an earthquake, and many temples collapsed mysteriously. The most terrifying portent of all was the fire that broke out in the Temple of Jupiter Capitolinus in the year of Sulla's return from Greece. No one ever discovered the cause of the fire. Sulla ordered the temple rebuilt on the lines of the former temple, though with much greater splendour of detail, and almost his last act before his death was to arrange for a contribution to the building fund. For the old statue of Jupiter made out of captured Samnite armour, he substituted a statue in gold and ivory on the model of Olympian Zeus, a sign, if any were needed, that Greek influence was dominant. Sulla did not live to see the completion of the new temple, which was finally consecrated in 69 B.C. by Catulus. The old temple had been burned to the foundations, and all its treasures including the Sibylline books were destroyed. The new temple proclaimed the coming of a new era.

For a few more years the Republic continued its halting existence, haunted by the ghosts of Marius and Sulla. Inevitably there would be a continuing dictatorship; inevitably the ancient forms would be found wanting. It was a time of wars and civil wars. The Roman general Sertorius had transformed Spain into his private preserve; Mithridates was renewing his conquests in the east; the Cretans were in revolt; pirates infested the seas; there were slave uprisings which threatened to become general uprisings, bringing about the downfall of Rome. Sulla had left behind him four good generals. They were Metellus, Lucullus, Pompey and Crassus. Altogether these four generals celebrated seven triumphs, and in the single year 71 B.C. all of then enjoyed triumphs.

Of the four generals Metellus was the oldest, a corpulent, amiable man given to luxurious habits, but without guile. Sent to Spain to put down the rebellion of Sertorius, he proved ineffective and two years later he was still calling for reinforcements. Pompey disliked him, and brought an army to Spain, hoping to win a quick victory over the Spanish rebels who were being commanded by a general of quite astonishing brilliance. He fought a pitched battle with Sertorius near the Sucro River, and would have been defeated if the army of Metellus had not come to his rescue. Sertorius was defeated. "If the old woman (Metellus) had not come just in time," Sertorius complained bitterly, "I would have whipped that young stripling back to Rome." Despite his real brilliance in the field Sertorius was not proof against traitors in his own ranks. He was murdered in 72 B.C. by Perpenna, one of his generals. Sertorius had been enjoying constant communication with Rome and the traitor came to Pompey with letters purporting to document the alliance between Sertorius and powerful forces in Rome. Characteristically Pompey tore the letters up without glancing at them, and ordered the death of Perpenna.

Metellus returned to Rome to enjoy a triumph he only barely deserved, while Pompey remained in Spain for a few more months putting down the last flickers of rebellion. It so happened that his return to Italy coincided with the last stages of the Spartacist revolt which Crassus was putting down. Crassus was well-born and wealthy, a good part of his wealth coming from his friendship with Sulla, who permitted him to buy up in a glutted market the houses and possessions of the men on the proscription lists. He was wily, avaricious and totally corrupt without possessing any vices; and he had a natural genius for organization. He organized the war against

Spartacus with almost terrifying efficiency, bringing against the rebels all the resources which a civilized state can command.

Spartacus had been a Roman soldier, but being reduced to slavery, he became a gladiator. He led the revolt of a small group of gladiators who escaped from Capua to Mount Vesuvius, where they were joined by great numbers of slaves. Thracian by birth, Spartacus had hoped to lead his forces to the security of Thrace, but his undisciplined *banditti* could not tolerate the thought of leaving Italy unplundered, and valuable months were lost in skirmishes. At last by sheer force of character Spartacus succeeded in welding together an army which at one time numbered 120,000 men. Six legions were raised to fight them, but it was not until Crassus took the field that they felt the full weight of Roman arms. Crassus destroyed their army, and the remnants were rounded up by Pompey, who appeared providentially to win an easy victory over men who were already in full flight. Six thousand slaves were captured and crucified along the road from Capua to Rome.

There was little honour in the Spanish victories, and less in the victory over the Spartacists, for treachery played a part in both. Lucullus, too, won a triumph that year for a victory over the Bessi, a Thracian tribe. It seems to have been an unimportant frontier campaign. Not one of the four triumphs of 71 B.C. were of any great importance, but three of the *triumphatores* were to go on to accomplish great victories. One dedicated himself to a life of fabulous luxury, two died miserably on foreign soil, but not before they had demonstrated the Roman power in the furthest reaches of the east.

Lucullus had been Sulla's chief of staff, a brilliant tactician, a man of extraordinary charm and persuasiveness. In 74 B.C. he received the conduct of the war against Mithridates, and for eight years of arduous campaigning he carried the offensive against the east. He succeeded in trapping the gigantic army of Mithridates beneath the walls of Cyzicus, and the king is said to have lost 200,000 soldiers to famine, disease and Roman arms before he fled with the remnants of his army by sea. In the decisive battle of Cabira in 72 B.C. the Roman cavalry scattered the entire Pontic army. Lucullus went on to cross the Euphrates and marched against Tigranocerta, the capital of Tigranes, king of Armenia. He reached the city on October 6, 69 B.C., the anniversary of the disaster at Arausio. Lucullus was reminded that this was a black day, one on which no battle should be fought. "Then I shall engage the enemy," he replied, "and I will make it a good day." After the battle Lucullus announced his own losses: five men killed, 100 wounded. He reported the enemy dead as: 100,000 infantry, and almost their entire cavalry. It is just possible that he was telling the truth.

In the summer of 68 B.C. Lucullus went on to attack the Armenian capital at Artaxata, but his march was delayed by continual skirmishes and interrupted by fierce snowstorms. He wintered at Nisibis, and there learned that the small detachments left in Tigranocerta and Pontus had been destroyed. There was nothing to be done but to turn westward, for his soldiers were now weary of marching and countermarching throughout Asia. His enemies in Rome were not idle. There were speeches in the Senate asking why he was perpetuating the Asian wars, and why his soldiers were wearing out their lives guarding his carriages and camels, laden with gold and precious goblets. At last he was recalled, and his command was given to Pompey, but he was permitted to enjoy a triumph.

The triumph of Lucullus consisted of a careful and elaborate display of treasure such as the Romans had rarely seen. The customary great procession of soldiers was omitted, for Pompey had allowed him to return with only 1,600 soldiers of his private guard. Plutarch says there were only a few horsemen in full armour, ten chariots armed with scythes, and about sixty of Mithridates' officers and relatives. The rest of the triumph was given over to the spoils —110 beaks of ships, a gold statue of Mithridates six feet high, a shield set with precious stones, twenty loads of silver vessels, and thirty-two loads of golden cups, armour and money, all carried by men. The most imposing treasure was carried on the backs of mules —golden couches, ingots of silver, nearly three million pieces of silver coin. Afterwards he feasted the city and all the villages around.

After his triumph his character changed. The stern and gentle soldier became a sybarite, superintending his own extravagance so extravagantly that he sometimes forgot in which of his many palaces he was staying. He possessed 200 purple mantles, ate from plate adorned with jewels, and cultivated his palate by tasting all the rarest and most costly foods. At the same time he built a famous library, which he threw open to any Greeks who cared to visit it, and gave splendidly to charity. When he died, he was remembered as an elder statesman who had surrendered all his ambitions to the task of living luxuriously and quietly, harming no one, giving advice to all who asked for it. Suddenly he became popular, and the people flocked around his body, saying he deserved to be buried in the Campus Martius like the ancient kings. Perhaps they remembered that he had conquered two kings in battle and therefore deserved a royal burial, but it is more likely that they remembered his regal presence and the regal luxury of his later years.

While Lucullus faded into opulent obscurity, Pompey went from triumph to triumph. First he swept the Mediterranean clear of pirates, while a certain Metellus of the great family of Caecilii Metelli was attacking the pirate stronghold at Cnossos in Crete. Inevitably there was friction between the two commanders. Pompey ordered Metellus to withdraw, and when this demand was refused, he landed his own troops on the island, and for a few days there was a confused civil war fought between the armies of the two commanders. Pompey seems to have realized that he was acting highhandedly, and pursuing a course of action that would bring him little credit in Rome. Finally he withdrew; Metellus went on to conquer the whole of Crete, and was granted a triumph and the title of Creticus. Florus tells us that it was a miserable triumph, shorn of all splendour; Pompey had used his influence to prevent the Cretan chieftains from appearing in the triumph.

This was Pompey at his worst, thirsting after the smallest triumphs, feverish for glory and determined to prevent others from achieving it. But once the quarrel with Metellus was concluded, he showed himself to be a bold and singularly venturesome general. Long ago he had promised himself the conquest of the east. It was due to his political manœuvres that Lucullus was recalled in the midst of his campaigns, his wars unfinished. Pompey assumed the *imperium*, regarding himself as captain-general of the east even before he set foot in Asia. In the spring of 66 B.C. he invaded Pontus, and on the frontiers of Armenia caught up with the army of Mithridates. On a dark night, before the moon rose, he launched his attack from the heights when the enemy was asleep. The enemy was thrown into confusion, and they were all the more confused when the moon rose at last, blinding them with its brilliance. That night the last levies which Mithridates led against Rome melted away, and the king himself was in full flight.

Pompey turned his attention on Armenia, but rumours of the massacre at the frontier had gone before him, and Tigranes, king of Armenia, decided to throw himself upon the mercy of the conqueror. Near Artaxata he rode up to Pompey's camp and would have ridden up to the general's tent if a lictor had not reminded him that it was permitted to no one to enter a Roman camp on horseback. So Tigranes went humbly on foot, and threw himself down before Pompey's tribunal and placed his diadem in Pompey's hands. It was an astonishing moment: for no other eastern prince had ever humbled himself in such a way before a Roman general.

Pompey permitted Tigranes to retain his kingdom on payment of 6,000 talents. Then he returned to Pontus to receive the submission of Mithridates' governors and to take possession of the royal treasury. He might have returned to Rome to enjoy a triumph, but Syria and Judaea beckoned. Syria became a Roman province, and the legions marched into Judaea, to take Jerusalem by storm. About this time there came news that the seventy-three-year-old Mithridates, the greatest and wisest of the Pontic kings, had taken poison, and when the poison failed to do its work, he committed himself to the mercy of a Gallic chieftain, who stabbed him to death. His last words were a pathetic request to be killed quickly to avoid the disgrace of being led in triumph.

Pompey had tasted victory; he was at his best when he was victorious. When he entered Jerusalem, he went straight to the Holy of Holies, but removed none of the sacred treasures. To the Jews he showed himself as a benevolent monarch, anxious not to show disrespect to their religion. Judaea became a Roman dependency under the rule of the high priests.

Pompey saw himself in those days as a new Alexander, and planned to march through Arabia to the Red Sea: a plan which Alexander had contemplated during the last days of his life. He had conquered Spain and looked out on the Atlantic; now he would conquer the entire east and look out upon the Indian Ocean. Suddenly he decided to return to Pontus, the scene of his earlier victories, to receive the submission of its prince, who sent presents and the embalmed body of Mithridates together with the Pontic regalia. He spent the winter in Ephesus, and nearly every day kings, princes and ambassadors came to wait upon him.

In Rome men feared his return, thinking he would march with his army to the city and appoint himself dictator. He surprised the Romans by dismissing his soldiers at Brundisium, telling them to appear at his triumph, but otherwise he asked nothing of them. He was flushed with victory, but curiously humble. With only a few friends, unarmed, he made his way to the capital. "It was as though," says Plutarch, "he were returning from a pleasure trip."

This triumph of Pompey exceeded in splendour any that had gone before. There were to be greater triumphs later, more imposing displays of captured treasure, more fearful evidence of ruined empires, but no one else ever returned to Rome with the proud boast that he had conquered the world, and led nearly 300 kings and princes in his triumphal procession to prove it.

This time there was no need to demand a triumph: it was offered gratefully by the Senate. Everyone was jubilant. As Pompey rode to Rome after leaving his army in Brundisium, he was met by successive processions, first of youths, then of citizens, finally of senators, who announced that they were "lost in wonder over his exploits, for no one had ever before vanquished so powerful an enemy and at the same time brought so many nations under subjection and extended the Roman rule to the Euphrates". As Pliny commented many years later, he had conquered Asia, but this was not so important as the fact that he had found Asia a remote province on the frontiers of the empire and made her a central dominion.

The triumph took place on September 28 and 29, 61 B.C. There was, of course, not enough time to display all the treasures brought back from the east, and only the most important ones were shown during the processions. Pliny records the inscription on one of the banners which was borne in procession on the opening day. It read:

> Pompey the Great, having rescued the seacoast from pirates and restored to the Roman people dominion of the seas, now celebrates a triumph over Asia, Pontus, Armenia, Paphlagonia, Cappadocia, Cilicia, Syria, Scythia, Judaea, Albania, Iberia, Crete and the land of the Basternae, and he has won victories over King Mithridates and King Tigranes.[1]
>
> (*Natural History*, VII, xxvi.)

There were other banners listing the treasure acquired from the captured cities, and still more which listed ships, cities and kings in haphazard order, as though in such a triumph it had become impossible to evaluate the dazzling tokens of victory. The historian Arrian recorded the inscription on one of the banners:

> Ships with brazen beaks captured: 800
> Cities founded in Cappadocia: 8
> Cities founded in Cilicia and Coele-Syria: 20
> Cities founded in Palestine: Seleucis.

> Kings captured: Tigranes the Armenian, Artoces the Iberian, Oroezes the Albanian, Darius the Mede, Aretas the Nabatean, Antiochus of Commagene.

This list represents only a part of the spoils: there were many more kings, and many more captured cities. Altogether Pompey claimed to have founded thirty-nine cities and to have captured 900 towns. But to the eyes of the Romans these claims were of small moment compared with the heaped gold, silver and jewels shown

---

[1] To this list Plutarch adds, Media, Colchis, Mesopotamia, Phoenicia, Palestine and Arabia.

in the treasure-carts, and perhaps even these were less intimidating than the banner which proclaimed that "Pompey the Great has triumphed over the world".

Displayed in the procession were the customary paintings depicting the chief events of his campaigns. There were paintings of Tigranes and Mithridates, and many paintings depicting the Mithridatic war, culminating in the king's flight by night and his death. There was a solid gold bust of King Mithridates eight cubits high, and another of King Eupator of the same dimensions. There was a bust of Pompey made entirely of pearls. There was a fantastic number of two-horsed carriages filled with captured weapons and the beaks of ships, and the ornaments of the triumph included the throne and sceptre of Mithridates and the couch of Darius, the King of Kings. Pompey himself rode in a chariot studded with gems and wore around his shoulders a cloak which he claimed to be the cloak of Alexander the Great, though Arrian doubted whether Alexander's cloak could have lasted over so many years.

More than 300 important prisoners, many of them kings and princes, walked in front of Pompey's chariot, and it was accounted in Pompey's favour that he ordered none of them to be chained. Among them was Aristobulus, the king of the Jews, and the wife, five sons and two daughters of Mithridates. All wore their national costume. None were executed, and all except two, Tigranes and Aristobulus, were set free afterwards, given costly presents and allowed to return home. Tigranes and Aristobulus appear to have been executed at a later date.

Inevitably special honours were paid to Pompey. He was permitted to wear the laurel wreath of the *triumphator* at the public games and to wear the robe of the *triumphator* at horse races. But he seems to have despised these outward manifestations of power and long afterwards it was remembered against him that he had divested himself of his military apparel and all marks of rank immediately after the triumph. Velleius Paterculus records that he was authorized by the tribunes to wear his golden crown and the full dress of the *triumphator* at the games, and to wear the crown and the purple-bordered toga at the theatre, and he refused both offers. The Romans regarded such refusals as acts of impropriety, and according to Cicero "his popularity was doffed with his raiment".

For many more years Pompey was to dominate the Roman stage, but never again did he receive the fierce affection of the Roman people. There were many reasons for this change. He was proud and sometimes overbearing; he had conquered the world and enjoyed three triumphs, and he despised the lesser efforts of lesser men. The whole economy of Rome had been changed by the triumph. He had brought 20,000 talents into the treasury, and raised the national revenue from 200 million sesterces to nearly 300 million, with disastrous effects on the money-market. Two years later, in July 59 B.C., at the games held in honour of Apollo the actor Diphilus said of him: "By our misfortunes thou art great—*Nostra miseria tu es magnus.*" It is just possible that Pompey was aware of the truth behind the allegation.

With understandable exaggeration Pliny spoke of Pompey's triumphs as equalling the brilliance of those of Alexander the Great, Dionysus and Hercules. No one had ever conquered in so many lands, or brought so much treasure to Rome, or shown so much indifference to glory once he was in power. He was not blinded by his own brilliance so much as terrified by it. In Asia his mind moved like quicksilver, for there was no one strong enough to oppose him, but in Rome he was at the mercy of every clique, and strangely hesitant. He saw himself as another Pericles, employing the influence he had won as a soldier to dominate the Roman scene, but his temper ruled against compliance with the mob and the senators distrusted him. Within twelve months of his triumph he stood almost alone, the victim of his own victories.

He may have known even in those early days that his star was falling. The rising star was a young red-headed orator, who at the age of twenty had won a civic crown for saving a soldier's life at Mytilene and whose chief claim to fame was his ability to borrow money and spend enormous sums on public games to increase his own popularity. He was lean as a hawk, and very charming in his cold impersonal way. He was a nephew of Marius, and once Sulla was seen to look fixedly at the boy and say: "I see many Mariuses in that child." Caius Julius Caesar was to be more murderous and more destructive than Marius had ever been.

7

THE TRIUMPHS OF CAESAR

IN THE summer of 61 B.C. Julius Caesar seemed to have exhausted all his hopes of advancement. He was thirty-nine, tall and slender, with a long thin face and dark piercing eyes, graceful and white-skinned, with something feminine in his appearance, in his mannered speech and careful ease. Brilliant and indolent, he had climbed all the rungs of the ladder: he had been military tribune, magistrate, judge, commissioner of buildings: finally by out-bribing all other candidates he had received the appointment of Pontifex Maximus. He was a man on whom there had fallen the shadow of many scandals, and he was heavily in debt—his debts amounted to the incredible sum of 830 talents, representing nearly £350,000. Part of this money had been spent in bribing high officials to appoint him governor of Further Spain. He was long past the age reached by Alexander when he was conquering the world.

That summer, as he prepared to travel overland to Spain, a change came over him. He, who once rode in a litter even when making the shortest journey, now rode on horseback. He, who once felt ill at ease except in the most delicate costumes, took to wearing the heavy bronze cuirass of a soldier. He, who liked polite society and intrigues, the company of beautiful women, all the formal and exquisite luxuries of Rome, now set his heart against them. Deliberately and methodically he was training himself for leadership, hardening his fleshy body, submitting himself to a course of rigorous apprenticeship to war. He had never commanded an army. He had never possessed real power. Now at last in middle age he was determined to set out on the path of conquest.

The pattern of his subsequent victories was revealed in those first Spanish campaigns. He fought strenuously, ruthlessly, with a cold intellectualism, driving his men hard and completing in a few weeks the subjugation of the tribes. He placed the Spanish banker, Lucius Cornelius Balbus, in charge of his supply trains. He fought close to his soldiers, and seemed completely careless of danger, and was never happier than when leading a forced march over impassable territory. He destroyed the Lusitanians, captured their treasure, and was able to pay off a good part of his debts. Then he returned to Rome to enjoy a triumph.

According to the law a returning general must remain outside the city walls to await the approval of the Senate for a triumph. Caesar had powerful friends in Rome, who wanted him to stand for the consulship, but a prospective candidate for the consulship had to attend meetings of the Senate and make himself available to the senators. He was in a quandary. He asked whether he might be elected by proxy, but this was refused, largely at the pleading of the younger Cato. He decided to gamble on the consulship and abandon the triumph. Dion Cassius says he abandoned it because he foresaw that as consul "he would be able to distinguish himself by even more numerous and memorable feats enabling him to obtain an even more brilliant triumph". His friends in Rome had done their work well, and he received the consulship.

For Caesar the consulship was only the stepping-stone to the great command which awaited him at the conclusion of his term of office. It was arranged that he should assume the governorship of Cisalpine Gaul and the command of the three legions stationed there; and since no troops could legally be stationed in Italy, the commander of these legions was in a position to dominate Rome. To further his own power, Caesar married his daughter Julia to Pompey, and when he left for the north the consuls were his own father-in-law Lucius Piso and Aulus Gabinius, a close associate of Pompey. Pompey and Caesar together would rule the Romans and all their colonies.

For nine years Caesar carved out an empire for himself in Gaul. He was constantly on the march, constantly putting down rebellions and extending the Roman dominions. A succession of savage campaigns demonstrated his talent for massacre. The poet Lucan speaks of him as "furious for war"—*in arma furens*—and impatient to cut bloody swathes through the enemy. "He would rather burst open the city gates than have them opened for him," says Lucan. "He preferred to ravage the land with fire and sword than to receive the farmer's permission to cross it peacefully. He detested an unguarded road, or to parade like a peaceful citizen." When Gaul and all its vast wealth fell to him, he invaded Britain, apparently in the hope of gathering a great treasure of British pearls, supposed to be especially valuable. He did obtain enough pearls to cover a breastplate, which he dedicated to Venus Genetrix, but his two brief explorations of Britain were of doubtful value: many years were to pass before the British were finally subdued.

Travelling continually, now wading across the Thames, now arranging a treaty of peace with obscure German tribes, Caesar was still, with Pompey, the ruler of Rome. His power rose from the possession of great armies scattered from the Rhine to the Pyrenees, and he had no illusions about the employment of these forces for his own advancement. Rome was astonished to learn that there was an entire legion of Gauls, wearing feathers in their helmets. He knew already that the ultimate power was in his hands, although following a meeting at Luca in 56 B.C. he claimed to share it with Pompey and Crassus, his old protector.

Crassus was the weakest link: affable, shrewd, a born intriguer, permanently dazzled by the brilliance of Caesar. He was almost sixty when he set out for the east to take up the *imperium*. He talked hopefully of the exploits he was about to perform, and ridiculed the conquests of Lucullus and Pompey. He spoke of subduing the Bactrians and the Indians and advancing like another Alexander to the ocean which lies beyond India, but his departure was ill-starred. When Aemilius Paulus set out against King Perseus, vast crowds accompanied him to the gates of Rome, and so it was with nearly all the other generals who set out for the east. But only a few friends bade Crassus farewell, and the tribune Ateius, who detested him for his avarice, publicly called down a curse upon him, consigning him to Hades.

Crassus was fifty-eight when he set out to conquer the east. One day his hands shook at the sacrifice and he dropped part of the offerings. He smiled and said: "Behold the infirmities of age!" It is doubtful whether the joke amused the soldiers who were compelled to follow him into Mesopotamia. Repeatedly he was warned against advancing into unknown territory; the omens were inauspicious; the soldiers complained at the heat, and were close to rebellion. The Parthians had spies everywhere. Suddenly they sprang at him. With banners waving silk and gold, the sweeping clouds of Parthian cavalry appeared; suddenly they tossed their cloaks away and revealed themselves in brilliant armour. Crassus ordered a charge, but the Parthian cavalry wheeled to avoid the brunt of it, and then attacked the frightened legionaries at their leisure. It amused them to aim at the feet of the Romans, who found themselves transfixed to the ground, and at their hands, which they nailed to the shields. In despair Crassus fled to the fort of Carrhae, but the Parthians followed him and demanded a parley. His soldiers were cowardly and hoped he would sue for terms, and so with a small staff Crassus set out to meet the Parthian general Surenas, who received him with honour and presented him with a sumptuously caparisoned horse. The feeble and bewildered old man was abruptly lifted on the saddle, while the grooms began thwacking the horse, urging it in the direction of the Parthian lines. Crassus realized too late that he was being tricked. One of his officers ran forward and killed the groom, and then they were all fighting. In the mêlée Crassus was killed, and a little later his head and right hand were sent as a present to Orodes, King of Armenia, who would have preferred to celebrate a triumph over a living Roman.

Having defeated Crassus, Surenas celebrated a triumph. It was a mockery of the Roman triumph. Caius Paccianus, a Roman prisoner who closely resembled Crassus, was made to wear female dress, set on horseback, and ordered to answer only to the name of Crassus or to the title of *imperator*. In front of him, on camel-back, rode trumpeters and lictors whose *fasces* were transformed into trophies with sacks of captured coins hanging on the staves and the still-bleeding heads of Romans transfixed on the points of the axes. Afterwards came the Seleucian camp-followers singing scurrilous songs about the effeminacy and cowardice of the defeated general, who was well-known for his unusually strict moral behaviour and who was never remarkable for his cowardice. Unwittingly the richest of Romans had brought a disastrous defeat to Roman arms.

Never before or since was there such a massive mockery of the triumph.

The Romans were stunned by the defeat at Carrhae, but for the moment there was very little they could do to retrieve their honour in the east. Pressing matters in Italy engaged their attention. The duumvirs were at loggerheads, each of them hoping to seize supreme power: Pompey in Rome, Caesar in Ravenna, were assuming the postures of wrestlers, each about to hurl the other to the ground, perfectly aware that the sound of a fall would shake the world. Both were sick men: Caesar suffered from epilepsy, Pompey from strange bouts of nervous exhaustion which left him incapacitated for months on end. One had conquered Spain, the Mediterranean and the east, the other had conquered Gaul. Neither had any love for the other. "With all their demonstrations of affection, their declarations of a firm alliance," wrote Cicero, "I am sure it will end in open warfare." A few months later Cicero returned from his governorship of Cilicia, and the world was presented with the strange spectacle of a brilliant orator spending his days wearily moving from one villa outside Rome to another, because a triumph could not be granted to one who had entered the city, and of all human rewards this was the one he wanted most. Meanwhile the Romans held their breaths. The two giants were preparing to tear at each other's throats.

At dawn on January 12, 49 B.C. Caesar crossed the flooded Rubicon. Pompey had boasted: "Wherever I strike the earth of Italy with my foot, legions will come forth!" From the beginning Caesar had the advantages of speed, position and numbers. He marched against Brundisium where Pompey and the consuls had taken refuge, intending to sail for Epirus; and when Pompey crossed the Ionian Sea with his fleet, Caesar followed him. At the battle of Pharsalia in Thessaly, the flower of the young Roman aristocracy, which had followed Pompey, was decisively defeated; over a hundred military standards were captured; and Pompey fled. Appian gives a hair-raising account of how the opposing armies, after invoking the gods and sounding their trumpets, marched towards each other "in stupor and deepest silence". It was as though they knew from the beginning that the destiny of the world would be decided on this obscure plain in Greece.

Caesar had won the east. In this single battle, fought against great odds, he had ensured for himself the place which Pompey had once occupied in the imaginations of the Romans. With Pompey dead—he was murdered while coming to shore in Egypt by one of his own centurions—there remained for Caesar only a leisurely mopping-up campaign. Reaching Egypt, he destroyed the army of Ptolemy and killed Achillas, who had plotted the death of Pompey. He marched into Pontus and destroyed the army of Pharnaces, the son of Mithridates the Great, four hours after sighting it. In North Africa Scipio and Cato, aided by King Juba of Numidia, hoped to rally all Africa to the lost cause of Pompey; but the war was already over when Caesar marched against them.

While Caesar was still in Africa, the Senate decreed thanksgivings in his honour lasting forty days, and went on to implore him to accept every honour they could think of. They begged him to ride in a triumphal chariot led by four white horses, reminding him that white horses had drawn the chariot of Camillus. Another decree doubled the number of his attendant lictors, and still another appointed him censor for a period of three years. He was appointed dictator for a period of ten years with absolute power over the legal machinery of the state and over the army.

The senators amused themselves by adding smaller honours to greater. Caesar was empowered to open the games at the circus. When legislative matters were discussed, Caesar was permitted to express his views before anyone else. His image in ivory was to be borne in procession among the images of the gods and set up in the

Temple of Jupiter Capitolinus opposite the seat of Jupiter himself, and elsewhere a bronze statue was to be erected to him, showing him standing on a terrestrial globe, and bearing the inscription *Caesar the demi-god*. According to Dion Cassius many more honours were granted to him, but since he refused many of them the historian contented himself with relating only those which the conqueror accepted as worthy of his position.

Returning to Rome, Caesar showed himself master of the situation. He addressed the Senate with disarming gentleness, praising them for their good deeds during his absence and assuring them that he had no intention of punishing them and he begged them to put aside all thoughts that he would employ the army against them. On the contrary they were to regard the army as guardians of their authority: henceforth the army would be the obedient servant of Caesar and of the Senate. He raised the subject of the immense riches he had acquired by forced contributions to his treasury during his campaigns, and he swore that he had kept none of this money for his own use. He explained that some of the money had been spent on the war, but much of it was reserved for the use of the senators, who could distribute it as they pleased either for the adornment of the city or to pay the costs of the administration. There would be no levy on the rich, and no new taxes. "I have no intention of causing any hardship," he declared. "We have sufficient income from present taxes, and therefore it is my purpose to be rich *with* you rather than to deprive anyone of his possessions."

The voice of the cooing dove was later heard in the Forum, where Caesar addressed the people, promising them everything they asked for, invoking the gods to witness that he was a man of peace whose only fault was that he cared too much for the safety of the Romans. But something in his manner suggested that he had other purposes in mind, and when the speech was over it was observed that the people were still restless and ill-at-ease, wondering what enormity would be committed upon them. Caesar enjoyed the spectacle of blood and they asked themselves whether they were to be the next victims of his insatiable love of conquest.

When the speeches were over, Caesar set about preparing his triumphs. He permitted himself four triumphs: *ex Gallia, ex Aegypto, ex Ponto* and *ex Africa*. To these triumphs he devoted the same careful attention to detail which characterized his campaigns. To make a more striking impression he arranged that the triumphs should follow one another at intervals of a few days. He established his headquarters near the Villa Publica, and there he lived while waiting for the inevitable day when, having enjoyed his triumphs, the Senate would solemnly invite him to take up residence within the city. Here he assembled all the treasures and spoils from the conquered countries, and here the joiners and carpenters set to work to provide the innumerable carts, show cases and wheeled platforms which would display his trophies to their best advantage. He paid particular attention to the design and workmanship of these vehicles, and ordered that different materials be used in each triumph. The carts were inlaid with citron wood for the Gallic triumph, with tortoise-shell for the Egyptian triumph, with acanthus wood for the Pontic triumph, and with ivory for the African triumph. There were statues representing the rivers crossed by his armies, and vast canvases showing episodes from his campaigns were paraded through the streets. The most prominent prisoners were released from their cells and loaded with the chains they would wear during the processions. Among them were Princess Arsinoë, the sister of Cleopatra, and Vercingetorix, the half-forgotten Gallic chieftain who had surrendered to Caesar six years before at Alesia. With them was the boy-king, Juba II, who had reached Rome only a few days before.

The first triumph took place towards the end of June in the blazing heat of a Roman summer. Since the previous day the gates of the temples were thrown open, and all night the blue smoke of incense rose from the altars. Garlands hung on all the houses and public buildings. Crowds spent the night taking up positions in the streets or fighting for places in the huge Circus Flaminius, through which the triumphal procession would pass. Visitors were streaming in from all parts of Italy, attracted by the prospect of enjoying the feasts and games which Caesar had promised.

At dawn all the participants in the drama were assembled on the Campus Martius. The order of the procession followed the prescribed pattern, with the senators and magistrates in front followed by the musicians playing the traditional music of the triumph. After the musicians came the spoils from the conquered cities of Gaul: gold and silver ingots, weapons, banners, crowns of gold and statues removed from Gallic temples with their places of origin indicated by enormous posters. A huge painting, sumptuously framed, represented the subjugation of Marseilles. There followed statues of the Rhine, the Rhône and the Ocean in chains, carved out of pure gold to signify Caesar's expedition against Britain. After the statues came the white bulls with gilded horns destined for the sacrifice followed by Vercingetorix at the head of a group of Gallic chieftains. Seventy-two lictors, an unprecedented number, escorted Caesar, who wore a purple toga and a laurel

PROCESSIONAL TRIUMPH AT THE TIME OF AUGUSTUS

wreath. He carried a branch of laurel in one hand and a sceptre topped with a gold eagle in the other, and his face was painted the colour of blood. He showed no emotion. Expressionless, staring straight ahead, he seemed to be rapt in the contemplation of his own divinity; and he seems not to have heard the scurrilous songs sung by the mobs lining the street, by the soldiers who marched behind him and by the actors who ran beside his chariot and fearlessly taunted him. One of the songs referred to his youthful love affair with the handsome young Nicomedes IV, King of Bithynia, with whom, according to a widely believed legend, Caesar had played the female role, lying on a golden couch arrayed in purple. So they sang to the marching rhythm of the Roman legionaries:

> Caesar conquered Gaul, and Nicomedes Caesar.
> Look upon Caesar, conqueror of Gaul.
> But where is Nicomedes, conqueror of Caesar?

They sang another song to warn the Romans against the conqueror of so many wives:

> O citizens, watch well your wives:
>   We bring the bald lecher home.
> He made love to the women of Gaul
>   With money stolen from Rome.

There were many other songs, all of them malicious, but only once did he lose patience and stammer out an oath against the singers, who knew they were safe as long as he remained in his chariot. He could not descend and punish these evil-doers, as he had punished so many in the past. The chariot was his prison, and there would be no escape until he reached the Temple of Jupiter Capitolinus.

But in fact he did escape from the chariot long before he made the sacrifices. Though the chariot had been carefully overhauled and every precaution had been taken, it broke down at one of the most significant places of the processional journey. He was entering the Velabrum and passing the Temple of Fortune when he felt the floor of the chariot give way under him. There was a sudden jolt, he lost his balance and fell to the ground. He was unhurt, but angry; and the procession came to a halt while he inspected the damage. He saw that the axle-tree was broken and the chariot could no longer be used. Messengers were accordingly sent to obtain another chariot, while Caesar fumed, knowing that the story would soon be spread all over Rome and in a few days would have reached the furthest boundaries of the empire. Previously he had always known how to deal with similar emergencies. When he stumbled and fell on the shores of Africa, it was remembered that he exclaimed quickly: "I hold thee in my embrace, O Africa!" But no witticism came to his lips as he surveyed the damaged chariot, and when at last the new chariot was brought up, it was observed that he recited a charm before entering it, and for the rest of his life he recited charms before stepping on to any vehicle whatsoever and even when he rode on horseback.

The procession continued across the Forum, passing the place where in a few months a temple would be erected on the site where his body was put to the flames by a howling Roman mob, with the Temple of Castor and Pollux on the left and the gleaming Basilica Aemilia on the right, until it reached the foot of the Capitoline hill, where two roads branched off, one leading to the great temple and the other to the Mamertine prison. Here Vercingetorix was led away to be strangled, or according to another account to die of slow starvation after being let down by a rope into the darker of the two underground cells. Caesar stepped down from the chariot, and those who were close by observed that something very strange was happening. He no longer wore the appearance of a triumphant conqueror, but of a penitent; and instead of mounting the steps proudly, like a god about to present himself to another god, he was on his knees. Stranger still, he began to shuffle on his knees up the steps, paying absolutely no regard to his own dignity, and when he reached the top he showed not a flicker of interest in the statue of himself erected there, though everyone expected that he would spend some minutes gazing upon it. Perhaps by his humble behaviour on the steps he hoped to avert the nemesis which was threatening him, but it is just possible that he crawled up the steps because he was overcome by that minor form of epilepsy from which he suffered throughout his life.

When he reached the Temple of Jupiter Capitolinus, Caesar laid his laurel branch in the lap of the god and sacrificed the white oxen. There were prayers and hymns, and a great feast was laid out, and afterwards the *triumphator* was escorted by singers and slaves bearing torches to his house in the city.

The second triumph celebrated his victory over Ptolemy and Egypt. This time there were no incidents, and everything took place according to schedule. Enormous framed paintings represented the ignominious deaths of Achillas, the general of the Egyptian forces, and Ponthinus, the Egyptian eunuch who had plotted against him. There was the inevitable statue of the Nile and a replica of the Pharos of Alexandria with imitation flames issuing from the top. Princess Arsinoë, loaded with chains, was made to walk in the procession at the head of the little group of Egyptian captives; and the Romans murmured over the fate of a young princess in her sorrow, and perhaps they murmured because they knew that Caesar had brought Cleopatra to Rome and was living with her, and it was Cleopatra who had insisted that her hated younger sister should form part of the triumphal procession. Arsinoë was about thirteen and had five more years to live, being put to death by Antony at the instigation of Cleopatra when Antony and Cleopatra were ruling over Egypt. Arsinoë was not the first foreign princess to walk in chains in a triumphal procession, for Pompey's triumph after the war against Mithridates had been graced with princesses, but "it was unheard of in Rome," wrote Dion Cassius, "that a woman, formerly treated as a queen, had to walk in chains".

Caesar enjoyed his second triumph. Except for the murmurs which greeted the presence of Arsinoë, whom he had no intention of putting to death, everything went according to plan. There were wild shouts of applause at the sight of the paintings representing Achillas and Ponthinus, and for some reason no scurrilous verses were sung.

About a week later Caesar celebrated his third triumph over Pharnaces, King of Pontus, the son of the unfortunate Mithridates. An enormous panel represented the king running at the approach of Caesar's armies, and this was greeted with laughter. Among the show-pieces of the procession he displayed a banner bearing only three words, but these the most famous he had ever written— *Veni, vidi, vici*. They were the words of his report to Rome after the victory over Pharnaces' army. Suetonius hints that Caesar was superbly daring in allowing this banner to be shown, for hitherto all inscriptions shown during a triumph had referred to particular events in a war. These three words, floating above the procession, were almost sinister in their nudity and remorseless declaration of the conqueror's powers.

The fourth triumph over Africa presented delicate problems. He had triumphed over the armies of Scipio and Cato, allies of Pompey, in battles fought on African soil. Juba, king of Mauretania, had made common cause with the Pompeians and had been defeated in the least important skirmish of the campaign. Caesar therefore staged his African triumph largely in terms of his minor victories against Juba and the Mauretanians, but took care to introduce a number of significant panels showing the fate that befell the Pompeian generals. One panel showed Scipio slitting open his stomach before throwing himself into the sea. Another showed Cato tearing out his own entrails like a wild beast, and a third showed King Juba and the Pompeian general Petreius fighting a duel to the death in order to avoid execution at the hands of Caesar. These panels were intended as a warning to the Romans not to hope for any revival of Pompey's cause. Appian says the warning was effective, and Pompey's former supporters were heard to groan with fear and misery as the procession passed.

The five-year-old Juba II walked in the procession, wearing his chains proudly. He was not executed. He grew up to become one of the most learned of historians. He was about twenty years old when Augustus gave him Cleopatra Selene, the daughter of Antony and Cleopatra, for a wife, and then offered him the kingdom of Numidia. He died at the age of seventy, renowned for his scholarship and his wisdom as a ruler.

Caesar had reserved his most threatening gestures for his last triumph, but he was in no mood to carry his threats to a conclusion. On the night of his African triumph he entertained the Roman people at a tremendous banquet, perhaps the largest that has ever been given. Two-thirds of the population of Rome, amounting to 200,000 guests, sat at 22,000 tables set up in the public squares. The best wine and the best food were served. The feast lasted late into the night, and it came to an end only when Caesar, who had been dining with friends, was observed to be passing through the Forum Julium, which he had built and named after himself. He was lying in a litter, wearing slippers, with a wreath of flowers on his brow which was streaming with perspiration. Almost the entire populace of Rome rose to accompany him to his house, and the forty elephants which had taken part in the triumphal procession accompanied him. From their backs came the blinding illumination which lit his progress along the Via Sacra, for each elephant carried a huge flaming torch. That night the people of Rome, surfeited by the excitement of the triumph and the feast, slept soundly for the first time in many weeks.

Most of the Romans had feared the return of Caesar, but now they began to hope their fears were unjustified. Cicero, who had good reason to be afraid, wrote during the days when preparations were being made for the four-fold triumph: "We are all his slaves, but Caesar himself is the slave of circumstance. The truth is that he does not know what he is going to do." Cicero was wrong. Caesar knew exactly what he intended to do. He had decided for reasons best known to himself to rule justly and soberly, to heal the wounds of the empire and to enjoy a prolonged period of peace with only an occasional campaign to break the monotony.

Caesar's first task was to ensure the loyalty of the army. Accordingly he rewarded his legions with large donations. Each veteran received 24,000 sesterces, each centurion 40,000, while the military tribunes and the cavalry commanders received 80,000. Though the donations were unexpectedly large, the soldiers complained, saying that too much money had been spent on staging the triumphs and this money should have been spent for the veterans. Caesar feared rebellion in the ranks and decided to put an end to the complaints. He marched to the soldiers' barracks, and when one of the malcontents was pointed out to him, he ordered the man put to death on the spot. Two others were turned over to the jurisdiction of the pontiffs and according to Dion Cassius they were "slain in the sacrificial manner" by the *flamen* of Mars. Their heads were exhibited outside the temple of Mars, and there were no more complaints.

Caesar had promised the Romans a great series of memorable spectacles to follow the triumphs. The first spectacle was the solemn consecration of the Forum Julium, which he opened with great pomp even though the statue of Venus ordered from the celebrated sculptor Arcesilaos was unfinished: instead there was a clay model of Venus. Caesar attended the celebrations in the company of Cleopatra, whose image in pure gold—supreme homage paid to the Queen of Egypt by her triumphant lover—would soon look down on the Forum.

But this was only the beginning of an uninterrupted series of entertainments. For weeks on end the city enjoyed a perpetual holiday. The Forum was covered with immense silken veils to protect the people from the burning summer heat, and under these veils gladiators fought to the death, actors performed on travelling stages, and speeches were delivered in honour of the conqueror. For three days athletes wrestled in the Campus Martius. In the Circus Maximus, enlarged at both ends and provided with a water-filled ditch to protect the spectators, men and youths of equestrian rank presented a programme of chariot races and feats of horsemanship. An African big-game hunt was staged: it lasted five days and 400 lions took part. Fifty elephants were made to fight one another, and for the first time since its appearance in Caesar's triumph, the Roman people were presented with the amazing spectacle of a giraffe. There were sea-battles fought on specially constructed lakes between ships with two, three and four banks of oars. There were Pyrrhic dances executed by "the sons of the great families from Asia and Bithynia". Caesar could well afford these spectacles. In his triumphal processions, according to Arrian, he displayed 60,500 silver talents and 2,822 crowns of gold. The Roman holiday was being paid for out of the plunder of the conquered cities, the greater part of it coming from Alexandria.

While Caesar was still superintending the spectacles news came from his lieutenants in Spain that the Republicans were on the eve of an uprising under the son of Pompey. After only four months in Rome he marched into Spain, where he spent the winter in a bitter struggle against the rebels, who knew that no quarter would be shown to them and therefore fought with fanatic courage. At Munda, in the south of Spain, not far from Corduba, Caesar with 40,000 troops found himself confronting an army of nearly 80,000. There was a moment when his troops panicked, and the conqueror who had enjoyed four triumphs gave way to sudden terror at the thought of dying in this obscure corner of Spain. Weaponless, without shield, helmet or sword, he ran up to his men, screamed at them to fight, invoked all the gods, and ordered the fugitives back into their lines. The historian Florus says he had "the look of death on his face". Armed only with a shield borrowed from one of his attendants he led the charge against the enemy. Faced by this unexpected attack, the enemy lines wavered and soon they were in full flight. "It was," says Velleius Paterculus, "the most bloody and perilous battle of his career." To his companions-at-arms Caesar admitted: "Today I, who have so often fought for victory, fought for my life," and it was no more than the truth.

As usual Caesar showed no mercy. According to *De bello Hispaniensi* the young Pompey lost 33,000 men on the battlefield and most of the survivors who took refuge in Munda and Corduba were later put to death. When Caesar left Spain, there was no more Republican army, and Pompey himself was dead.

Once more the terrified senators vied with one another in heaping new honours upon him. He was proclaimed "Father of his country", and a statue was erected for him in the temple of Quirinus, bearing the inscription: *To the invincible god*. It was decreed that every temple of Rome and all the towns of the Republic should possess his statue. There were to be circus games and processions in which his image would be carried alongside that of Victory. Because Caesar had restored peace to the world, a new temple in his honour was to be built and called "the new Concord"; every year festivals would be held there in his honour. Another temple dedicated to Liberty would preserve the memory of Caesar as the great Liberator. The anniversaries of his birth and his victories were to become holidays. His person was declared sacrosanct and inviolable, and the senators swore to defend him at all

times with their lives. Nothing remained but to deify him, and
this was done. Caesar accepted these honours, even the honour of
deification, calmly, regally, as though he felt they were due to him,
and apparently he never suspected that the senators in their determination to rid themselves of him were secretly mocking him and
drawing him ever closer to disaster. By September Caesar, the divine
Julius, was preparing for his very earthly triumph. Once again he
employed the ruse he had employed so successfully in his triumph
celebrating the conquest of Africa. Spanish prisoners in chains
would appear in the procession, though the war he fought in
Spain was a civil war fought against the armies of young Pompey.
He promised that his fifth triumph would be as magnificent as any
of the others, and gave orders that the litters and carriages bearing
the spoils should be decorated with polished silver.

The Spanish triumph took place in October. Crowds of foreigners
had come to Rome, and Caesar arranged to have stage-plays
describing his victories performed in a multitude of languages, an
idea which commended itself to Augustus who imitated it in his
own triumphs. Once again Caesar supervised all details of the procession, only to discover that the people, like the senators, were
too frightened by the display of naked power to enjoy the spectacle.
One person was not afraid. The chariot was passing the benches
reserved for the people's tribunes, those high magistrates whose
persons were inviolate, when Caesar observed that one of them
failed to rise and salute him. Caesar was beside himself with anger.
He stopped the chariot, recognized the offender as Pontius Aquila,
and shouted: "O very powerful Tribune Aquila, is it your purpose
to take the Republic from me?" Aquila remained silent; the procession went on its way; and for days afterwards Caesar was heard
muttering, whenever anyone asked a favour of him: "Of course
you will first have to ask the permission of Pontius Aquila."

After the triumph came the feasts and the games, but the cooks
failed to produce the food expected of them and five days later
Caesar gave another and better feast for the people of Rome.
Stage-shows were given at the games, and Caesar insisted that
Decimus Laberius, the famous author of mimes, should perform
in one of his own pieces, though he was a member of the equestrian
order, had never acted on the stage, and was of an age—he was
over sixty—when he might be expected to enjoy his leisure.
Laberius dared not defy the command of the deified Julius, but
revenged himself by delivering a prologue in which he complained
bitterly over this new honour heaped on his bent shoulders. Why,
he asked, had this excessive good fortune (*fortuna immoderata*)

come to a man too old to enjoy it, with neither grace nor beauty to commend him? Ah, it would be better to have summoned me when I was younger and more supple, and therefore more easily bemused by the grandeur of the occasion and more likely to bend before Caesar. Now the years choke me, and I am no more than a tomb bearing only a name—*Sepulcri similis nihil nisi nomen retineo.*

But this was only the beginning of an astonishing performance in which all the resources of an old playwright's wit and passionate anger were focused on the figure of the dictator who sat in a special box and wore a crown adorned with rays. As the play unfolded the audience was rewarded with a whole series of improvisations on the theme of Caesar's rise to power and the Roman loss of liberty. The most crushing line of all crystallized in a single marmoreal sentence the terrible uncertainties of the time:

> *Necesse est multos timeat quem multi timent.*
> He must fear many whom so many fear.

When they heard these lines the audience turned like one man to watch Caesar. They saw him flush angrily, but soon there were more taunts, more ringing rebukes hidden within the text of the play. Caesar could nearly always master his anger, and though he refused to give Laberius the palm of victory, he paid him his fee, amounting to 500,000 sesterces. The palm of victory was awarded to a young and very beautiful Syrian actor who had often entertained Caesar privately.[1]

According to Plutarch, the fifth triumph alarmed the Romans more than any of the others. Caesar was celebrating his victory over the Romans. By celebrating his victory over the young Pompey he was celebrating the end of the Republic, which still existed in theory, though Caesar was dictator and might soon be king. Everyone was aware that dark and sinister forces were at work: and all the corruptions of autocracy were working upon the state. Trembling, they waited for "the night of the long knives".

In those last five months of his life Caesar had little time for revenge. Like Alexander on the eve of his death in Babylon, Caesar in Rome was toying with the thought of one last supreme campaign to crown his career and bring the whole world to his feet. Plutarch says there had occurred to him a strange and wonderful plan of leading his army against Persia and then along the shores of the Caspian Sea till he reached Scythia, returning in a great circle through what is now southern Russia into Germany and

[1] Macrobius, *Saturnalia*, II, 7. Macrobius draws a wonderfully rounded portrait of the old actor Laberius, and gives the complete text of the bitter prologue.

France, and so to Italy, when he would have completed "the circuit of his empire, bound on all sides by the ocean". To prepare for his invasion of Persia he sent his engineers to cut a canal through the isthmus of Corinth. That winter—it was the winter of 45 B.C.— he was perfectly serious about his determination to conquer the world, and at the same time he seems to have lost his joy in conquest.

He was ageing rapidly and suffered more and more from those brief attacks of epilepsy which always occurred when he least expected them. More honours were heaped on him: in honour of his birth the month Quinctilis was changed to July, and an additional college of the Luperci was established in his name. He was given a golden throne in the Senate and his image was carried in processions with the images of the gods. But the honour he coveted most was always a triumph, and there was reserved for him the rarest triumph of all, unlike any enjoyed before. He would enter Rome on horseback, wearing the royal purple toga and the high red boots of the ancient kings. He would come alone, with only a small escort, without prisoners or any pomp, a triumph in which Caesar would be divorced from his conquests, shining in his own undivided splendour. The divine Julius, wearing the robe of a king, would take triumphant possession of his royal city.

The occasion for the triumph arose during the last days of January when there took place the traditional Latin festival (*Feriae Latinae*) on the Alban Mount, sacred to the Latins from time immemorial. Here all the tribes of the Latin League congregated annually to sacrifice at the temple of Jupiter Latiaris, and here, too, conquering generals refused a triumph by the Senate were allowed to enjoy an *ovatio*. Caesar was called upon to attend the festival in his dual role of *pontifex maximus* and as dictator, but chose to appear in the garments of a dictator. He performed the sacrifices at the Alban Mount and rode back to Rome to enjoy the last of his triumphs. Never before him had any conqueror been allowed to ride on horseback into the city: even the great Marcellus had been compelled to enter Rome on foot. Crowds gathered in the streets and voices were heard hailing him as king. Caesar was pleased, until he heard the murmurs of the opposition party. "I am no king, but Caesar," he shouted, and there for a while the matter rested. Some of those who had hailed him as king were rounded up and imprisoned as disturbers of the public peace.

Caesar continued to toy with the thought of assuming the title and dignity of king. It was whispered that a mysterious passage in the Sibylline oracles meant that only a Rome ruled by a king would be able to defeat the Persians. At the festival of the Lupercalia in

February Mark Antony, running naked in the Forum, placed a laurel crown laced with the white ribbons of a diadem on Caesar's head; and Caesar had sense enough to throw the crown away. "I am no king," he said. "The only King of the Romans is Jupiter." He ordered the laurel crown carried to the Temple of Jupiter Capitolinus and hung there as a trophy, and commanded that there should be inserted in the records of the Republic the statement that on the fifteenth of February the Romans presented a diadem to Caesar, and he refused it.

The Republic was dying of loss of blood, of terror and perplexity and the weariness that came from so many wars; and Caesar too was dying. Dreaming of a world empire and preparing the greatest campaign he had ever undertaken, he sent sixteen legions across the Adriatic and chose the date, four days after the Ides of March, when he would join his army. He planned to leave Rome for at least two years. He seems to have known there was a conspiracy against his life, but when he was warned not to appear in public without his guards, he answered: "It is unlucky to keep watch all the time—only those who are afraid do it." So he went to his death as fearlessly as he had lived, believing in his star to the last.

Caesar's murder was attended by many ironies. The leader of the conspirators was Marcus Brutus, a former governor of Cisalpine Gaul and the foremost orator after Cicero of his time, a man widely believed to be Caesar's illegitimate son. Those who had murdered him had only a few months before sworn to defend his life. After the battle of Pharsalia the Romans had thrown down the statues of Pompey, and it was Caesar who ordered them restored. He was stabbed to death below Pompey's statue. For weeks there had been strange premonitions of disaster; soothsayers had whispered in his ear that he should behave cautiously; horses were seen to weep on the Rubicon; doors opened of their own accord. To all these warnings Caesar had answered with a smile of calm disbelief. Once he was asked: "Which death is best?" and he answered: "That which is least expected." And so it happened that he died at the foot of Pompey's statue on the eve of the expedition which would have made him emperor of the world.

One final triumph was reserved for him: a funeral more splendid than any known up to this time. Venus had been his guardian goddess, and so a temple of Venus made of pure gold was erected to house his funeral couch. All Rome came to the Forum to see him lying in state, red with the blood of his twenty-three wounds. While the Romans were debating whether to light the funeral pyre within the sacred walls of the Temple of Jupiter Capitolinus, two men armed with swords and javelins set fire to the couch with torches, and then everyone was heaping dry branches and benches on the flames. Women tossed their jewels into the pyre, and the musicians and actors who had taken part in his triumphs removed the embroidered triumph-costumes they had put on for the occasion, tore them to ribbons and hurled them into the flames. The veterans of his wars tossed their shields and swords into the fire, which burned all night. Relief and sorrow and exaltation marked the faces of the onlookers. They could not believe that the tall, thin, nervous man who had ruled over them for so long had gone from them. They watched the sparks flying upwards, and when the flames had died down, they searched among the ashes for his bones, which were carried reverently away.

So died Julius Caesar, descendant of gods and kings, a man more corrupt than any of his time, stern and unyielding in his determination to acquire supreme power, dedicated to glory, contemptuous of fame. Of all the *triumphatores* he was the one who wore the painted robes with the greatest sense of being born to them. So that he could enjoy his five triumphs he had killed, according to Pliny, 1,192,000 men in battle and fought fifty wars, and half the population of Rome had perished. The price was too high. In the days to come the Romans searched for a leader who would bring them peace and a little charity.

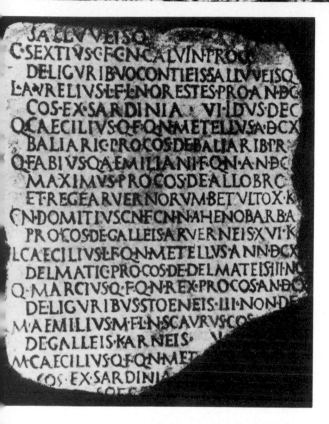

ROMVLVS·MARTIS·F·REX·AN[
[D]E·CAENINENSIBVS·EM[A]
[M]ARTI·[O]·F[E]

SA·LVVEISQ[
C·SEXTIVS·C·F·CN·CALVINPROC[
DE·LIGVRIBVOCONTIEISSALVVEISQ[
L·AVRELIVS·L·F·NOR·ESTES·PRO·AN·DC[
COS·EX·SARDINIA·VI·IDVS·DEC
Q·CAECILIVS·Q·F·Q·N·METELLVS·A·DCX[
BALIARIC·PROCOS·DEBALIARIBPR[
Q·FABIVS·Q·AEMILIANIF·Q·N·AN·DC[
MAXIMVS·PROCOS·DEALLOBR[C
ET·REGEARVERNORVMBET·VLTOX·K[
CN·DOMITIVS·CN·F·CN·NN·AHENOBARBA[
PROCOS·DEGALLEISARVERNEISX·VI·K[
L·CAECILIVS·L·F·Q·N·METELLVS·A·NN·DCX[
DELMATIC·PROCOS·DE·DELMATEISIII·N[
Q·MARCIVS·Q·F·Q·N·REX·PROCOSAN·DC[
DELIGVRIBVSSTOENEIS·III·NONDE[
M·AEMILIVS·M·F·L·N·SCAVRVSCOS[
DEGALLEIS·KARNEIS·V[
M·CAECILIVS·Q·F·Q·N·MET[
COS·EX·SARDINIA[

Inscriptions from the Consular and Triumphal Annals, found in the Forum in the sixteenth century. The first (*above*) records the triumph of Romulus over the Caeninses and Antemnati. The second (*left*) celebrates triumphs by three members of the Metelli family, that of Q. Caecilius Metellus over the Baleari in 122 B.C., L. Caecilius Metellus over Dalmatia in 117 B.C., and M. Caecilius Metellus over Sardinia in 115 B.C.

(Museo Dei Conservatori, Rome.)

The engraved bronze cista from Praeneste, showing a triumphal procession and sacrifice of the third century B.C.

Silver cup from Boscoreale, probably illustrating the triumph of
Tiberius over Pannonia in A.D. 12. The original reliefs may have
adorned the Arch of Tiberius. (*Top*) The *triumphator* standing in the
quadriga, clasping an eagle-crowned sceptre and laurel branch
while an attendant holds a crown over his head. (*Bottom*) The white
ox, adorned with fillets and triangular crown, is led to the sacrifice
by the *victimarius* and the *popa*, who carries the sacrificial axe over
his shoulder

Silver cup from Boscoreale. The whole of the second side of the cup
depicts the scene before the temple of Jupiter Capitolinus. (*Top*)
The *triumphator* (much damaged) stands at the left of the tripod altar
attended by a priest, a flute-player, guards and lictors. (*Bottom*) The
sacrifice takes place before the garlanded temple. It is the moment
just before the sacrifice, with three *victimarii* holding the ox down
and the *popa* about to strike

(The Louvre, Paris.)

The Arch of Triumph of Galerius, at Salonica.
(Royal Greek Embassy.)

The Arch of Triumph of Trajan, at Benevento.

(*Alpina.*)

Relief from the Arch of Titus, with the spoils from Jerusalem.

Apotheosis of the Emperor Antoninus and the Empress Faustina, from the Vatican Museum.

Relief of a sacrifice in front of the Temple of
Capitoline Jupiter, now in the Louvre.

Marcus Aurelius entering Rome in triumph, from a bas-relief.

(Museo Dei Conservatori. *Alinari.*)

Probus

Augustus

FOUR ROMAN EMPERORS

Caracalla

Commodus

Relief depicting the triumphal entry of Alfonso I of Aragon into
Naples on June 2, 1442, on the walls of the Castel Nuovo, Naples.

(*Anderson*)

Triumph of Caesar, by A. Andreini. Engraving
based on lost panel by Andrea Mantegna.

Triumph of Chastity. School of Mantegna.

Triumph of Love. School of Mantegna.

(Both from National Gallery of Art, Kress Collection.)

"The Triumph of Death". Fresco by an unknown Catalan artist, in the Palazzo Abbatelli, Palermo, Sicily.

The Trumpeters, from Mantegna's Triumph of
Caesar at Hampton Court.

(Reproduced by gracious permission of Her Majesty the Queen.)

Brown sardonyx gem representing the triumph of a Christian emperor, possibly Constantine the Great

(Sommerville Collection, University Museum, Philadelphia.)

8

THE TRIUMPH OVER THE WORLD

WHEN Caesar died, the most powerful man in Rome was Mark Antony, who at the time of the murder was standing only a few steps away from the conspirators. He quickly borrowed some clothes from a slave, and hurried away to his house on the Carinae in disguise, while the conspirators made their way with drawn swords to the Temple of Jupiter Capitolinus to discuss what should be done now that Caesar was dead and there was no logical successor. It was a time when only the boldest could hope to survive, and the man who would take Caesar's place needed audacity almost to the point of insanity. Antony was bold. Elegant, handsome, prodigal with his wealth, superbly at ease with soldiers in the camp, resembling Hercules from whom according to a family tradition he was descended, he took command of the situation; and after he had read Caesar's will to the people with its promise of generous gifts and obtained possession of Caesar's papers and private property, the way to supreme power lay open to him.

At that moment power could have been snatched from him by only one man, Marcus Aemilius Lepidus, Caesar's Master of the Horse, whose soldiers were now encamped in the Forum. Velleius Paterculus says of him that he was *omnium vanissimus*, the most fickle of mankind, but in fact he was a man with considerable gifts, who moved cautiously and could be bribed. Antony bribed him with money and the title of *pontifex maximus*, and went on to bribe the Senate. He promised an end to the dictatorship. He promised the veterans land in the Campagna, and he offered the conspirators commands in the conquered territories after having engineered a promise from the Senate that none of them should be punished "for the sake of peace". He was promising all things to all men when Octavian, Caesar's grandnephew, arrived in Rome from Apollonia in Epirus, where he had been studying military affairs with Agrippa, his constant companion.

Octavian was eighteen, golden-haired and white-skinned, the possessor of a grave and disturbing beauty. He was delicate and often ill, and he had been ill when he followed Caesar to Spain, taking part in the savage campaigns against the Pompeians. Caesar was especially attracted by the boy's courage. Mark Antony despised the boy. Himself the son and grandson of *triumphatores*, it amused him to point out to his friends the lowly origins of the claimant to the powers of Caesar, saying that Octavian was descended on his mother's side from a great-grandfather of African birth who once kept a perfumery shop and then a bakery at Aricia, while his paternal great-grandfather was no more than a humble rope-maker. It may have been true, but to despise Octavian was folly. Mark Antony treated him as an impostor, refused to grant him his inheritance, claiming that it had already been spent and in any event belonged to the Roman people, and he refused to help Octavian punish the murderers of Caesar. Octavian swore vengeance.

It was a quiet vengeance, very slow, very cautious, very astute. Octavian had the nimbleness of youth, while Mark Antony at forty after years of dissipation lacked any kind of elasticity. Octavian's aim was to inherit the empire of Caesar. For this purpose he was prepared to subordinate all other considerations: he was even prepared if necessary to form an alliance with Mark Antony.

That summer and autumn Rome remained on the edge of civil war. But to fight a civil war effectively large armies are required, and neither Octavian nor Mark Antony possessed any large forces. Suddenly deserting Rome in the depth of winter Mark Antony took command of three Macedonian legions which had recently arrived from the east and marched north in the hope of raising a much larger army in Cisalpine Gaul, that vast territory extending from the Alps and including the entire Po valley. Octavian, with a small army of veterans from the Campagna, marched after him. At Forum Gallorum and later at Mutina there were fierce battles, and Mark Antony was defeated. He abandoned Italy and made his way over the Alps to Gaul, hoping to attract to his command the Roman legions in the richest province of the empire. There were at this time two Roman armies in Gaul, one commanded by Marcus Aemilius Lepidus, the other by Lucius Munatius Plancus, once Mark Antony's secretary, famous for his wit, his intelligence and his treachery. Plutarch says that Mark Antony simply presented himself in the camp of Lepidus and received an ovation from the soldiers, taking over the command immediately, and Plancus, realizing which way the wind was blowing, joined forces with him soon afterwards. He had left Italy a fugitive, and was now returning at the head of seventeen legions. The army of Gaul was about to hurl itself against Italy.

Rome was in a panic. The senators were appalled by the prospect of a civil war more terrible than the last, and cast around for a

formula that would satisfy the conflicting claims of Octavian and
Mark Antony. They could find none until Quintus Pedius, another
of Caesar's nephews, who had been elected consul alongside
Octavian, suggested the formation of a triumvirate with Octavian,
Mark Antony and Lepidus as supreme rulers of the state. The
senators were delighted by this simple and dangerous solution to a
problem which had hitherto defied any reasonable solution, and
in October 43 B.C. the triumvirs met on a small island on the Reno
River not far from Bologna, each of them with an escort of five
legions armed to the teeth. For three days they discussed quietly
and in complete seclusion how they would divide the *imperium*.
Lepidus was a distinguished soldier, but distrusted by his troops;
he counted for little. The real battle was between Octavian and
Mark Antony, both of whom had assumed heroic proportions in
the eyes of the people. They were no longer men; they were legends.
No one would dare to dispute their decisions, even the most terrible
decisions. The triumvirs permitted themselves the luxury of killing
off all the people they disliked, sometimes for the most trivial
reasons; and 300 names were listed as enemies of the state, to be
killed secretly, in the middle of the night, without warning. The
Sullan and Marian massacres were being repeated, but with one
great difference: the triumvirs gained nothing by the massacres.
Once more we are presented with a meaningless sacrifice in honour
of a triumph.

Some of the Republicans whose names did not appear on the
proscription lists thought the massacre was a small price to pay for
an era of settled peace. Others foresaw that the reign of terror
might be continued indefinitely. Quintus Pedius, the consul, was
shown a preliminary death-list amounting to only seventeen names
and announced that these deaths were necessary for the salvation
of the state, and the next day died of a broken heart. As Caesar's
grand-nephew he had been permitted to enjoy a triumph shortly
before Caesar's last triumphal entry into Rome. Among those who
were proscribed was Cicero, who was riding in a litter by the seashore when Antony's hired assassins caught up with him, and cut
off his head and hands, which had written so many books and
speeches. Cicero's head and hands were nailed to the rostrum by
Antony's orders, to put fear in the hearts of his remaining enemies.
Three sophisticated and talented rulers were giving way to primitive savagery. "They let their anger and fury overcome their sense
of humanity," says Plutarch sombrely. "They showed there is no
beast so savage as a man possessed of power answerable only to his
own rage."

October passed, and then it was November with the triumvirs safely established in Rome, dividing the spoils between them. Among those spoils was the power to grant triumphs without consulting the wishes of the Senate, and Antony insisted that triumphs should be granted to the two generals who by joining forces with him had permitted him to threaten Rome and so allowed him to enjoy his present high pinnacle of power. Accordingly a triumph was granted to Plancus on December 29, and another to Lepidus on December 31. Plancus had been permitted to add some names to the death-lists, and included his own brother. Lepidus did the same. Plancus claimed to be celebrating his victories in Gaul, and Lepidus his victories in Spain, but no evidence about any victories won by them has survived, and it is more likely that they were granted triumphs as rewards for their treachery. Velleius Paterculus records a punning song sung by the soldiers who marched in the triumph:

> *De Germanis, non de Gallis*
> *Duo triumphant consules.*

Germanus can mean "German", but it can also mean "brother": and the bitterness of the sally was not lost on the triumvir Lepidus, who issued an edict commanding the people to rejoice and be merry under pain of proscription. But the people continued to curse the *triumphatores*, and the soldiers continued to sing their song.

Lepidus had some reason for objecting violently to the song. He had in fact put the name of his brother, Paulus Aemilius, on the death-list, apparently on the command of Mark Antony, but he had also taken care to warn his brother in time. Plotius, the brother of Plancus, was less lucky: he was killed by hired assassins.

Plancus was the evil genius of the conspiracy, always pulling strings, always employing flattery to advance his position. He flattered Cleopatra outrageously, but he was equally flattering to Caesar. His surviving letters show him to be a wit, and Trebonius, the conqueror of Marseilles, admired his witticisms and published a collection of them. It is recorded of him that he once danced naked, his body painted blue, his head encircled with reeds, wearing a fish's tail. In the end he became censor, a post equivalent to that of a judge of the Supreme Court: it was a strange appointment for a man who had committed all the crimes on the calendar. "There were no charges he could make against young men, or hear others make, which he had not committed himself," says Velleius Paterculus; and it seems to have been no more than the truth.

Plancus continued to exert his malign influence during the years of the triumvirate and the early years of the principate. In 42 B.C. he flattered Octavian by rebuilding the Temple of Saturn at the foot of the Capitoline hill in his honour, and when Octavian finally assumed supreme power and was searching for a memorable name by which he might be known it was Plancus, says Suetonius, who suggested the name Augustus, meaning "consecrated". Earlier he had been appointed governor of Asia Minor by Mark Antony. He stole Mark Antony's will from the Vestal Virgins and transmitted it to Octavian, and he was in Alexandria when the triumvir was enjoying his days of dalliance with Cleopatra, acting as master of ceremonies in their court. Inconstant and treacherous, his only admirable achievement lay in the founding of the city of Lyons.

We would recognize the treacherous Plancus if he entered the room, but we would be hard pressed to recognize the two generals who were granted triumphs in 42 and 41 B.C. One was Publius Vatinius, commander of the army of Illyria with headquarters in Dyrrhachium (Durazzo), a political adventurer whose public appearances were chiefly reserved for the law courts. Cicero attacked him in a violent speech during the trial of Milo, but he was later defended in court by Cicero on Caesar's urging. He must have been a good soldier, for Dyrrhachium was an important base against the Republican army which Brutus had gathered in Macedonia. Publius Vatinius claimed a triumph on the grounds that he had won a resounding victory against the Republicans—it was the first time that any general had ever claimed a triumph for fighting against Romans—and Mark Antony rewarded him by permitting him to ride in triumph on July 31, 42 B.C.[1] Some excuse for the triumph had to be invented, and so it was claimed to be in honour of a victory over the Illyrians.

The other *triumphator* was Lucius Antonius, the younger brother of Mark Antony, a strange tormented man, who envied his brother's power and looked for every opportunity of assuming power in his own right. The opportunity came in the late summer or early autumn, when Octavian marched over into Greece to join forces with Mark Antony against the armies of Brutus and Cassius; there followed the battle of Philippi, in which the Republican armies were destroyed, and the Republic perished, never to revive. Octavian was ill—he took very little part in the fighting and had to be carried across Greece in a litter—and Lucius Antonius must have reasoned that a heaven-sent opportunity had been given him.

[1] Dion Cassius suggests that Vatinius not only did not win any victories over Brutus, but his soldiers went over to the enemy "since they hated him and despised him by reason of his disease." (*Roman History*, XLVII, 21).

He was consul; he was in a position to raise his own legions; and he foresaw a time when he would be able to divide the empire with his brother. The much-married Fulvia, who was the wife of Mark Antony and the mother-in-law of Octavian, became his mistress, and it seems to have been Fulvia who suggested to Lucius Antonius that he should mark his accession to supreme power by celebrating a triumph. Hers was the most powerful voice in Rome. Her favour was courted by the Senate. In her person was represented the power of the triumvirs, for Lepidus was her slave, only too ready to obey her will, and her family connections with Octavian and Mark Antony gave her the right to speak in their name. Accordingly this dazzling and beautiful woman made it known to the Senate that she believed the time was ripe for granting a triumph to her lover, and on January 1, 41 B.C. he celebrated his triumph in honour of a victory over an Alpine nation, though he had never in fact possessed a command in the Alps. It amused him to follow the example of the great Marius by riding in procession on the official opening day of his consulship, and to assume an air of almost excessive humility—he is the only *triumphator* known to have refused to wear the heavily embroidered robes of his office. The real triumph, however, belonged to Fulvia. Dion Cassius describes the triumph with unusual bitterness:

> So Antonius celebrated a triumph over a people he claimed to have defeated, although in truth he had done nothing to deserve a triumph and had never commanded an army in these regions, and it was in fact Fulvia . . .[1] In the following days she assumed a prouder air than he did, and she had of course far more reason —to arrange for a triumph for someone else is a more worthy thing than to receive a triumph at the hands of another.

> Lucius Antonius therefore donned the robe of a *triumphator*, rode in the chariot and performed all the other rites appropriate to the occasion, but it was Fulvia who gave the impression of being the originator of the spectacle, employing him only as her performer. The triumph occurred on the first day of the year, and Lucius prided himself, as Marius had done before him, on holding it on the first day of his consulship. Furthermore, he even prided himself on being superior to Marius, saying he had voluntarily put aside all the trappings and had assembled the Senate while wearing civilian clothes: something which Marius had done only unwillingly. He claimed too that almost no crowns had been granted to Marius, while he himself had been awarded many, especially by the people, tribe by tribe—an honour con-

[1] There is a break in the text at this point.

ferred on no other *triumphator* in the past. In fact he owed this honour, too, to the influence of Fulvia and the money he had lavishly scattered among many people.

(*Roman History*, XLVIII, 4.)

The triumph of Lucius Antonius, with its parade of humility and its blaze of unmerited crowns, was one of the most astonishing spectacles ever presented to the Romans: it was the first occasion in history at which a man received a triumph by the favour of a woman.

The subsequent career of Lucius Antonius only emphasized his natural depravity and keen desire to take possession of the empire, even if it meant taking it from the hands of Fulvia. That redoubtable woman, who was not afraid to appear among the soldiers with a sword at her side, making speeches to them as though she were their general, was in fact the successor of Julius Caesar as the unchallenged master of Rome. When Octavian returned from Philippi, he found himself challenged by Fulvia and the entire Senate; he had almost no troops; and he was in danger of arrest. His instinct was to go at once to the heart of the trouble, and he deliberately provoked a quarrel with Fulvia by sending back to her mother the wife he had married only a short while before, saying he had not touched her and she was still a virgin. From that moment there was war between Fulvia and Octavian, with all the advantages on the side of the young general, who was adored by his troops. Fulvia panicked and fled to Praeneste with the senators dancing attendance upon her, while Lucius Antonius led his army northward, hoping to occupy the whole of northern Italy and gather together a force which would once more make him master of Rome, this time by force of arms, not by permission of Fulvia.

The consequences of his march to the north were disastrous. He reached Perusia (Perugia), and there called a halt. He decided to put the city in a state of defence and wait for the reinforcements which Fulvia had promised him. None came. There was a drought in Umbria; the slaves in the city were dying of starvation, and the army itself was reduced to living on small rations. Lucius Antonius was completely pitiless. To save food, and to prevent the enemy from seeing the funeral pyres which would ordinarily have to be lighted over the bodies of the dead slaves, he gave orders that the dead and dying should simply be shovelled into the earth. Octavian came up with a large army and besieged the fortress, which was forced to capitulate; and his soldiers would have looted the city if someone had not fired it. The city was in ashes. For some unexplained reason Lucius Antonius was pardoned, but the senators who accompanied him in his northern march were summarily executed. Dion Cassius tells the story that some 300 of the defenders were captured, brought back to Rome and sacrificed on the altar of Julius Caesar in the Forum. It is not an improbable story. Some very solemn and terrifying act was needed to celebrate a total victory against the rebels, and it was just such an act as the young Octavian might be expected to commit. He could not celebrate a triumph over his own countrymen, but he could at least grant himself the pleasure of a public hecatomb, and he could also enjoy the panoply of a *triumphator* without taking part in the public ceremony of triumph. Dion Cassius relates that the Romans gave themselves up to merry-making as soon as they heard the news of victory, and when Octavian returned from Perusia "they conveyed him in a triumphal dress into the city and honoured him with a laurel crown, giving him the right to wear it on every occasion at which *triumphatores* had worn them in the past" (*Roman History,* XLVIII, 16). This meant that Octavian could appear at the theatre, at games and even in the Senate wearing the star-studded dress of victory, but it also meant that he was sitting in the undisputable seat of power. He was enjoying the supreme triumph—the triumph which went beyond all other triumphs, even the final triumph of Julius Caesar, because it dispensed with the triumphal machinery. He was twenty-one, and all of Rome was at his feet.

There remained a long and cautious mopping-up campaign, a slow but inevitable victory over the Pompeians who had raised an army in Sicily, and over Mark Antony who was already surrendering to the charms of Egyptian luxury, for he had already sailed in a flower-decked ship along the Cnidus River with Cleopatra and taken up residence in her palace in Alexandria. Fulvia had escaped to Greece, and was no longer a menace—she died the following year at Sicyon near Corinth. Lepidus had received the governorship of Africa, where he was to remain in obscurity for five years before being recalled to put down the Republican uprisings in Sicily, and failing in the attempt he was to spend the rest of his long life as a state prisoner, a triumvir reduced to penury. Brutus once called him *homo ventosissimus*, "a most weather-cocky man", and his life proved the disadvantage of following the fashionable winds.

Meanwhile Octavian showed no desire to quarrel with Mark Antony. Even if he had wanted war, the Romans were too exhausted to fight. They wanted peace and were prepared to enforce their demand: crowds followed Octavian in the street, clamouring for the peace so long denied to them. Fulvia's death paved the way to a reconciliation, and soon feelers were being thrown out to Antony, suggesting another meeting like the former one on the island near Bologna, in which the dictators would once more divide the power between them and celebrate their reunion with an exchange of gifts, marriages, triumphal processions. The meeting took place in Brundisium in the summer of 40 B.C. Once more the empire was divided, with Octavian receiving Spain, Gaul, Sardinia and Dalmatia, and Antony receiving "all the lands that belonged to the Romans across the Ionian Sea, both in Europe and Asia". It was arranged that Mark Antony should marry Octavia, Octavian's chaste and beautiful sister, to cement the alliance. They were in a gay mood. There were banquets and much entertaining. Dion Cassius says that Octavian entertained "in the military and Roman way", meaning perhaps that he was inclined to be formal, but Mark Antony entertained "according to the Asiatic and Egyptian manner", suggesting that he delighted in the panoply of the occasion. Then the two conquerors of the world returned to Rome to share a triumph for having made peace with one another.

Apparently, it was a full-scale triumph with all the appropriate pageantry, but there were no prisoners, for they were not celebrating a war but the coming of peace. Both the Barberini fragments and the Capitoline records describe it as an *ovatio*, but it is unlikely that the two conquerors performed the formal *ovatio* on the Alban Mount, for the purpose of the triumph was to publish the peace between them and the ceremonies at the Alban Mount were associated only with war. Dion Cassius says they entered Rome on horseback "as though at a triumph" and were later granted the garments of the *triumphator* and attended the festivals on golden thrones. The Capitoline records describe it as a real triumph *quod pacem fecit*. The nature of the triumph had been changing rapidly since Julius Caesar broke the traditional pattern. In a few more years Octavian was to change it again so completely that it was to bear the marks of his particular conception of the triumph to the very end.

The solemn treaty at Brundisium was an event of vast and incalculable magnitude. Henceforward for 350 years, except for one day's fighting in the streets of Rome, there was to be peace in Italy. In honour of this peace Virgil wrote his Fourth Eclogue celebrating the coming birth of a child who would inherit a world at peace, and dedicating the work to his patron and benefactor, the gentle Caius Asinius Pollio, who had saved the property of the poet in Mantua from confiscation. Among the Romans there was so great a demand for peace that when it was learned that Octavian intended to destroy the armed forces of the Pompeians in Sicily, both the *triumphatores* were stoned by crowds on the Via Sacra, and the threatened war was postponed.

Meanwhile the triumphs continued: not the great tradition-breaking triumphs of the unchallenged Caesars, but the lesser triumphs of generals who fought on the frontiers of the empire. One such triumph was granted to Lucius Marcius Censorinus on the first day of his consulship in 39 B.C. after victories in Macedonia, but little is known about his campaigns. A more significant triumph was granted in October of the same year to Caius Asinius Pollio, whose friendship with Virgil was only one of his many claims to fame. This extraordinary man combined the talents of a poet, a historian, a general and a superb negotiator with an almost magical talent for survival. The poet Horace said of him that he walked with a bold and firm step over the volcanic ashes of the civil war. He feared no one. He played a dubious role in the adventures of Lucius Antonius. He was a close friend of Mark Antony, but he was also in the trust of Octavian, and together with Maecenas, the great patron of the arts, he was one of the two men most responsible for bringing about the treaty of Brundisium. Something of his temper can be observed in the letter he wrote to Octavian, who offered him a command. "No," he replied, "my services to Mark Antony are too great, and his kindness to me too notorious. I must keep aloof from this war—and be the prey of the conqueror" (*Velleius Paterculus*, II, lxxxvi). After Brundisium he was attached to the staff of Mark Antony, and fought a brief campaign against the obscure Illyrian tribesmen known as Parthini. He was granted a triumph in October, 39 B.C., and thereafter retired to private life to cultivate the arts, write tragedies and open the first public library. He was thirty-seven at the time of his triumph, and he lived to be eighty.

The battles fought by Caius Asinius Pollio were of no particular importance, but in the following year there was celebrated a triumph which made the Romans deliriously happy, and once again it was due to an officer on Mark Antony's staff. By a strange quirk of fate the *triumphator* had himself appeared in a triumphal procession before—as a prisoner carried in the arms of his mother in the triumphal procession of Pompeius Strabo, the father of Pompey the Great, in 89 B.C. Cicero says that as a boy he was a mule-driver for an army bakery. No other *triumphator* ever came from such lowly origins as the man who was the first to win a decisive victory over the Persians for the Romans.

Publius Ventidius Bassus was born in the province of Picenum on the Adriatic coast. He first came into prominence when Julius Caesar discovered his military talents and employed him in Gaul, where he executed his commissions so well that he rose to high rank, becoming first tribune of the commons and then praetor. After the assassination of Caesar, he allied himself with Mark Antony, and when Octavian invested Perusia, Ventidius Bassus brought up his army and attempted diversionary tactics. After Brundisium Antony sent him to Asia to make war on the Parthians, then being led by a renegade Roman officer, Quintus Labienus, who had taken part in the conspiracy against Julius Caesar and afterwards escaped to the east. In a series of quick campaigns in Syria and Cilicia Ventidius Bassus routed Labienus and a Parthian army under Prince Pacorus, and went on to occupy Palestine and to fight an inconclusive battle against Antiochus I, King of Commagene. His major achievement consisted of three pitched battles against Parthian forces, all of which he won handsomely, thus pushing back the frontiers of Parthia to Mesopotamia and Media. His victory was all the more desirable because the Romans still remembered vividly the defeat of the army led by Crassus.

Antony was in Athens when the news of the victories first reached him, and he immediately announced victory celebrations. Public feasts were held throughout Greece, and special games in honour of the victory were held in the stadium, with Antony acting as chief steward, wearing a white gown and white shoes, and when the wrestlers were locked together, it was Antony, acting as superintendent of ceremonies, who parted them. He decided to lead an army and join Ventidius Bassus, and he was already on the march when he learned the full details of the victories—Prince Pacorus had been killed in battle, Labienus had been caught and put to death, and a vast number of prisoners had been captured. Antony seems to have been annoyed; his lieutenant had been only too successful; and Ventidius Bassus was deprived of his command. Inevitably a complete report was sent to Rome, and just as inevitably Antony claimed a triumph for himself, as commander-in-chief of the army of the east responsible for the defeat of the Parthians. The Senate however decided upon a fairer distribution of honours. It granted Antony a triumph, to be enjoyed by him whenever he saw fit to return to Rome, but it also proclaimed that Ventidius Bassus deserved a triumph; and the senators noted that Prince Pacorus had been killed on the anniversary of the death of Crassus. Vengeance against the Parthians, so nicely timed, delighted the Romans, and accordingly they rejoiced as the triumphal procession wound through the streets with the former slave arrayed in

the majesty of a *triumphator*. Ventidius Bassus had fought one of
his major battles among the foothills of the Taurus mountains, and
the triumph was celebrated *ex Tauro monte et Partheis*. It took
place on November 27, 38 B.C. Both Antony and Octavian seem to
have been a little piqued by the resounding victory over the Parthians, for the Romans were busily whispering in their satiric way
that the two conquerors who had divided the world between them
were luckier in their lieutenants than in their own persons.

This was a triumph which could not be refused: it belonged to
the rare number of triumphs magnificently deserved, of which
there were perhaps no more than twenty through the centuries.
The next triumph, granted by Octavian, was a deplorable affair
celebrated by a commander for putting down an obscure uprising
in Spain.

Gnaeus Domitius Calvinus was a capable officer, one of Julius
Caesar's best generals, who had led the centre at the battle of
Pharsalia. He was known for his brutality. Sent to Spain to quash
the rebellion of the Cerretani in the Pyrenees, he had won an easy
victory after one of his officers and about two hundred men fell
into an ambush: the legionaries fled and scattered in the surrounding countryside. Calvinus refused to proceed with the campaign
until these legionaries were rounded up. He sent messengers out to
summon them on the excuse of granting them a free pardon, and
when they were brought together he ordered every tenth man to
be killed, including the ranking centurion who had been in command at the time. "In this way," Dion Cassius remarks dryly, "he
acquired a reputation for discipline." He had, of course, acquired
this reputation long before, and the incident provided only one
further example of his exquisite brutality. Having punished his
soldiers, he went on to punish the enemy, bringing fire and sword
to the foothills of the Pyrenees. There were no further uprisings
among the Cerretani.

Returning to Rome, the general enjoyed his dubious triumph,
and with the spoils set about the task of perpetuating his name.
The Regia, the official residence of the Pontifex Maximus on the
Forum, had been destroyed by fire. He rebuilt it in solid marble,
paying for it with the gold captured in Spain, and then suggested
to Octavian that the new Regia should be adorned with statues
from the east. Octavian had a special affection for Alexander the
Great and possessed four of the great statues which once supported
Alexander's tent. Calvinus wanted them to adorn the Regia, the
physical embodiment of his triumph, and requested them on temporary loan. Two of these statues were lent to him, and the two

others were placed before the temple of Mars Ultor. When some time later Octavian asked for the statues back, Calvinus showed the full extent of his cunning and his treachery by complaining that he had not enough workmen to remove them and Octavian could, if he wished, send his own workmen to fetch them. Octavian was trapped. If he sent workmen to remove the statues, it would be whispered all over Rome that he was committing sacrilege. For more than two hundred years the lavishly decorated Regia with the statues remained on the Forum, to perish at last in the Great Fire of A.D. 191.

Octavian had promised peace: inevitably there was war. The Pompeians in Sicily refused to obey the will of Rome. They possessed a powerful fleet, and their ships raided the coast of southern Italy at will. They were in a position to intercept the corn-ships from Egypt, and sometimes did so. Octavian decided therefore to build a fleet at least as powerful as theirs, and lost the greater part of it in a sea-battle in the bay of Cumae near Naples. In his despair he sent for Agrippa, who was in Gaul, having just quelled a rebellion by the Aquitanians. Agrippa was offered a triumph, which he refused on the grounds that it would be dangerous and unseemly to celebrate a triumph at a time of national misfortune. He was a superb technician, and succeeded in the space of a year in building a fleet more powerful than any the Romans had ever possessed before; and by digging a canal between Lake Lucrinus and Lake Avernus and then providing an outlet to the sea, he was able to establish his naval base in a land-locked harbour safe from attack.

Octavian was in a mood of quiet despair. He had always paid particular attention to omens, and that year the omens were more than usually unfavourable. Near Rome blood had fallen from heaven, and the birds had carried the blood far and wide, scattering it all over Latium. To Octavian an even more dreadful portent occurred when his wife Livia was sitting in her garden, and an eagle flew overhead, dropping in her lap a white bird which carried a sprig of laurel with the berries still on it. There were long and learned discussions about the meaning of the portent, which seemed to be intended to convey a direct message from heaven. Almost alone Livia believed that the dropping of the laurel sprig was an auspicious sign: she planted the sprig of laurel, and in later years, when the sprig became a grove, the laurels of Livia were twined into crowns for the heads of *triumphatores*.

In spite of the omens, Octavian decided upon war against the Pompeians in Sicily. Three fleets converged upon the island, with "that weather-cocky" Lepidus leading the fleet from Africa. Another fleet consisting of 130 ships had been supplied by Mark Antony in exchange for 20,000 legionaries for his promised invasion of Parthia; but Antony was notably absent. After weeks of confused and bitter fighting, Octavian seems to have lost heart, and he was about to abandon the campaign when a fish leapt out of the sea and fell at his feet—a portent of more than usual magnitude. Agrippa won a naval battle off Mylae; and Lepidus for no reason that anyone has understood razed Messina to the ground, an act that horrified Octavian who immediately set about punishing the *pontifex maximus* and did not rest until Lepidus threw himself at the dictator's feet and begged for mercy. Octavian displayed little knowledge of strategy, and lost too many battles for comfort. The real victors were Agrippa, whose victory off Mylae was rewarded with a gold crown decked with the miniature beaks of ships, and Lucius Cornificius, who fought a long and successful rear-guard action against the Pompeians and for the rest of his life was permitted, whenever he dined abroad, to ride home by torchlight on the back of an elephant. Some years later he was awarded a triumph for victories in Africa.

Octavian had won the war which the Romans hoped they would never have to fight, and Octavian, as commander-in-chief of the invasion forces, must have felt the need to celebrate a triumph if only to demonstrate to the Romans that he had indeed won a victory which brought peace to Italy. Legend said that the news of the victory reached Rome in a way which was entirely supernatural. An obscure soldier was suddenly "seized by the god", and after saying and doing many strange things he was seen to run up the steps of the Capitoline hill and lay his sword at the foot of the statue of Jupiter Capitolinus, as a sign that weapons would be no longer needed. A few days later the soldier's prescience was confirmed by the arrival of Octavian's officers in Rome.

Such was the story told at the time, and there is every reason to disbelieve it. We need not disbelieve Dion Cassius's account of the shower of honours heaped on Octavian. It was not enough to grant him a triumph: every imaginable tribute was offered to him. He was granted statues and addresses of praise, the right to a front seat at the spectacles, an archway surmounted by trophies and the privilege of riding into the city on horseback; he was permitted to wear the laurel crown on all occasions, and to invite his family and children to a banquet within the sacred walls of the Temple of Jupiter Capitolinus on the anniversary of his victory, a day to be celebrated with thanksgivings in perpetuity. Some of these honours he had already received; some he refused out of modesty; still others were added when he showed an understandable reluctance to have too many honours heaped on him. The machinery of the triumph with its strict regulations and careful apportionment of privileges was giving way to a rag-bag of honours. It is possible that Octavian enjoyed most the honour, granted to none before him, of being permitted to sit with the tribunes, those inviolate magistrates who guarded over the welfare of the city. In later years Octavian was honoured with two more triumphal arches, but of these only the foundations remain.

With Octavian's triumph over Italy, it is possible to detect a strange weakening of the triumphal machinery: as though this machinery was unable to bear the weight of honour. Caesar had claimed honours which were for the most part clear-cut and well-defined, designed for a deliberate purpose. The honours showered on Octavian suggest flattery and a fearful gratitude by a people who dared not look him in the face. Like Caesar, Octavian was beginning to possess the quality which was later known as *terribiltà*: some god-like power drove him, and the people, afraid the tyrant might become a monster of tyranny, were concerned to appease his restless spirit.

In Alexandria Mark Antony was living in a state of permanent splendour interrupted by occasional forays and marauding expeditions against Armenia and Parthia. He had succumbed to the East. He dressed in flowing robes with an oriental dagger at his belt, permitted himself to be seen in public reclining on a golden couch, and allowed sculptors to represent him in the shape of the gods Osiris and Dionysus, while Cleopatra appeared as the goddess Isis and as Selene, goddess of the moon. Only one thing was needed to complete his pleasure: an oriental triumph with kings and captives passing in procession before his queen, himself in the robes of an oriental *triumphator* presiding over the festival. It was an easy task to invade Armenia and capture the reigning king by a ruse, and then to lead him to his fortresses one by one in the hope that he would reveal where his treasure was hidden, but Artavasdes was not a man who took easily to servitude. Mark Antony made him wear silver fetters, thinking it beneath the dignity of a king to be bound with thongs, and then drove back to Alexandria with his prisoners.

When the news of Mark Antony's Alexandrian triumph reached Rome, there were expressions of horror. This triumph was regarded as an obscene parody of the triumphs known to the Romans. It was bad enough that Antony rode through the streets in a chariot with the Armenian king, his wife and children stumbling before him, not victims of honourable war, but of deceit. Far worse was the place set aside for Cleopatra who sat on a high throne of gold raised upon a platform of silver, assuming the place of Jupiter, as she received the gifts of the captives. It pleased the Romans that when the Armenian king was brought before her, he refused to do homage or address her by any name except Cleopatra. All kinds of favours were promised to him if he would beg for mercy, but this too he refused. He was roughly handled, but not killed, and remained a prisoner of the court.

A few days later Antony announced the creation of a new Empire of the East, to be ruled jointly by Cleopatra and her children. The occasion was a feast in honour of his victories held in the gymnasium in Alexandria. Antony and Cleopatra sat on their thrones, and below them were the thrones of their children, the twins Alexander Helios and Cleopatra Selene, both six years old, and the two-year-old Ptolemy Philadelphus. There was also the twelve-year-old son of Cleopatra by Julius Caesar, called Ptolemy Caesar or Caesarion. Antony seems to have completely abandoned his responsibilities to Rome, and acting as proconsul and triumvir he distributed kingdoms to Cleopatra and her children like someone drunkenly scattering jewels among his friends and intimates.

To Cleopatra, whom he named "Queen of Kings", went Egypt, Cyprus and Coele-Syria, and Caesarion, who bore the title of "King of Kings" became co-regent. Armenia, Media, Parthia and the unconquered territories beyond the Euphrates went to Alexander Helios, Cleopatra Selene became queen of Cyrene, and Ptolemy Philadelphus was appointed ruler over Phoenicia, Cilicia and Syria. The children were dressed in the appropriate costumes— Alexander wore the Persian tiara, and Ptolemy Philadelphus wore a Macedonian bonnet with a diadem and the Macedonian cloak of purple wool like the one worn by Alexander the Great. The new kings and queens were surrounded by bodyguards wearing the costumes of their countries. On coins stamped for the occasion were inscribed the words: CLEOPATRAE REGINAE REGVM FILIORVM REGVM—*Cleopatra Queen of Kings and her Sons who are Kings*. Cleopatra had won a signal victory, and to celebrate it she wore the costume and attributes of Isis, with a sistrum and winnowing fan in her hand and the sacred knot at her breast. Antony abandoned his role of emperor, and assumed the role of a god. Putting aside his golden sceptre and purple robe studded with huge gems, he wore the costume and attributes of the god Dionysus, a crown of ivy on his head, the thyrsus in his hand and buskins on his feet:

his gown was shimmering gold. The Romans might reasonably wonder what a Roman consul was doing in that costume.

At first, when news of the Alexandrian triumphs reached Rome, it was deliberately hidden from the people. Octavian seems to have been puzzled, scarcely believing that such a monstrous change could have taken place in Antony's character, but when Plancus revealed Antony's will with its enumeration of the princely gifts to Cleopatra and her children, he realized that *hubris* was working on the character of the lordly triumvir and soon his lust for power would drive him to madness. "He is a delirious player on the cymbals," Octavian said a little later. "He is giving away islands and whole parts of continents as though he were master of the earth and the sea."

In Alexandria Antony had celebrated two triumphs, but since the Romans accounted them as triumphs *against* Rome, they were never included in the official roster. His triumphs were overwhelming ones, shaking Rome to her foundations. In that same year three obscure triumphs were celebrated between June and October. The first went to Titus Statilius Taurus, who had command of one of the armies in Octavian's first unsuccessful invasion of Sicily and who later covered himself with glory in a raid against Antony's cavalry at Actium. This triumph was granted for his conquest of the two Africas. The second triumph went to one of Antony's men, Caius Sosius, governor of Syria and Cilicia, who crucified King Antigonus and placed Herod on the throne of Jerusalem. His triumph was granted for his conquest of Judaea, and he remained in Rome as Antony's chief representative in the capital. At Actium Caius Sosius commanded the left wing of the fleet against Octavian. He was taken prisoner and later pardoned. The third triumph, held on October 13, went to Caius Norbanus Flaccus, who had been consul in 38 B.C. and received his triumph for some obscure victories in Spain, the happy hunting-ground for those who desired the honour of a triumph without incurring very much risk.

But all these were minor triumphs, of so little importance that they provoked hardly a ripple upon the Roman imagination; and we know little or nothing about the circumstances of these triumphal processions.

Then came the battle of Actium on September 2nd, 31 B.C., only three years after Antony had celebrated his triumphs over the east. Octavian was now master of the world.

No conqueror ever moved more cautiously. It was almost a year before Octavian felt strong enough to enter Egypt and to demand, as the price of his victory, that Cleopatra should surrender herself and her treasure to the conqueror. Antony was dead. He had promised himself he would die on the battlefield, but in fact he killed himself by falling on his sword in Cleopatra's palace, and he died in her arms. While Cleopatra herself was still hesitating whether to live or to die, there came a messenger from Octavian, Cornelius Dolabella, who warned her that in three days she would be taken to Rome to decorate the triumph. *"Non triumphabor,"* she answered. "I will not be drawn in the triumph." From that moment her decision was made. When Octavian had visited her, she gave him every indication of her desire to live, but she had already made secret preparations for her death. On the following day, wearing her royal robes, attended only by her waiting women Charmion and Iras, she killed herself by baring her arm to the bite of a sacred serpent hidden in a basket of figs.

With the death of Antony, Octavian had no more enemies worthy of his steel. Only Caesarion, the son of Julius Caesar by Cleopatra, could claim to inherit the power won by his father. The boy had been sent into hiding in Ethiopia, but he was summoned back and killed by orders of Octavian, who claimed to be the adopted son of Julius Caesar and could not therefore tolerate the presence of a contender to the throne. The other children of Cleopatra were left unharmed.

Though Agrippa sent messages from Rome, urgently recalling him to the capital, Octavian enjoyed a triumphal progress through Egypt, Palestine, Syria and Asia Minor. It was a slow and stately progress, interrupted only by receptions for the kings of the territories now to be administered from Rome: the powers of Herod, appointed by Antony, were confirmed. Once again the senators discussed the nature of the triumph which would be offered to the world-conqueror. It was decided to permit him the enjoyment of a triple triumph on three successive days, first over Europe, then over Asia, and lastly over Africa and Egypt. Once again Octavian was permitted to wear the triumphal insignia on all public occasions. There was to be a quinquennial festival in his honour, his birthdays were to be commemorated with religious rites, and the day of his victory at Actium was to be marked in the calendar as one of the auspicious days. The priests were ordered to remember him in their prayers, especially the prayers for the Senate and the Roman people. A further decree proposed that Octavian should be invested for life with the *potestas tribunitia.*

Octavian superintended his three triumphal processions with quite extraordinary care. This triumph was so great that the usual order of the procession could be safely dispensed with: for the first time the senators were to follow, not to proceed the *triumphator*. For the first time, too, the Vestal Virgins were to go forth in solemn procession and conduct the conqueror into the city. This was to be the greatest of all triumphs, but an oddly discordant note was struck from the beginning. Aemilius Paulus, Pompey and Julius Caesar had each enjoyed triple triumphs, and it was inconceivable that Octavian should enjoy a lesser one. There had been a battle at Actium, followed many months later by a skirmish in the outskirts of Alexandria. These were decisive engagements, and well worthy of a triumph. But how was it possible, out of two successful campaigns, to celebrate a triple triumph?

Octavian himself or the senators solved the problem by invoking the minor campaigns against the Pannonians and Dalmatians, which were also campaigns against the surviving Republicans in Illyria. Accordingly the first triumph celebrated the conquest over the tribesmen, and was designed as an *hors d'œuvre* to the two more splendid triumphs that followed. The first triumph took place on August 13, 29 B.C., and was followed by the triumph in honour of Actium the next day. There was a display of naval trophies, but care was taken to avoid any direct reference to Antony. For his part in the naval victory Agrippa was given a sea-blue banner in lieu of another naval crown.

The third triumph was the most magnificent the Romans had ever seen. Here were displayed the spoils and treasures removed from Egypt, including two strange animals no Romans recognized —a rhinoceros and a hippopotamus walked in the procession. There were pictures representing the Nile and Egypt; there were hundreds of statues from Egyptian temples; there was a painting of Cleopatra with a serpent coiled over her arm, as she lay in her death-throes upon a royal couch. Among those who saw the paint-ing was the twenty-two-year-old poet Propertius, who remembered with a feeling of terror the impression aroused in him by the painting:

> I saw her arms bitten by the sacred snakes,
> And the hidden way of sleep stretched forth her limbs.

But though the immense painting was carried in the triumph, no attempt was made to remove the statue of Cleopatra which Julius Caesar had placed in the temple of Venus Genetrix. There she reigned supreme, while in the procession she was an object of horror and execration. The hated enemy had fallen, but some-thing of her power still remained to haunt the Roman people, who saw in her the symbol of all the luxurious vices of the East.

Two of Cleopatra's children were led in chains. They were the twins, Alexander Helios and Cleopatra Selene, eight years old and appealingly handsome. They were allowed to walk with Octavian up the steps to the Temple of Jupiter Capitolinus, and were not consigned to the Mamertine prison.

So the strange procession with its black men and elephants and carts laden with treasure passed through the streets of Rome, while the senators followed the triumphal chariot, mingling ignominiously with the soldiers. There were other innovations. In the past a slave or an attendant in the chariot held a crown over the *triumphator's* head: this time Octavian wore the crown, which was rayed and glittering with gems. Yet to him the most important innovation may have been the branch from the sacred laurel grove which Livia had planted near her villa at the ninth milestone of the Via Flaminia, and which he carried in his right hand throughout the procession. After the procession this sacred branch was replanted, to be used again in further triumphs. The green branch was in some strange way regarded as the continuing emblem of the triumph.

With Octavian in his chariot rode two children clothed in white robes. One was the fourteen-year-old Marcellus, Octavia's son, destined if he had lived to be the successor to the throne: the other was the thirteen-year-old Tiberius, the son of Livia by a former husband, who inherited the throne, although he possessed none of the blood which flowed through Octavian's veins.

The Romans were awed by the sight of the royal treasures which accompanied the Alexandrian triumph. This money was to be used to finance a vast programme of public buildings, and one of the more unexpected results of the triumph was to make ready money so abundant that the rate of interest fell and the value of real estate sky-rocketed. The Alexandrian treasure produced inflation.

For the Romans, too, this triumph was the most memorable of all. Those three days of triumph later came to be called *feriae augustales*, and still later they were known as *ferragosto*. Today on August 15, the anniversary of the triumph over Cleopatra, Rome still keeps holiday. Shops, banks and offices are closed; even the Sistine chapel is barred to visitors; and Roman holiday-makers celebrate the defeat of an ancient empress of Egypt by going on picnics in the Abruzzi mountains. Six centuries after the triumph the Roman Catholic Church pronounced the day a church holiday, celebrating instead of the death of Cleopatra the anniversary of the Assumption of the Virgin Mary into Heaven.

For a few more years triumphs were to be awarded to Roman generals, but a change was already in the air. It seems to have been Agrippa who suggested that the triumphal procession should be reserved for the emperor alone. To the *triumphator* there would be given all the outward manifestations of a triumph—the laurel crown, the ivory staff crowned with a golden eagle, the curule throne, the two triumphal garments known as the *tunica palmata* and the *toga picta*, and even the triumphal chariot. These they would be allowed to keep and bequeath to their descendants, and at their funerals their images would appear robed in the triumphal garments, but the procession would be forbidden to them.

Octavian planned other changes. Still oppressed by the memory of the murdered Julius Caesar, he built a forum in his own honour and vowed a temple to Mars Ultor—Mars the Avenger. This new temple would supersede the Temple of Jupiter on the Capitol, becoming the centre of a new cult. Here the *triumphator* would deposit his insignia after each triumph. In the imagination of Octavian the triumph was to be performed before the shades of Julius Caesar. In much the same way prisoners captured in ancient times by the Chinese were presented in the Ta Miao temple in Peking to the shades of the imperial ancestors.

Octavian did not content himself with building the gigantic temple to Mars Ultor, the first temple to Mars ever erected within the walls of Rome; he also restored and enlarged the temple to Jupiter Feretrius on the Capitol, supposed to be the most ancient in Rome. He was in fact continually building and restoring temples, and the approaches to the Capitol were becoming uncomfortably crowded. The temple to Jupiter Capitolinus, however, had remained unchanged since its restoration by Sulla except for the addition of the statue of Jupiter which looked down upon the Forum from the platform outside the temple. By a strange coincidence the statue was put up on the day of the discovery of the Catilinarian conspiracy in 63 B.C., and Cicero, speaking from the Rostra, was able to point to the new and gleaming statue as the saviour of the city, the protector of the Roman state.

Octavian, as he surveyed the world in the early years of his principate, seems to have abandoned the worship of Jupiter as the most powerful of the gods; he prayed instead to Apollo and Mars. For a few more years he permitted his generals to observe triumphs—Suetonius says he permitted thirty triumphs, but only eight are recorded between 28 B.C. and 19 B.C. Thereafter triumphs were reserved for the emperor and for members of the imperial family.

The last of the triumphs enjoyed by a general not a member of the imperial family was granted in 19 B.C. to the banker Lucius Cornelius Balbus for his victories over the Garamantes and other African peoples. Balbus had been an intimate friend of Julius Caesar, and the chief supplier of his army during the early Spanish campaign. He was a skilful administrator, a great lover of philosophy, and after Maecenas the greatest patron of letters in his time. Suetonius tells the story of how Balbus forcibly prevented Caesar rising to receive an important deputation, believing that Caesar was more than half divine and therefore not to be inconvenienced by anything so unimportant as a deputation. The last of the Roman generals to triumph was not even a Roman citizen by birth, but a pure Spaniard who was born in Gades (Cadiz) and acquired Roman citizenship late in life.

That year Octavian, now known throughout the world as the Emperor Augustus, also enjoyed a triumph, though it was one which never appeared in the official list of triumphs. Since acquiring power he had spent half his days abroad, inspecting his empire, leaving the government in the safe hands of Agrippa. Now, after spending two years in the east, he returned to Rome bringing with him the bronze eagles lost at Carrhae, and now restored by the Parthians: the eagles had come into the possession of his stepson Tiberius, who in turn had given them to the Emperor. The Romans were overjoyed, and Augustus was permitted to enter the city through an arch especially erected in his honour, riding at the head of his legions. The bronze eagles were deposited in the still-unfinished temple of Mars Ultor; and there were many who regarded the occasion as greater than a triumph.

While Augustus took very little interest in the formal triumph and after his great triumph of 29 B.C. never celebrated one, he occasionally permitted himself the luxury of entering the city in procession, improvising on the theme of the triumph, as Julius Caesar had done before him. There were no sacrifices and no prisoners, but the procession was otherwise hardly distinguishable from a triumph. Coins were struck to honour the pacification of the Parthians; there were donations to the soldiers, gifts to the people, special prayers were offered in the temples. Six years later, after a progress through Gaul and Spain, there was a similar procession, and this time the emperor climbed the steps to the Capitol and solemnly placed on the knees of the statue of Jupiter a laurel wreath. He had long since put formal triumphs behind him, but it was a triumph in everything except name.

As he grew older, he became more and more interested in the ancient Roman past. His own place in Roman history was assured, but he gave the impression of being a man determined to seek for his own origins in antiquity. At some time in the winter of 18/17 B.C. he ordered that the names of all the consuls and *triumphatores* who had exercised power since the founding of the city be inscribed on the walls of the Regia in the Forum. The *fasti consulares*, which also included a brief notice of memorable events from the beginning of the Republic to the time of Augustus and was subsequently kept up to date until A.D. 13, covered the west wall and part of the south wall, while the *fasti triumphales* covered the remaining space on the south wall. When the site of the Regia was discovered in 1878, fragments of the *fasti* were found exactly where Augustus had ordered them to be inscribed. They have since been removed to the Conservatori Museum in Rome, where they can be seen today. The first fragment of the *fasti triumphales* reads simply:

ROMVLVS.MARTIS.F.REX.ANN / / / / /
DE.CAENINENSIBUS.K.MAR.
/ / / / /MARTIS.F.REX.II

Romulus, son of Mars, king in the year . . . (triumphed) over the Caeninenses on the kalends of March, and for the second time . . .

So the long list of *triumphatores* continues, with many breaks, until the time of Augustus himself. The letters are very small and deeply incised, and some of them still bear traces of the red paint which once embellished them. Unfortunately this record of the triumphs cannot be completely relied upon. It has no high claim to credibility, being no more than an official compilation reflecting the historical knowledge of the time. Two more fragments from other *fasti* have since been discovered, but they add little to the information carved on the walls of the Regia.

Often ill, always strangely detached from matters of this world, Augustus became increasingly enamoured of peace. Three times in his long reign the doors of the temple of Janus, closed only twice in the entire history of Rome up to his time, were ceremonially closed by the emperor himself. As he saw his own strength declining, he came more and more to look forward to the time when it would be possible to surrender his burdens to his nephew Marcellus or to his stepsons Tiberius and Drusus. Marcellus died young; Drusus died; then there was only Tiberius, thin and tall, with his small mouth and enormous eyes, to contend for the throne after Augustus's death.

The emperor was a long time dying. Long before his death he had become a symbol of unity, a legend so powerful that he seemed to have no life of his own. There is a story that in his later years

Augustus showed his quixotic temper by sometimes standing outside his palace with unkempt beard in beggar's robes, gravely
accepting the coins tossed to him; and perhaps these occasional acts
of humility had their source in penitence. He lived simply, disliking display. The violent ambitions of Tiberius disturbed him,
and he seems to have been relieved when his stepson abandoned a
military career for self-imposed exile on the island of Rhodes after
waging a series of bitter campaigns in Gaul, Germany and Pannonia. Suetonius says he was granted an ovation and a triumph for
these campaigns, but no details of this triumph have survived.

In those early years, while he was still finding himself, Tiberius
always gave the impression of a ruthless, efficient, superbly well-
equipped machine. He went about the business of acquiring power
with a strange methodical ruthlessness, killing off all rivals, possessed of an unswerving confidence in his destiny. On the day when
his long exile came to an end, an eagle perched on his house in
Rhodes, and then he knew he would triumph again.

Tiberius triumphed altogether three times, but the greatest
triumph was the last. This took place on January 16, A.D. 12, after
his victories over the Pannonians. On that day the throne of the
seventy-four-year-old Augustus stood at the foot of the Capitoline
hill, and when the triumphal chariot approached the throne
Tiberius dismounted and prostrated himself before his stepfather.
It was a touching moment, for Tiberius was thereby ascribing the
victory to the emperor, now grey-haired and grey-bearded, with
rheumy eyes, no longer the young lithe prince which the world
remembers from the statues made in his youth. Tiberius was in a
relenting mood. He did not order the execution of the Pannonian
prince Bato, who had allowed him to escape when his army was
trapped. He sent the prince instead to Ravenna, after loading him
with gifts; and afterwards he gave a banquet at a thousand tables
to the people of Rome.

This triumph, or perhaps an earlier one, was recorded in a monumental sculpture long since lost, which is reproduced in miniature
on a small silver cup found at Boscoreale. It is an astonishing work
of art, by far the most subtle and evocative of all sculptured representations of a triumph. Two episodes are shown: the procession
with the imperial chariot and the actual sacrifice before the garlanded temple of Jupiter Capitolinus: and the artist has successfully evoked the sense of an endless sacrifice in this round frieze
crowded with figures, with solemn gestures and significant movement. So well has the artist depicted the scene that we almost
hear the voices of the participants.

We see Tiberius standing in the gilded chariot, an attendant behind him supporting the golden crown, the eagle-crowned sceptre and the laurel branch in the *triumphator's* hands. Following the chariot come the soldiers in short tunics, bearing laurels over their shoulders, one of them with a golden *torque* round his neck as a sign of his especial bravery. The lictors bearing the *fasces* march beside the four horses, some gazing back in reverence towards Tiberius. All through the composition of the triumph there is the subtle play of backward gazing faces and those which look impassively forward, steeled to the discipline of the procession. So the youth running behind the haunches of the ox swings his body round and turns his face upward in contemplation of the *triumphator's* glory, while the other youth, who bears an axe on his shoulder, studies the strange knot he has tied in the ox's halter. The ox is the most rounded and well-modelled figure in the entire frieze, a heavy beast with short legs, decked with fillets and ribbons, wearing the sacrificial crown between its golden horns, seemingly unaware of the presence of the youth tugging at it, leading it forward. There is a grave stateliness in the procession, which moves quietly, gathering the momentum which will explode into violence in the last scene of all.

On half a cup the artist has represented fourteen figures, four horses and an ox. In a kind of deliberate shorthand—for much has been left out—he has suggested the mood and the tempo of the procession; shown how the soldiers and lictors held themselves in procession; given us a close view of the chariot; described the strange loneliness which attends the sacrificial ox; painted the *triumphator* in stern magnificence.

On the other side the same figures are represented. We see the *triumphator* wearing the cuirass, with a military cloak thrown over his shoulders. An acolyte, dressed in a tunic, plays on the flute. Incense rises from the tripod, while the *triumphator* declaims the appropriate prayers in the presence of the lictors. The artist has deliberately represented the most solemn moment of the triumph: the moment of prayer which is also the moment of sacrifice.

No one ever represented the sacrifice better. Before the garlanded temple, the wide-winged eagle of Jupiter filling the pediment, the kneeling *victimarii* pull the ox's head to the ground. One holds a triangular knife, ready to slit the victim's throat; a youthful *popa*, like a young Hercules, prepares to strike at the victim's skull with an axe, while another attendant watches in trepidation. The tranquil temple on its raised platform looks down on the scene in silence: the composition of the garland and pediment suggesting an enormous wide-open eye. We see the gilded tiles, the bricks of the double platform, the marble columns receding into the distance: there is no doubt about the setting. The artist has deliberately isolated the axe-head and given the scene of the sacrifice a monumentality which seems strange when we remember that the figures are only a few centimetres high. No other relief describes the sacrifice with such effortless power.

The triumph of A.D. 12 was the last to take place in Augustus's lifetime. The emperor was already dying of the wasting disease which finally killed him. During his last year he composed the long account of his stewardship which was found carved in marble at Ancyra. He wrote: *Twice I triumphed with an ovation, three times I celebrated curule triumphs. Although the Senate decreed me additional triumphs I set them aside. In my triumphs there was led before my chariot nine kings or children of kings.* With these last words he saluted Alexander and Cleopatra, the children of Cleopatra whose statue was borne in the procession of his Egyptian triumph.

When he died, most of his sins were forgiven him. At his funeral his image, wearing the triumphal garments, was displayed over his coffin. Once again, and for the last time, he rode in his triumphal chariot, or so it seemed: but in fact it was a golden image of the emperor arrayed in the *tunica palmata* and the *toga picta,* holding the sceptre and the laurels, who passed in procession. Soldiers guarded his coffin, as it was borne through the *porta triumphalis.* It was a kind of triumph in reverse, for the names of all the conquered nations were written on standards and flourished before him. His body was burned on the Campus Martius and the ashes were placed in the mausoleum he had built in his own honour. And the people, seeing so many soldiers gathered around the body of the dead emperor, asked whether he had done any wrong to be defended when he was dead.

Tacitus said of him that he had brought peace to Rome, "a peace stained with blood". Maecenas once called him a common hangman, and the philosopher Seneca spoke of his clemency "which arose out of weary cruelty". He was a man of moods, stern, gentle, unassuming, intolerant of all opposition, at once the most pacific and war-like of emperors. For another hundred years the Roman people were to pay bitterly for the long peace he had brought them: he had saved the empire, but only at the price of enslaving the Romans. Tiberius reaped what he had sown; and the shadow of the long-dead emperor fell across all the remaining years of Rome.

9

THE TRIUMPHS OF MAD EMPERORS

WITH the death of Augustus the Roman empire lost its reason for existence. He had built the empire in his own image: like him, it suffered from a wasting disease and survived by repeated acts of will. After him there came only the slow and exhausting process of degradation. Three hundred years were to pass before the pagan-Christian Constantine infused the empire with a new spirit.

Augustus had killed the triumph: it had become in his reign no more than one of the many imperial processions, a gesture in honour of his own divinity. He had built the vast temple of Mars Ultor and ordered that the triumphal mystery should take place there, but in fact it continued to take place on the Capitol. Triumphs continued to make their way through the streets of Rome, but very rarely: altogether there were only twenty-one triumphs between the death of Augustus and the rise of Constantine. The original strength had departed. There was something feverish and ghostly in all the triumphs that came afterwards.

Almost Tiberius was a ghost. He was fifty-six when he became emperor, a grave, silent man, who walked stiffly and seemed plunged in permanent melancholy. Pliny calls him *tristissimus hominum*, the most melancholy of men. No inner fire warmed him. It was a face wasted with misery, though sometimes even after he became emperor those enormous eyes would open wide and reveal their beauty and from his small mouth there would come a lapidary phrase. He had survived all those who had better claims to the throne, and to the end he wore the look of "a man who has survived".

There was bitterness in him: the consuming bitterness of a man who came to power too late to enjoy it. He took no pleasure in his empire, shuffled off responsibilities whenever possible, and did nothing to extend the frontiers of Roman power. After his accession he never led an army, and Suetonius says he allowed his generals to put down rebellions "only reluctantly and of necessity". Consequently there were few occasions for triumphs and the presentation of triumphal *regalia*. Disliking display he forbade the use of the triumphal robe in the circus.

When Augustus died, Germanicus was in Gaul, but hearing of a mutiny in the army of the Rhine he hurried to Germany and by soft words succeeded in quelling it. He was then twenty-nine, a singularly gentle and kindly soldier, with none of the mysterious reserve which characterized his uncle. He wrote comedies. He enjoyed talking with soldiers in the camp. He was at ease with poets, lawyers and men in all walks of life. He could probably have made himself emperor, for the soldiers he had saved from mutiny begged him to put himself at the head of the army and march on Rome. Germanicus refused, and even threatened to kill himself if they persisted in their disloyalty to the emperor. To give the soldiers something to do, he led them in a quick campaign against the German tribes to the east of the Rhine, which was so successful that Tiberius, who feared the growing power and fame of his nephew, offered him a triumph. Germanicus accepted the triumph, but went on fighting. He fought a pitched battle against Arminius, the leader of the German confederacy, recovered the eagles abandoned by Varus, and solemnly buried the dead legionaries who were still lying where they fell in the Teutoburg forest. At last the patience of Tiberius was exhausted. Too many victories were being won by his nephew, who was abruptly recalled to Rome to take part in his long-promised triumph.

This was the only triumph celebrated during the long reign of Tiberius. It took place on May 26, A.D. 17, and all Rome came out to witness the event. The triumph was in honour of victories over the Cherusci, Chatti, Angrivarii and other tribes in the lands between the Rhine and the Elbe, but to the Romans these victories were less important than the recovery of the eagles, the presence of Germanicus in their midst, the knowledge that the German wars were temporarily over. They hurried out to meet him when he was twenty miles from Rome, and it was observed that the Praetorian Guard was especially conspicuous among the welcoming-party, a fact that was undoubtedly reported to Tiberius with unhappy consequences. Germanicus rode in the triumphal chariot with five of his young sons by Agrippina, among them the boy who had been nicknamed Caligula, "the Little Shoe", by adoring legionaries. There were the usual painted reproductions of battles, pictures of the mountains and rivers over which the armies had fought. There were carts filled with the spoils of war. Arminius was still at large, but his wife Thusnelda had been captured, and she walked before the triumphal chariot, carrying in her arms a baby born in servitude. But the people of Rome had eyes only for the conqueror, who was unusually handsome as he stood in the ornamental robes of a *triumphator* in a chariot so crowded that there was no room for the public slave who normally whispered into the conqueror's ear that he was only mortal. There was about him, as he rode through Rome, something which suggested mortality. Drusus, his father, had died young. His uncle, Marcellus, had also died young. Tacitus says they watched him passing before them and murmured among themselves: *Breves et infaustos populi Romani amores*. "How brief and ill-starred are the loves of the Roman people."

Germanicus may have guessed how brief and ill-starred his life was to be when he saw the hastily-erected triumphal archway on the Capitoline steps commemorating the recovery of the lost standards, designated not with his own name, but with that of Tiberius. The emperor, in fact, was assuming responsibility for the victories. Having refused all titles previously offered to him by the Senate, he now accepted the title of Germanicus, implying that he was himself the conqueror of Germany. But he remembered to make a present of 300 sesterces to every Roman citizen in honour of the triumph, saying he did this in the name of his nephew. It was a surprising act of charity on the part of a man rarely noted for his charity. The *ornamenta triumphalia* were awarded to the three generals, Aulus Caecina, Lucius Apronius and Caius Silius, who had brilliantly assisted Germanicus in his campaigns.

Germanicus was allowed to remain only a few months in Rome. In the autumn he was sent to the east to assume control of the disaffected provinces of Syria, Judaea, Commagene and Cilicia, with the powers of an imperial governor. Tacitus, who tells the story in tones of sombre tragedy, believed he was sent to the east to remove him from the Roman scene, but Germanicus himself, exhausted by the German wars, seems to have delighted in the prospect of a long and not too troublesome sojourn in countries where he could resume his archaeological interests and study at the feet of scholars. He crossed the Adriatic in a storm, and at Actium offered sacrifices on the battlefield, where his great-uncle Augustus had fought against his grandfather Antony. Then he visited Troy, sailed into the Black Sea, paused briefly in Thrace and Byzantium, made his way to Armenia, where he appointed a new king, and spent some leisurely months in Egypt, sailing up the Nile and studying the antiquities. He admired the Pyramids, listened to the voice of the image of Memnon, and showed his solicitude for the Egyptians by opening the granaries and reducing the price of corn. Everywhere he went, says Tacitus, he put aside the demeanour of a prince. He walked about in the loose robes of a Greek philosopher, in sandalled feet, without guards, and was gentle with everyone.

He was mistaken, however, if he thought he could make a peaceful progress. Everywhere he went he was dogged by the presence of his *adjutor*, a man sent to spy on his movements and report to the emperor. This was Gnaeus Piso, an aristrocrat of boundless ambitions who apparently hoped by a judicious use of his reportorial powers to assume the position occupied by Germanicus. He was married to Plancina, the daughter of the perpetually treacherous Minucius Plancus. Germanicus returned to Antioch from Egypt, to find Piso in full control of the army. Piso was dismissed, not without considerable trouble, and soon Germanicus, who had been in remarkably good health, fell unaccountably ill. It was rumoured that he was poisoned. Human bones, spells and incantations, together with cinders smeared with blood, were found beneath the floors of his palace. Germanicus himself was sure he had been poisoned, but he was troubled by the thought that Piso should have used a slow poison when it was so evident that he wanted power quickly. "Poison is such a tedious affair," he said. "Why poison me, when he wants the province and the legions in great haste?" But the poison was quicker than he thought, and he died a few hours later. Naked, he was laid on the funeral pyre in the forum of Antioch, and Agrippina, the mother of his nine children, took his ashes to Rome.

No one ever discovered whether Germanicus was deliberately poisoned by Piso, but all the evidence pointed to his guilt. And there was some evidence which pointed to the guilt of Tiberius.

When the news of Germanicus's illness reached Rome, the whole city was plunged into grief. The same night there came the report that he was recovering, and immediately there was a general rush to the Capitol by people who wanted to celebrate his recovery with sacrifices. So many people were hurrying there with torches and sacrificial victims that the gates were all but torn off, and Tiberius was awakened from sleep by the sound of voices chanting: "Rome is safe, our country is safe, for our Germanicus is safe."

Tiberius took no part in the funeral ceremonies. As always he was strangely remote and forbidding, alone with his ghosts on the Palatine. He granted the most splendid funeral, ordered the centurions and tribunes to carry the urn on their shoulders all the way from Brundisium to Rome, and permitted the Romans to throng in vast numbers around the funeral cortège to the mausoleum of Augustus. Afterwards he allowed to Germanicus the honours which would have been paid to a dead emperor. Triumphal arches were erected in Rome, on the banks of the Rhine and on Mount Hermon in Syria, with inscriptions recording his achievements, and how he *died for the Republic*. His statues were set up in various cities, and sacrifices were made before them. His bust was placed in libraries and in public galleries, a cenotaph was raised in the forum of Antioch where his body was burned, and in the suburb of Epidaphne where he died a commemorative mound was raised.

In that same year died Arminius, the German chieftain, who destroyed the army of Varus. He was killed by men of his own tribe, who were sickened by his assumption of dictatorial powers. In the following year Piso died by his own hand during the course of his trial before the Senate, leaving a message imploring Tiberius not to punish his children.

For Tiberius the death of Germanicus was a matter of little importance; he felt no grief, and had long ago removed himself from the world of intelligible government. Not mad but close to madness, he allowed power to fall into the hands of his minister, Sejanus. Battles were fought on the frontiers, and from time to time there were awards of *ornamenta triumphalia* by the senators. One such award was given to a certain Camillus, described by Tacitus as "an inexperienced soldier who enjoyed the honour without harm, since he lived an unambitious life". Of Poppaeus Sabinus, who received the honour in A.D. 26 Tacitus says: "He rose from a poor family, and for twenty-four years exercised command over important provinces, not from any remarkable ability he possessed, but because he was equal to the task and not too great for it." Tacitus, the patrician, admired humility in others.

For twenty-three years Tiberius ruled without ever governing and murdered without ever knowing why. There was about all his crimes, which were innumerable, the sense of a man consumed by his own carelessness, his own indifference, his own desperate need for quietness. For the last eleven years of his reign he simply retreated from life into the magical island of Capri, where he might have found quietness, if quietness were possible. He died at the age of seventy-eight of old age and misery, his death hastened by poison administered perhaps by Caligula. It had been a strange reign. Tacitus describes it as "a time of peace wholly unbroken or only slightly pricked, deep gloom in the capital, and an emperor careless about the forward march of his empire".

Caligula, the son of Germanicus, possessed none of his father's virtues, and in his four-year reign proved only what the Romans already knew: that absolute power corrupts absolutely. He was twenty-five when he came to the throne, and almost his first task was to sweep the works of Virgil and Livy from the libraries on the grounds that Virgil had no learning and Livy was an incompetent blunderer. Two years later he built a bridge of boats across the bay of Baiae and rode across it, wearing the jewelled breastplate of Alexander the Great, his sword by his side, his shield on his arm and a crown of oak-leaves on his head. He was followed by his army, and when he reached Puteoli he gave the order for the charge and entered the city like a conqueror. The next day he rode back across the bridge in a triumphal chariot, wearing the clothes of a charioteer at the games in the Circus. This triumph was adorned with prisoners: some Persians who had been living quietly in Rome. The army followed, and the musicians played. At the centre of the bridge Caligula halted, and addressed his soldiers with a long harangue on the subject of the great victory they had just accomplished and declared that the exploits of Darius and Xerxes were trifling compared with his own magnificent enterprise. Then he gave donations to his soldiers and promised them a banquet, remaining all the while on the bridge, very drunk and happy as he gazed at the boat-loads of holiday-makers who had come to see him in his glory.

For the first time an emperor's triumph had slipped over the thin border-line which separates glory and madness.

Caligula had been on the throne for only a few months when he declared himself a god, and placed in his own temple a life-size statue of himself in gold. Every day the statue was dressed in his discarded clothes; priests uttered prayers; the proper sacrifices were offered. He had a nice taste in sacrificial victims, and urged those who wished to worship him to offer up flamingoes, peacocks, guinea-hens, woodcock and pheasants. Suetonius says that every night he invited the moon to his embraces, and every day he whispered secrets into the lips of the massive statue of Jupiter Capitolinus. Once he was heard to say to the god of triumph: "Lift me, or I will lift thee!"

His vices conspired to drive him mad. He said once that he possessed the unshakeable rigour of the Stoics, but this rigour amounted to no more than a strenuous search for disaster; and he regretted that no earth-shaking and terrible events happened in his reign. In this he was wrong. He was himself an earth-shaking event, possessed of an illimitable delight in pure evil. Nero's sins were smaller.

Caligula perverted the triumph when he crossed the bridge of boats; he perverted it again when on an impulse he decided to invade Britain, marched his legionaries from Lyons to the Channel, boarded a trireme, and suddenly gave the order to his legionaries to collect seashells, saying they were "the spoils of ocean". These spoils were then solemnly despatched to Rome, and the senators were ordered to offer them to the treasury of the Capitol. For this invasion of Britain, so singularly unsuccessful, he demanded and received the honour of a triumph, and led his army through the streets of Rome, riding in a chariot and leading before him a handful of prisoners and deserters. These deserters were Gauls with their hair dyed red, to make them more nearly resemble Germans; he ordered them to learn German speech and to take Germanic names. But when he reached Rome, it disturbed him to see the senators coming out to meet him and he abruptly postponed the triumph and announced that he would be content with an ovation. So he entered Rome and scattered coins prodigally among the spectators, while the Gauls with dyed hair walked before him. It was his birthday, August 31, A.D. 41. Four months later, while walking through the vaulted passage-way which led from his palace to the Circus, he was stabbed to death, and all Rome sighed with relief.

They said of Caligula that brilliance often shone through the darkness of his mind, and they might have said the same of his successor, the Deified Claudius, the younger son of Drusus, who was the brother of Tiberius. He was fifty-one when he came to the throne, much against his will. He was a scholar, author of *Tyrrhenica*, an immensely learned study of Etruscan origins, now lost. He wrote a history of Carthage, and another of Rome from the battle of Actium in forty-one books, and the memorials of his own times in eight books. He wrote comedies and a treatise on dice-playing. Livy had been his tutor; scholars surrounded him in his youth; and he would have been perfectly happy to spend his time in libraries. He was fine-boned and handsome, but suffered from a kind of palsy, so that his head wobbled on his neck and his legs sometimes gave way under him. Suetonius says he was majestic in appearance "when sitting still, and especially when lying down".

It is the habit of scholars suddenly raised to positions of power to enjoy it to the uttermost. Claudius modelled himself on Augustus, and set about extending the bounds of his empire. Since the time of Julius Caesar no Roman had set foot on Britain, famous for its tin-mines and pearls. He decided to conquer it. Aulus Plautius, who held a high command in Gaul, was ordered to make a preliminary reconnaissance in A.D. 42, the year after Claudius came to the throne. Accordingly a three-pronged attack was launched from the Lowlands, and Aulus Plautius crossed over into Kent. There was little opposition until one of his armies under Flavius Vespasianus, the future emperor, reached the Midlands. Claudius himself, after receiving preliminary reports, decided to take over supreme command in Britain. He sailed to Marseilles, marched across Gaul to Boulogne, where a fleet was waiting for him, and soon he was receiving the submission of the tribes. It was a quick and painless conquest—according to Suetonius no battles took place during Claudius's stay in Britain. Six months after setting out he was back again in Rome. The Senate had once offered him the *ornamenta triumphalia*, which he refused as beneath his imperial dignity. Now, having conquered Britain (or a small corner of it), the Senate hurriedly convened to grant him a triumph. He was so delighted that he invited the provincial governors to attend and pardoned some exiled enemies of the régime so that they could see him in his glory. His wife Messalina rode in a carriage behind his chariot. A number of generals who had taken part in the British campaign received the *ornamenta triumphalia*, and they were permitted to ride behind the empress, also in carriages. One officer was receiving the honour for a second time, and for him a new honour was created—he was permitted to ride a caparisoned horse while wearing a tunic embroidered with palms. Only one incident disturbed the calm celebration of the triumph. Corpulent and ungainly, the emperor stumbled at the foot of the Capitoline steps, and two officers of the court had to hold him up at each side as he made his slow shuffling way to the Temple of Jupiter Capitolinus. No one knows whether he fell from nervousness, or from an attack of palsy, or in conscious imitation of Julius Caesar, the only other *triumphator* who crawled up the steps.

There was no end to his enjoyment of the triumph. He gloried in his new title of Britannicus. The Senate ordered arches to be erected in his honour in Rome and Boulogne, bearing his trophies. He set a naval crown on the gable of his palace as a sign that he had subdued the ocean, and he ordered the erection in Camulodunum of a large and splendid temple in his own honour; and the name of Camulodunum was changed to Colonia Victricensis, the Colony of the Conquering Claudius. The most distinguished Britons were invited to enrol themselves in the college of the Claudian Flamens,

A few months later the unwelcome news reached Rome that the British under Caractacus were in full revolt. The conquest was in fact no conquest at all. There were more battles, and it was not until A.D. 47 that Aulus Plautius was able to announce that Britain was pacified. Claudius summoned him to Rome for an ovation, which in this case seems to have been a modified triumphal procession through the streets of Rome, without the usual procession to the Alban Mount. Claudius showed great warmth. He felt no jealousy over the exploits of the commander-in-chief of the Roman forces in Britain. The emperor himself invested him with the *ornamenta triumphalia,* the laurel crown and the *triumphator's* robe, presenting him with these honours outside the city. Suetonius says the emperor walked on the general's left as they went to the Capitol and back. Probably they walked together, for it is unlikely that the emperor should walk while the general rode in a chariot.

After Aulus Plautius no other person not a member of the imperial house received an ovation.

After nine years of fighting Caractacus was captured, put in chains, and with his wife and brothers brought to Rome. Claudius seems to have debated with himself whether he would hold another triumph, but finally decided upon a spectacular display, an altogether new kind of triumph, without the usual procession through the streets. It took place outside of Rome, on the plain facing the camp of the Praetorian Guard, and a vast concourse of Romans was invited to watch the grand spectacle of the captives and the trophies of war passing before the emperor, who sat on a throne with his wife beside him. It was observed that Messalina wore a general's cloak and was assuming a position unusual in the wife of an emperor. Caractacus was brought before the throne. He was in chains, but held himself like a king. Tacitus has preserved, or invented, the speech in which Caractacus demanded without any show of humility that his life should be preserved, reminding Claudius that there would have been no triumph if he had not fought the long war against the Roman legions. He was immediately pardoned, his chains were removed from him, and he seems to have spent the rest of his life in honourable captivity. To Publius Ostorius Scapula, governor of Britain, went the *ornamenta triumphalia.* He died a few months later, worn out, it is said, by the fatigues of office while the dangerous and long-drawn-out war with the British tribes continued.

Claudius delighted in receiving honours, and he delighted in giving them. He gave the *ornamenta triumphalia* to a boy, Lucius Silanus, who was affianced to his daughter. So many people received the honour that the legions sent a humble entreaty to the emperor requesting that generals in command of armies close to the frontiers be awarded the same honour, to prevent them from seeking pretexts for war. Once the triumphs themselves had been devalued by granting too many of them, it was perhaps inevitable that the *ornamenta triumphalia* should suffer the same devaluation.

After a reign of fourteen years Claudius was poisoned by his fourth wife, Agrippina. He richly deserved to die, but he hardly deserved Agrippina, the shrewish and murderous mother of Nero by a former husband. In a pleasant fiction the philosopher Seneca imagined the Deified Claudius spending his after-life in Hell, playing with a bottomless dice-box.

In the veins of Nero there flowed the blood of Augustus, Agrippa and Germanicus. He possessed all the talents except one—he never understood the meaning of moderation. In his youth he had something of the delicate beauty of Augustus, but soon the face grew heavy to the point of travesty with dewlaps and fat jowls and a small mouth riding arrogantly above a jutting chin. This malodorous, pot-bellied, spindle-legged ruler of the world had three aims in life—to be a great singer, a great lyre-player and a great poet. Almost as soon as he became emperor he set about reciting his verses in public, and ordered them to be engraved in gold in the Temple of Jupiter Capitolinus. He hoped to be remembered as an emperor of peace, thought of withdrawing the army from Britain, and did everything possible to avoid making military decisions. He enjoyed no military triumphs, but deliberately sought to transform the triumph into its poetic equivalent. To his generals he gave the *ornamenta triumphalia* without seeming to care whether they won any victories, and Suetonius observed with horror that he gave it to men below the rank of quaestor, and even to knights, and sometimes granted it to people who had never fought at all.

He was a man, says Tacitus, who lusted after the incredible—*incredibilium cupitor*, and all his triumphs were incredible. He had none of the insane barbaric grandeur of Caligula, who gloried in being a god and ordered divine honours to be paid to him. Nero was of the earth, earthy: Caliban in the robes of a king. His triumphs accordingly were the expressions of his arrogance and petulance, his yearning for the unattainable, his lust for murder, his delight in art: and the triumphs were painfully boring. Only once did he show a spark of divine arrogance, and that was when he ordered the erection of an arch of triumph in his own honour on the Capitol, to celebrate some imagined victories over the Persians. He celebrated his first triumph over the murder of his mother, Agrippina.

It was an unusually unpleasant murder, and Nero suffered some pangs of conscience after it had been committed. There were nightmares, visions of the furies with their blazing torches, and for a few days an overwhelming sense of grief. Then at last, reassured by his friends that the murder of Agrippina would be regarded in Rome as an act of piety towards the state, Nero returned to discover the rewards of murder. All Rome welcomed him. The senators put on their holiday robes to greet him, with their wives and children; the streets were thronged with seats raised against the houses to accommodate the multitude of spectators. "They watched it as they would watch a triumphal procession," says Tacitus; and indeed it was more than the simple entry of an emperor into his city. Nero greeted the people he had enslaved, and went on to perform sacrifices at the Temple of Jupiter Capitolinus exactly as though he were a *triumphator*. A similar triumph seems to have taken place after he murdered his wife Octavia, the daughter of Claudius and Messalina, who was asphyxiated in a steam-bath.

Nero's triumphs followed no accepted pattern. He celebrated a triumph over Tiridates, king of Armenia, who was induced to come to Rome with a safe-conduct, to receive the diadem from the hands of Nero. Wearing the robes of a *triumphator*, Nero sat on a curule chair in the Forum, against a display of military standards. All round him, guarding the temples in the Forum, were the soldiers of the Praetorian Guard in full armour. A sloping ramp led to the throne, and the Armenian king was led up the ramp to prostrate himself before Nero, who raised him up and kissed him and then removed the turban from his head, replacing it with the jewelled ribbon of the tiara. A high official who could speak in Armenian translated the words of the king and recited them to the great crowd which had assembled in the Forum. A little later the same scene was enacted in the theatre, where after prostrating himself the king was permitted to sit by Nero's side. The soldiers acclaimed Nero as *imperator*, and the emperor walked up the Capitoline steps to deposit a laurel crown on the lap of the god as a sign of his triumph. Nero seems to have been particularly delighted by the coming of King Tiridates, and to impress his visitor he ordered the roof of the Pantheon to be covered with gold leaf. At his command this was done in a single day.

After this imaginary triumph he ordered that the door of the temple of Janus should be shut, "since there was no more war in the world".

There were many wars, but Nero seems to have been unaware of them. When Gnaeus Domitius Corbulo, after distinguishing himself in campaigns against the Parthians, returned from the east, he received instead of a triumph the order to kill himself. Nero, living in the imaginary world of perpetual triumph, could not brook the presence of a real *triumphator*. He gave the *ornamenta triumphalia* to those who served him, not to those who were rivals. About this time he was giving the greatest honour known to the Romans to panderers, informers and the slavish servants of his court.

There remained the prospect of a triumph so great that the world would be astonished. Such a triumph had been won only once in human history by the Greek Periodonicus, who won the whole circle of the Greek games. Nero decided to make his way to Greece and win, if not all the games, at least as many as an emperor might win with decency. In A.D. 66 he set out for Greece, and soon after his arrival ordered that the games usually performed at intervals of five years at Olympia, Nemea, Delphi and Corinth should take place during his stay. He won all the games he contested. He even won the chariot race after falling with his chariot and horses to the ground. There was a moment when he began to speak in the authentic tones of Caligula. He ordered his herald, a man of consular rank, to proclaim: "The Victor, Nero Emperor, crowns the people of Rome and the whole world which belongs to him." He won altogether 1,808 prizes, and was almost delirious with joy as he returned to Italy to celebrate his single-handed triumph over the greatest athletes, singers, actors and flute-players of his time.

He disembarked at Naples, where he ordered part of the city wall to be razed following the Greek custom whenever the victor at the Sacred Games came home. In the same way he entered Antium, where he was born, and Albanum, where he had his favourite residence on the shores of the Alban Lake, and Rome, where he expected to receive the most violent applause. He was not mistaken. For his entry into Rome he chose the chariot which Augustus had used in his triumph nearly a hundred years before, and he wore a Greek mantle spangled with gold stars over a purple robe. The Olympic wreath was on his head, the Pythian wreath in his right hand, while a long procession of bearers carried the other crowns and wreaths he had won in Greece. Then came a procession of tall soldiers bearing on the tips of their spears advertisements proclaiming where he had won his prizes, and the names of his competitors, the titles of his songs and of the plays he had performed in. Victims were sacrificed in his honour all along the route, which was sprinkled with perfume, and the common people showered him with songbirds, ribbons and sweetmeats. Beside him rode the flutist Diodorus, a youth of great beauty. Five thousand applauders followed behind his chariot, shouting themselves hoarse as they declaimed that they were the attendants of Augustus Caesar and the soldiers of his triumph. Others had taken up their positions behind the spectators and were shouting at the top of their voices: "Hail, victor of Olympia! Hail, Pythian conqueror! Hail, Augustus! Glory to Nero Hercules! Glory to Nero Apollo! Thou art the one supreme victor! O voice divine! Blessed are those who hear thee!"

So the *triumphator* passed through the streets of Rome behind a team of milk-white horses, drowned in applause. To enable his

chariot to enter the Circus Maximus which was filled to overflow-
ing, one of the arcades had to be removed. The procession passed
through the Circus and made its way across the Velabrum and the
Forum to the Palatine. He had no intention of sacrificing at the
Temple of Jupiter Capitolinus, but instead offered sacrifices at the
Temple of Apollo built by Augustus on the summit of the Palatine.
Afterwards he entered his Golden House, recently completed,
where he carefully spread out his precious collection of crowns,
together with images of himself playing the lyre. He also had coins
struck showing himself as a lyre-player.

Only a few more months remained to him. Revolution broke out
in Gaul. Nero had always believed in the power of song, and now
composed songs of defiance against the rebel leaders. The songs
however were powerless to stop the irresistible march of his
enemies, and when the Senate issued an order that he should be
flogged to death as a public enemy, he fled in disguise. His last
words after he had stabbed himself in the throat were: "Such is
fidelity!" It was a strange statement from a man who had never
shown any fidelity throughout his life.

So died Nero, the last of the Augustan line, a silly man who murdered with the deftness of a child tearing the wings from a fly. His
death closed an epoch. Afterwards there were to be many triumphs,
but not until the Middle Ages were triumphs again conceived as
poetical improvisations.

After Nero came the deluge: two years of terror. "It was a time,"
says Tacitus, "rich in disaster, fearful in its wars, torn by civil dis-
turbance, and even in peace full of horrors." The young Nero was
followed by the seventy-three-year-old Galba, the richest private
citizen who ever came to the imperial throne. He had received the
ornamenta triumphalia during the reign of Claudius. Gouty, infirm, harsh with the harshness of the old, he was murdered in the
Forum after ruling less than a year. He was replaced by Otho, a reckless voluptuary, who sensibly killed himself after a rule of only
ninety-five days. "Beastly Vitellius", a heavy-set man with a limp,
ruled with magnificent ineffectiveness after being proclaimed
emperor in Germany, and when civil war broke out, did nothing
whatsoever except wait upon events. Tacitus described him brilliantly as a man who "buried himself in the shade of his gardens
like those slothful brutes which, given food, lie still and slumber,
abandoning the present moment and the immediate future and all
hereafter in the same oblivion". In the reign of Vitellius the
Temple of Jupiter Capitolinus went up in flames.

A civil war between the followers of Vetellius and those of

Vespasian was being fought within the city. The prefect of the city, Flavius Sabinus, an old man in his dotage, was the brother of Vespasian. When he saw his soldiers were in danger, he took refuge in the Temple of Jupiter Capitolinus. The Vitellians attacked, threw lighted brands into the temple, and waited for the Flavians to emerge from the burning building. But they did not emerge. The temple was filled to bursting with the statues of gods and heroes. Flavius Sabinus ordered them torn down to form a barricade, stamped out the fires, and hoped to remain in the temple until help arrived. The Vitellians simply tossed brands on to the roof, and soon the temple was gutted. Vitellius watched the blaze from the Palatine, and he seems to have known his end was near.

He was killed only a few days later by the soldiers of Vespasian, who found him hiding in a small store-room near the palace. His arms were bound behind his back, a rope was put round his neck, and a sword was kept under his chin, to prevent his head from drooping. Then he was dragged naked along the Via Sacra to the Forum, where the bystanders pelted him with dung and shouted out that he was an incendiary and a glutton. Once he murmured: "I was your emperor!" but these words only delighted his enemies, who tortured him unmercifully and at last stabbed him to death at the Wailing Steps on the Aventine and then flung his body into the Tiber. As he was being dragged through the streets, he may have reflected that he was following part of the route of the triumphal procession.

The successor to the throne was Vespasian, a man of lowly birth, who won the *ornamenta triumphalia* in Britain under Claudius, and rose to great prominence only when he was sent by Nero to the east to conduct a war against the Jews. He was a good soldier, coarse in speech, solidly built, with a thick neck, heavy nose, small restless eyes, a round bald head. Suetonius says he had "the expression of one who is straining at stool". Yet in fact he never showed any uneasiness and passed through life as effortlessly as any peasant. Proclaimed emperor in Alexandria, he made his way by slow stages to Rome; almost his first task was to rebuild the Temple of Jupiter Capitolinus.

On June 21, A.D. 70, under a cloudless sky, the solemn rites were performed with the emperor in attendance. The area of the temple precincts was encircled with fillets and garlands. The Vestal Virgins sprinkled the holy place with pure water; a sow, a sheep and a bull were sacrificed; prayers were addressed to Jupiter, Juno and Minerva and all the tutelary gods; the great foundation stone was laid in place. The new temple was to be higher and more imposing than the old. The second temple was made largely of wood. This one was to be almost entirely of marble.

While the temple in Rome was being rebuilt, the temple in Jerusalem was being attacked by Vespasian's son Titus, who had been left in command of the four legions in Syria. Titus had none of his father's coarseness. He was graceful, gentle, affectionate. A skilled horseman, a brilliant letter-writer, Titus had inherited his father's military skill, and was determined to excel as a general. He was twenty-eight. Towards the Jews he was completely pitiless. After a long siege Jerusalem fell. The old and the infirm, with the women and children, had crowded into the great court facing the Holy of Holies, and were slaughtered by the maddened Roman soldiers, exasperated by the endurance of the Jews. The stairs of the temple ran with torrents of blood, and the Antonia fortress went up in flames. Titus himself hoped to save the Temple, but arrived on the scene too late. Soon the whole Upper City vanished in the flames, and soon there was nothing left of Jerusalem except the blazing ruins. According to Josephus there were more than a million victims.

The capitulation of Jerusalem took place in August, and in October, at Caesarea, Titus celebrated the eighteenth birthday of his younger brother Domitian by staging games in which the captured Jews served as gladiators forced to fight against wild beasts: 2,500 Jews lost their lives in the games. Titus went on to Berytus (Beirut), and staged more games. Then he returned to Rome to discover that the Senate had decreed a triumph for him and another for his father.

At first it was decided to hold two separate triumphs, but better counsels prevailed. The young Titus and the ageing Vespasian held their triumph together, riding together in the same chariot, with Domitian riding beside them on a magnificent horse sumptuously adorned. Orosius, the Christian historian, saw a peculiar blessedness in the appearance of father and son together. "Of all the 320 triumphs which had been held since the foundation of the city," he wrote, "none was so fair and strange as this spectacle, which saw father and son riding in the triumphal chariot after their glorious victory over the people who offended the Father and the Son."

It was a triumph to rival all previous triumphs, glittering with so much stolen treasure that it seemed to pass "more like a river than like a procession". Before dawn the soldiers marched to their meeting-place near the Temple of Isis and Serapis in the Campus Martius. Deeply attached to this temple, Vespasian and his son spent the night there. At dawn the emperor of the prince appeared before the soldiers clad in the traditional purple robes and wearing laurel crowns, sitting on thrones in the temple portico and receiving the acclamations of the army, and later in the Octavian Walks receiving the senators and magistrates and members of the equestrian order. They were unarmed, and wore gowns of silk. The shouting was so loud that Vespasian had to raise his hand for silence. In this sudden silence he rose, covered his head with his mantle and offered up prayers, and his son did the same. Afterwards Vespasian made a brief speech, and then dismissed the soldiers to enable them to take breakfast. There were sacrifices to the gods whose statues stood before the *porta triumphalis,* and at last the procession set out along a circuitous route, passing first through three theatres on the Campus Martius—those of Marcellus, Balbus and Pompey—so that the spectators, who had been crowding the streets since dawn, would have an opportunity to see it.

The triumph was remarkable for the presence of innumerable wheeled platforms, two or three storeys high, which displayed in great detail the conquest of Jerusalem. Josephus speaks of immense tapestries "woven in gold" which portrayed the life-like images of battle. He describes these tapestries as he saw them with his own eyes:

> On one was to be seen the devastation which struck a peaceful nation; on another there were the entire armies of the dead; and on others we saw people in flight or led into captivity. We saw huge walls laid low by engines and powerful fortresses overwhelmed. Here was a scene depicting the crumbling of the defences of a populous city, with a foreign army pouring through the walls. Everywhere a deluge of blood, the hands of the weak and afflicted stretched out in supplication, fire-brands pouring into temples, houses collapsing, and their owners buried in the ruins. And after pictures suggesting the overwhelming desolation and horror came others showing rivers flowing through a land which was not at all peaceful and cultivated, and the waters from the river were not supporting man or beast—these rivers flowed through a land given over to flames.
>
> (*De Bello Judaico,* VII, 5)

A novel element was introduced to these travelling stages: the *tableau vivant.* Against a backcloth representing the stricken cities the captives played out their roles; on each platform the governor of a Jewish city stood in chains. The spoils were generally heaped haphazard in the carts, but everyone could see the treasure taken from the temple—the seven-branched candlestick, the golden table of shewbread, and the silver trumpets. The prisoners were roped together, and at least one of them, the redoubtable revolutionary leader Simon bar Gorias, was flogged throughout the whole length of the procession. At the Capitoline steps he was led away to the Mamertine prison and put to death.

Vespasian seems to have delighted in the procession more for the sake of his sons than for any honour it brought to him. Suetonius records that he was exhausted by the slow and tiresome procession, and was heard to complain: "It serves me right for being such a fool as to want a procession in my old age," and he protested that he had never had any ambition to enjoy a triumph. We do not know the exact date of the triumph, though it was probably in the summer of A.D. 71, and it is likely that Vespasian was oppressed by the dust and the heat.

That summer the door of the temple of Janus was closed for the first time since the end of the German wars under Augustus—the Senate had refused to sanction Nero's closing of the door after the accommodation with Parthia. For the first time in living memory there was peace throughout the empire. The heavy, slow-witted peasant had succeeded where the aristocrats had failed.

For ten more years Vespasian continued to rule with rough benevolence and sturdy commonsense. Nero's Golden House was torn down, and the space given over to public baths. He had no taste for self-glorification: there was an end to poetic improvisations. The one luxury which Vespasian permitted himself was the Temple of Peace which he erected to house the treasures he had gathered from the east, but he kept the most precious of his treasures—the Tablets of the Law and the purple veils from the sanctuary of the Holy of Holies—in his own palace. The Temple of Peace was erected in A.D. 75, and both Pliny and Herodian attest to its magnificence.

About this same time, on the ridge of the Velia, at the summit of the Via Sacra, there were being laid the foundations of the triumphal archway designed to commemorate the victory over Judaea. Today it dominates the Forum. It is astonishingly well preserved, very quiet in the immensity of the Forum, glittering in the valley beneath the Palatine, owing its survival to a series of accidents. Originally it stood nearer the site now occupied by the church of S. Francesca Romana; Hadrian removed it to make way for the Temple of Venus and Rome. During the Middle Ages it was half covered with rubble. So it remains, very gentle and delicate, blending magnificently with the rubble-strewn landscape all round it.

The Baths of Titus have vanished, but the Arch of Titus, especially at sunset, has the air of having been built yesterday. Titus is shown in relief, crowned by Victory and driving in a triumphal chariot driven by Roma. Opposite is another relief showing the captives and the spoils: the Jews walking in huddled silence, bearers holding up the golden table of the shewbread and the heavy seven-branched candlestick. The inscription reads: SENATVS POPVLVSQVE ROMANVS DIVO TITO DIVI VESPASIANI F VESPASIANO AVGVSTO. *The Senate and People of Rome to the Deified Titus Vespasian Augustus, son of the Deified Vespasian.*

The arch combines delicacy with a brooding heaviness. Only a few years or months separate it from the grotesque Colosseum with its piled Doric, Ionic and Corinthian columns. There, finally, delicacy was overwhelmed by immensity, by the crushing weight of impalpable stone.

The homely Vespasian died after a ten-year reign, shouting in his delirium that an emperor should die on his feet. He possessed the ancient Roman virtues of sternness and generosity. His younger son, Domitian, who came to the throne after the short reign of Titus, never showed any generosity and was stern to madness. He forbade everything except the worship of himself and the building of triumphal arches in his own honour. He was another Nero, morose and solitary, living in dreams, murderous to his intimates, still more murderous towards his casual acquaintances. He murdered for the pure joy of murdering, without compunction and apparently without regret. He said once that both Vespasian and Titus owed their accession to him, but he never explained how this came about. He liked to be called *"dominus et deus"*. Once he wrote about a rebellious tribe in Numidia: "I forbid the Nasamones to exist." He might have gone on to forbid the existence of the Romans except that it pleased him to celebrate games at immense cost, presiding over them in Greek costume, and wearing a coronet of gold laced with figures of Jupiter, Juno and Minerva, the presiding deities in the Temple of Jupiter Capitolinus. His thoughts were often of that remote and forbidding temple: he was himself present in the temple when it was set on fire.

Dion Cassius describes Domitian as "a man filled with passionate boldness and dissembling". Tacitus says he dissembled even in his triumphs, for it was widely believed that the prisoners who paraded before his chariot after his summer campaign against the Chatti in Germany were actors clothed in the appropriate costumes and provided with yellow wigs. In honour of this campaign Domitian gave himself the title of Germanicus. This triumph seems to have taken place in September, A.D. 84. After the victories of Julianus in Dacia, Domitian enjoyed another triumph in A.D. 91, assuming the title of

Dacicus, and he erected an arch in his own honour near the *porta triumphalis*. He was so overwhelmed with his victories that he filled the Capitol with his own statues, invited the entire Roman nobility to feast with him, and ordered that a colossal equestrian statue of himself in gilt bronze be erected in the Forum. It was rumoured that the spoils heaped in the carts were actually treasures taken from his own palace. It may have been true. He had Nero's effrontery, and something of Caligula's thirst for divinity. He erected so many arches "with trophies and chariots in relief" that someone at last scratched the Greek word *arkei,* meaning "enough" on one of them. The Romans were weary of Domitian long before he was dead.

Domitian himself seems to have wearied of life long before the end. Dion Cassius tells the strange story of how he celebrated a funeral feast in honour of his Dacian victories, inviting the most respectable members of the nobility to share it with him. They came to a strange apartment where everything was given over to funereal darkness:

> Here everything was black, the ceilings, the walls, the pavements, and the rows of bare stone couches. The guests were introduced at night without their attendants, and they all saw at the head of their couches pillars like tombstones where their own names were graven, with cresset-lamps, like those which hang in tombs, suspended above them.
>
> Presently there came a troop of naked boys, painted black, who danced around with horrid movements, and then they stood very still before the guests with offerings of food—those scraps of food which are commonly presented to the dead. The guests were terror-stricken, expecting at any moment to be put to death; and they were all the more convinced that death was coming to them when they realized the deathly silence of everyone in the apartment. It was like the silence of the grave, broken only by the sepulchral voice of Domitian as he spoke of the dead.
>
> (*Dion Cassius,* LXVII, 9)

It was, of course, the emperor's idea of a joke. He had no intention of killing his guests, only of frightening them out of their wits. When the lights came on, the naked boys had been washed and decently clothed, and were given as presents to the guests together with the silver cups and plates in which the funereal dinner had been served. It was a joke which lay very close to madness, and Domitian seems to have been quite mad during the greater part of his reign.

Once when Domitian saw some mushrooms on the table, he blanched, remembering how Claudius had died. "You may eat them," his father said, "for it is written in the stars that you will die by the sword." Domitian became so fearful of assassination that he ordered his palace hung with mirrors so that he could see whether anyone entered unannounced. In the autumn of A.D. 96, when he was forty-five and had reigned for fifteen years, a succession of strange auguries drove him frantic with despair. The Capitol was struck by lightning. The golden statue of the emperor on his arch of triumph was torn from its sockets. Never had there been such appalling thunderstorms. It seemed to Domitian that some vast and terrible judgment was about to be visited on him, and he was heard to say: "Something is about to happen which men will talk of all over the world!"

He was thinking perhaps of some mysterious and widespread conspiracy; of great wars breaking out; of still more terrifying prodigies. Once he dreamed that a golden hump grew out of his back, and he interpreted the dream to mean that the empire would be happier and more prosperous after his death. So it happened, but not in a way he could have foreseen. He was killed by a certain Stephanus, the steward of his niece, who had pretended for some days that he had injured his hand and in the bandages kept a concealed dagger. Domitian was reading when he was suddenly slashed in the groin. He called to one of his servants to bring him the dagger he kept under a pillow, but the dagger had mysteriously vanished. The emperor fought gamely. Almost his last act was to plunge his lacerated fingers into his assailant's eyes.

With the death of Domitian the line of the Flavian emperors came to an end. The experiment had failed. For a little more than 125 years the Romans had been ruled by princes who acted as though the empire was their private preserve, to be handed down as an heirloom to their descendants or the descendants of their wives. Only Augustus and Vespasian had ruled with responsibility: their triumphs were real triumphs, and their greatest reward was the enjoyment of an empire at peace. Both in their different ways had fought against the slow corruption of the times, unable to prevent it or even to recognize the evil in their midst.

For the most part the emperors who followed were wise and responsible men who looked around the world with anxious eyes. They moved with caution, perpetually troubled and oppressed by the presence of dangers which possessed no name. Few can have guessed that the Christians would inherit the Roman name and the power of the Caesars.

IO

REVIVAL UNDER TRAJAN

IN THE age of Nero and Domitian the Roman triumph disintegrated, becoming no more than a meaningless spectacle, attended by the odour of corruption. An ancient mystery, performed for eight centuries, had succumbed to weariness. The improvisations of Nero and Domitian assumed the form of poetic burlesques, but they were not the first to improvise on the theme of the triumph. Nero and Domitian simply divorced the triumph from reality.

How gravely the triumph had been compromised we know from the writings of the satirical poet Juvenal, who flourished towards the end of the first century. He laughed openly at the pretensions of conquerors who thought that trophies—a breastplate hanging on a tree-stump, a flagstaff from a captured galley or a prisoner sorrowing on a triumphal arch—belonged to the highest attainments of men. He poured scorn on the generals, whether Greek, Roman or barbarian, whose whole aim in life was to attend a triumph in their own honour. Whole countries were despoiled, and the conqueror himself endured untold hardship and danger in his thirst for glory: "So much more," says Juvenal reprovingly, "do they thirst for glory than for virtue." *Tanto maior famae sitis est quam virtutis.* So it had always been, but in his own day the thirst for glory had exceeded all human bounds. He was perhaps thinking of the triumph of Titus over the Jews when he wrote with bitter vehemence:

Old Democritus would have laughed his sides out,
And died of laughing, if he saw the conqueror
Raised on a high chariot in the dusty circus,
Robed in the gown of Jupiter, hitching on his shoulder
An embroidered toga dyed with Tyrian purple.
Then on his head a vast and sumptuous crown
So heavy it would break his neck unless
A public slave sweated under the burden:
And so the slave and master ride together
To keep the master free-from those deformities
Which come from pride. And there's his bird
Perched on an ivory staff; the horn-blowers;

The long parade of friends; the white-robed
Clients of the conqueror, endlessly paying
Respects and more respects, and being paid
In coin and dinner-doles . . .

(Satire, X, 34-46)

In the same spirit of contempt Propertius had spoken of lying in
a woman's arms in the upper storey of some building overlooking
the triumphal procession, and watching the trophies and banners
as they passed, amused by all the hubbub in the street. Persius
wrote with even more bitterness in a poem to his friend Bassus,
who was living in contentment in the Sabine hills:

Have you heard the news? The laurelled message came:
Another victory by Caesar over the flower of Germany,
And now we must rake cold ashes from the altars.
I heard Caesonia has ordered weapons
To grace the city-gates, and royal mantles,
And for the prisoners perukes of yellow hair,
And chariots, and statues of the Rhine.
Thus does she celebrate in honour of the gods,
And the presiding genius of our leader.
Myself, I have ordered
A hundred pairs of gladiators to celebrate this day.
Would you forbid me? Then at least be kind to me.
Play the game with me. Let us give
Huge donations of bread and oil and meat
To the hungry mob. Do you forbid me. Speak plainly.
"No," you say, "the neighbouring fields
Are still not cleared of bones."

(Satire, VI, 43-52)

Persius imagines himself a *triumphator* returning after the
campaign, offering largesse with open hands: two hundred
gladiators would provide a modest entertainment for the mob.
The yellow perukes of the prisoners were, of course, part of the
legend of the triumph, going back perhaps to the time of Claudius
and Caractacus. Persius never for a moment disguises his bitterness against the horror of the triumph, all the more horrible because the "uncleared fields" were never seen. To Persius, and to
many Romans, the triumph was beginning to wear the livery of
death.

The years of the meaningless triumph were nearly over: henceforward the triumphs were to be celebrated only on rare occasions,

and only when important victories were won. The maniacs passed; the engineers came in. Trajan, Hadrian and Marcus Aurelius were men who bore a troubled weight of responsibility; it would never occur to them that the empire was a plaything. Trajan in particular, with his modern face, his look of calm and unwearying attention, his brow furrowed, the lips pursed, everything about him suggesting a grave awareness of all the manifold problems of ruling an empire, belongs to the category of great emperors. Dante called him "the iris of the Eagle's eye, whose pupil is David". Dion Cassius said "he loved, greeted and honoured the good; the others he ignored". Everyone seems to have agreed upon his almost saintly character, forgetting that he was constantly at war and enjoyed all his battles.

Trajan was the son of a general who won victories over the Parthians and the Jews, and received the *ornamenta triumphalia* before being appointed proconsul of Asia. He himself was governor of Germany when he was called to the throne. He did not leave for Rome immediately, but waited until he had completely pacified the country; and though he had won many battles no triumph accompanied his return. Instead, he entered the city on foot, very humbly, a small escort riding beside him, and after only a few weeks in Rome he set out for Dacia where there was a revolt among the tribesmen. He returned to Rome in A.D. 103, celebrated a triumph and was given the title Dacicus—the first of three imperial titles granted to him by an adoring Senate.

We know nothing about the details of the triumphal procession. We know, however, a little about the days that followed. According to Dion Cassius, the triumph was followed by 123 days of games and gladiatorial displays in the Colosseum, and some 10,000 gladiators fought in the arena. Trajan had a passion for watching gladiators; spent much of his free time watching the contests; drank heavily; fell in love with one of the dancers in the pantomimes; and made plans for more wars against the unruly Dacians. Three years later, after another successful war against Dacia, he held another triumph. The great triumphal arch he built to celebrate his victory has perished, but some of the statues of Dacians which once embellished it were removed two centuries later by Constantine to grace his own arch of triumph. About this time Trajan gave orders for building the long graceful column, known as the Column of Trajan, which records in minute and loving detail along spiralling bands the long-drawn and hard-fought campaigns against Dacia. The sculptures are not pretty. They show the Romans massacring their enemies, carrying all before them. More impressive sculptures

decorate the arch at Beneventum, erected to celebrate the completion of the long military road from Beneventum to Brundisium.

In the history of the Roman triumph the arch at Beneventum
occupies a special place. None of the surviving archways are as
majestic as this, none so well-preserved. Built in A.D. 114 and only
completed after his death, it represents the apotheosis of the emperor, who appears as a man of almost Buddha-like calm, crowned
by fortune, presiding at the sacred rites, blessing the bread to be
given to the people and receiving from Jupiter the thunderbolt of
power. The emperor wears an air of strange reserve and power, god-
like in his calm, beautiful with the beauty of maturity. Again and
again the familiar face, little damaged by time, confronts the spectator, and he appears most wonderfully of all in a relief depicting
an imperial reception in the presence of Neptune, Hercules and
Bacchus. No one knows why these particular gods look down upon
the scene or why the reception is being held. It must have been a
very important reception, but the history of Trajan's reign is frag-
mentary: we can only assume they are representatives from three
Italian cities whose work met the favour of the emperor. Robed in
a voluminous toga, Trajan leans forward a little and presents his
visitors with a gift—a laurel wreath, a crown, no one knows what,
for time has eaten the gift away.

The significance of many of the reliefs remains mysterious, but
there is nothing in the least mysterious about the two large panels
and the long frieze which describe with abundant detail the entire
course of a Roman triumph from the moment when the *triumphator* receives the senators in the Campus Martius to the moment
when the sacrifice is offered in the Temple of Jupiter on the Capitol, the priests at their prayers, the axe lifted and the white ox
kneeling. No other sculptured representation of an entire triumph
has survived. A sculptor of superb power carved these reliefs,
showing how it was seen by men and by gods.

The gods preside, and their place accordingly is on the attic,
where we find Jupiter flanked by Juno and Minerva, the three
Capitoline gods, offering the thunderbolt to the emperor. Such an
offer, unprecedented in its magnitude, implies far more than a
triumph; it implies in fact the apotheosis of the emperor, henceforth to be regarded as one of the gods and equal to them in power
and majesty. Behind the three Capitoline gods, on guard and
watchful, are the lesser gods Hercules, Bacchus, Ceres and Mercury:
Hercules with his club, Bacchus with the grapes twined in his hair,
Ceres with her crown and Mercury with his winged helmet. On the
other side of the attic still another god appears: Roma herself,

standing under the archway of the *porta triumphalis,* an imperious
figure who places her hand on the shoulder of the young and imperious Hadrian, her kinsman. One might reasonably guess that
this relief was designed when Hadrian came to the throne: he is
altogether too prominent. On either side of Roma are the senators
who have just emerged through the gate to welcome and congratu-
late the emperor.

The triumph itself is depicted in a narrow frieze, encircling the
whole archway in a band nearly fifty feet long. Over a hundred
figures, smaller than life, appear, and perhaps half of them have
crumbled with age. Enough remains to give us a sense of a continuing procession. We see the delicately carved triumphal chariot
with the lictors walking beside it, the long cavalcade of prisoners,
some of them riding in ox-carts, and the sleek oxen wearing crowns
and fillets embroidered with flowers are escorted by the *victimarii,*
who will be responsible for sacrificing them—thickset, brawny men,
wearing leather aprons, naked to the waist. We see the sweepers,
the basket-carriers, the shield-bearers, the musicians, the senators,
all moving with the slow rhythm of the procession. Historical
accounts speak of the triumphal procession lasting from the early
morning to late afternoon, although the distance traversed was no
more than five or six miles. The arch at Beneventum supplies the
reason—no one hurries. These carved figures move at the leisurely
speed of perhaps a mile an hour. There is no hurrying, no crowding. The celebrants have time to turn and gaze at the onlookers;
they struggle under the weight of treasure; they stand and stare at
the people crowding the streets. They do not move with the precision of the massed soldiers and tribute-bearers on the great
apadana stairway at Persepolis. They are on holiday, and there is
no need for them to move like legionaries going into battle.

Under the archway there is a relief showing the emperor at the
most solemn moment of all. He stands veiled and wreathed with
oak leaves, attended by his body of twelve lictors. Grouped around
the altar of incense are two long-haired *camilli,* and the flute-
player has blown out his cheeks as he prepares to play a sacred
chant. The emperor is scattering grains of incense on the altar. The
victimarii are already at their work. One is pulling down on the
head of the sacrificial ox, holding it by the ear and the muzzle,
while another has lifted the sacrificial axe high above his head—the
axe will crush the ox's brains, and afterwards a knife will be drawn
across its throat. It is a scene very similar to the one depicted on
the Boscoreale cup, but here illustrated in greater detail and with
more dramatic intensity. All except the *victimarii* are calm, caught

up in a timeless moment, in a silence that is broken only by the mournful playing of the flute. Because they are in the presence of Jupiter they wear the crown of oak leaves and hold themselves with a becoming gravity. The design is purely Roman, with hardly a trace of the classical Greek spirit which informs the monumental carving on the attic. This is the moment they have been waiting for, the most solemn moment of the sacrifice. The laurels have already been deposited on the lap of Jupiter: the hymns have already been sung: there remains the agony of the sacrifice. At the moment when the dark blood spills from the neck of the sacrificial victim the emperor and all those around him will be in communion with Jupiter. So, wearing their high crowns, they gaze impassively into the world of the gods.

Such was the triumph of Trajan, sculptured by an unknown artist of formidable power. For a brief moment we see Trajan plain, and then he vanishes, being at once the best and least known of emperors: for there are only brief records of his reign and yet no other emperor was depicted so often by sculptors. He had reigned for nearly twenty years when he died of dropsy, or perhaps of poison, in Cilicia while returning to Rome after a long visit to the east. A great triumph was being prepared for him, and a triumphal arch was being erected, when there came the news of his death. His ashes in a golden urn were deposited beneath the great column which bears his name.

On his deathbed Trajan adopted his kinsman and principal commander Hadrian as the successor to the throne. As soon as he reached Rome Hadrian was given permission by the Senate to celebrate the triumph won by Trajan. He refused. Instead he ordered that the image of the dead emperor should be borne in triumph to the Capitol. Of all the innovations which from time to time have changed the course of the triumph this was the most moving, the most solemn, and the most deserving. Never again was a dead emperor to pass in triumph through the streets.

Trajan had left an empire at peace: Hadrian was determined to prevent any interference in the peace. He was singularly well-suited to enjoy it. Fair-skinned, with bluish-grey eyes, thick curly hair and a well-trimmed beard—he was the first of the Roman emperors to show himself bearded—he possessed all the talents. He had an expert knowledge of painting and sculpture, spoke Greek and Latin with equal proficiency, though with a Spanish accent, and to the end of his life remained boundlessly curious about everything that happened. Tertullian called him *omnium curiositatum explorator*. He liked to march bare-headed at the head of his army, and he spent the greater part of his active life on the march, inspecting his empire. He was responsible for few wars, and seems never to have enjoyed a triumph. "There were no campaigns of importance during his reign," says Aelius Spartianus, "and the wars he waged were brought to an end without arousing comment." His coins were stamped with the proud and rare words *Pax, Patientia, Justitia*. Such words aimed too high—he did in fact wage a terrible war against the Jews, putting to death, according to Dion Cassius, "five hundred and eighty thousand people not counting those who died from hunger and plague". But no triumphant army returned from Palestine to Rome, bearing vast booty. It is possible that there was nothing left in Palestine to pillage.

Hadrian wears a modern face, and possessed a peculiarly modern temper: troubled, adventurous, clear-headed, uncertain of his aims but supremely certain of himself. He was "in all matters various", said Aelius Spartianus. If he celebrated no triumphs, it was because he was too busy, not because he hated the sight of blood. His successor, Antoninus Pius, was the gentlest Roman since Numa, a tall handsome man who liked to quote the words of Scipio that it was preferable to save a single citizen than to slay a thousand foes. He would have thought a triumph a mockery of everything he stood for. When he lay dying at the age of seventy an officer asked him for the watchword of the day. "*Aequanimitas*," he answered, and then fell into the sleep from which he never awoke. Equanimity is not a quality one associates with *triumphatores*.

Trajan, Hadrian and Antoninus Pius were all superbly civilized men, but most civilized of all was Marcus Aurelius, the nephew of Antoninus. He too possessed all the talents. He was the only Roman emperor to possess any skill at painting. He boxed, wrestled, played ball and hunted well. He wrote angelically. He was a passionate student of philosophy, even when he was a boy. When he came to the throne he made his adoptive brother Lucius Verus his associate; it pleased him to divide his own power, and he seems to have liked Verus for his gaiety and elegance. Verus was a profligate, perhaps a murderer. When war broke out in the east, he made his way to Antioch and amused himself while the legionaries under Avidius Cassius fought a series of hard campaigns against the Parthians. Sura, Europus, Edessa and Nisibis fell. Ctesiphon was destroyed. Verus, completely corrupted, returned to Rome to enjoy a triumph, graciously suggesting that the co-emperor should enjoy it with him. To mark the occasion the two young sons of Marcus, Commodus and Verus, aged five and three, received the title of Caesar and took part in the procession. It was the autumn of A.D. 166. By winter the Romans were wishing the soldiers had never left the east to take part in the triumph, for the pestilence came with them.

Outwardly Verus appeared as a great general who had led the Romans to victory against the Armenians, the Medes and the Parthians. He was offered the titles Armeniacus, Parthicus Maximus and Medicus. With his aristocratic forehead and air of consummate nobility, he looked like a born leader of men; those who knew him well remembered that all his victories were won in the brothels of Antioch. With him when he returned to Rome was a vast company of harpists and flute-players, jugglers and entertainers and actors of all kinds. "He brought his actors from Syria as proudly as though they were kings to decorate his triumph," said Julius Capitolinus. "There were so many of them that one might be forgiven for thinking he had made war on them, instead of on the Persians."

Verus was a weakling who had a passion for feeding raisins and nuts to his favourite horse. His death in A.D. 169 was a relief to Marcus: that dazzling youth who showered gold powder on his hair was an emcumbrance to the proper management of the empire. Alone, Marcus showed himself at his best. There were revolts in Germany. He put them down sternly and went on to put down another uprising in Egypt, and returned to Rome to enjoy a triumph on December 23, A.D. 176, giving to every Roman eight aurei, one for every year of his absence from the capital. It was more largesse than the Romans had ever received from an emperor.

Marcus had two passions: philosophy and his son. As a philosopher he saw with astonishing clarity: as a father he was blind. Like Verus, Commodus was a magnificent dissimulator. In the presence of his father he showed himself as an accomplished prince, witty, luxury-loving, precociously intelligent. Away from his father he behaved like a brute. Sent to Germany to continue the war against the revolting tribesmen Verus abruptly returned before winning any victories and demanded a triumph, which his indulgent father gave him. This triumph seems to have taken place in A.D. 177, and there is a story that Marcus was so pleased with his son's prowess that he ran beside the triumphal chariot when it was driving through the Circus Maximus. He was fifty-six, and ageing rapidly; Commodus was sixteen, at the height of his beauty. Henpecked, hating Rome and hating war, happiest with his books and the secret *Meditations* which he wrote throughout his life with no intention of ever making them public, Marcus set out on his last campaign against the German tribesmen. He was in Vienna when the fever gripped him. In his delirium he was heard repeating the line of a forgotten poet: "Terrible is the work of war!" One evening, when he was asked for the watchword, he seems to have misunderstood the question, and answered: "Go to the rising sun, for I am setting." With his death the empire fell into the hands of a nineteen-year-old youth, who was already mad.

For nearly a hundred years, from the accession of Trajan in A.D. 98 to the death of Marcus Aurelius in A.D. 180, the Roman empire had enjoyed unbroken prosperity under emperors of astonishing insight; and now the luck was running out. Pliny during the reign of Hadrian had spoken of "the boundless majesty of the Roman peace"—*pacis Romanae immensa maiestas*. The peace survived, but the majesty was dimmed. Instead of the noble philosopher on the throne, there was a lunatic prince who celebrated on October 22, A.D. 180, only six months after his father's death, a completely imaginary victory over the German tribes. By the new emperor's orders there was held "a second most happy triumph over the Germans"—*triumphus felicissimus Germanicus secundus*. Commodus succeeded in introducing one innovation so extraordinary that it was never repeated. He invited his favourite catamite to ride behind him in the triumphal chariot. "It amused him," says his biographer Aelius Lampridius, "to turn around from time to time and kiss his beloved openly, repeating the performance later in the orchestra of the theatre."

Commodus, wildly insane, went from one enormity to another. He was all vice where his father was all virtue. He had Nero's passionate addiction to murder, and Nero's megalomania. It annoyed him that the world paid little attention to him, and he was determined that the world should pay for having overlooked his virtues. When he took part in gladiatorial shows, the crowd shouted: "You are the winner, the very first! You are the winner, from everlasting, O Amazonian, you are the winner!" He was called Amazonian because he liked to appear in female dress. One day he changed the name of Rome to Colonia Commodiana. On another day he remembered he had twelve names and there were twelve months in the year, and he gave orders that every month should be named after himself. The Senate and the fleet acquired his name; the Romans became Commodiani; for himself, wearying of all his other names and titles, there was the pleasant sobriquet: "Victor of a thousand gladiators." Then he wearied of this title, and contented himself with the appellation Hercules.

In the end, of course, Commodus had to be put away. He was strangled by his mistress Marcia with the help of the prefect of the guard and buried during the night against the will of the Senate, which would have preferred to see him publicly dragged by the hook. The Senate, deprived of its rightful victim, became hysterical with anger and published a decree which reads like a prolonged curse:

> With one voice we say: Let him be dragged by the hook.
> He who killed all men, let him be dragged by the hook.
> He who killed people of all ages, let him be dragged by the hook.
> He who killed men and women, let him be dragged by the hook.
> He who set aside the testaments of the dead, let him be dragged by the hook.
> He who despoiled the living, let him be dragged by the hook.
> We were the slaves of slaves!
>   (Aelius Lampridius, *Commodus Antoninus*, XVIII)

Servis serviimus. . . . Never was such a cry of despair spoken by the Senate. As though the madness of Commodus had been communicated to the trembling senators, they surrendered their power to the first strong man who emerged upon the scene. Pertinax was sixty, an experienced soldier who had held commands in Syria and Britain, a man capable of bringing about energetic reforms. Three months later the soldiers wearied of his determination to restore discipline, and murdered him in bed. His successor Julianus died just as unimpressively two months later. The real power fell to the hands of Septimius Severus, a large, heavy, plain-spoken African from Leptis, who was married to a Syrian wife. He was the first plebeian and the first African to rule the Roman empire.

Rome was jubilant at the prospect of an emperor who could keep order. Following a long forced march from his headquarters in Pannonia, Septimius Severus rode up to the gates of Rome in military uniform, but he changed into civilian clothing and entered the city on foot. The city was decked with flowers and laurels, and ablaze with torches and incense. The delighted Romans thought he was another Trajan, but in this they were wrong. Coarse, brutal, intoxicated with military affairs, he treated the empire as though it were a pasture for his army. Only an army of embattled legionaries ever received his commendation. He gloried in extending the bounds of the empire and sent his generals against Scotland, Greece, Mesopotamia and Persia: he celebrated their victories by assuming the titles Parthicus, Arabicus, Adiabenicus. He made war, says Aelius Spartianus, because he was possessed by a thirst for glory rather than for reasons of necessity—*gloriae cupiditate non aliqua necessitate.* Severity was his watchword.

His most notable achievements were his victories in the east. He received a triumph for his Mesopotamian victories in A.D. 196, but refused another following the conquest of Ctesiphon on the grounds that he suffered from gout and could not stand upright in the chariot: he gave permission for his twelve-year-old son Caracalla to hold the triumph instead. This triumph took place in A.D. 200 or 201, and in the following year the emperor began the construction of the huge arch which bears his name in the north-east corner of the Roman Forum, just below the Capitol, not far from the traditional site of the tomb of Romulus. We know from the coins of Severus and his son Caracalla that the arch was once adorned with a chariot drawn by six horses abreast, with figures of the emperor and his sons. It is a strange and troubling archway, not to be compared with the arch of Trajan at Beneventum or the arch of Titus.

On the arch of Severus we see the emperor entering Babylon, we see the great towers of the city and the siege engines, and then on the lower register we see him addressing his soldiers. There is no drama, no sense of continuity, no attempt to give meaning to the whole. Everything seems to be taking place inside a vacuum. There is the inevitable frieze of a triumphal procession, but the figures are wooden. It was as though the artist who depicted the triumph felt no reason to believe in its validity: only the prisoners and the strange winged victories seem to possess any reality.

Severus died at the age of sixty-five in York during an expedition against Britain, and for a brief period Caracalla and his brother Geta ruled jointly. After a particularly brutal murder—Geta was stabbed to death while taking refuge in his mother's arms—Caracalla became sole emperor, and almost his first task was to remove his brother's name from the arch below the Capitol. From the positions of the rivet holes patient decipherers have been able to discover that where the inscription now reads: OPTIMIS FORTISSIMISQVE PRINCIBUS—*To the best and strongest of Princes*, there were once the words: P. SEPT. LVC. FIL. GETAE. NOBILISS. CAESARI—*To Geta, the most noble Caesar, son of Publius Septimius Lucius.* So do the crimes of princes reveal themselves in rivet holes.

Caracalla was foolish and witless—*stultus et demens.* Like Commodus and Nero he suffered from imperial madness. Once when his mother wondered whether there was any money left in the treasury, he put his hand on his sword and answered: "Never fear, mother, there will be money as long as we have this!" His father's dying words were: "Enrich the soldiers, and scorn all other men," and Caracalla was determined to follow in his father's footsteps. He fought against the Alemanni, whose name first appears in his tory during his reign, and then invaded Dacia and marched against Parthia. He assumed the titles Alemannicus, Germanicus, Parthicus and Arabicus; and the son of Pertinax suggested that he should have added Geticus Maximus, after murdering his brother. He was murdered after a reign of six years and seems never to have enjoyed a triumph.

Caracalla was mad in the Roman fashion: stern, merciless, puritanical. Elagabalus, who claimed to be Caracalla's son, was mad in the Syrian fashion, vain, foppish, effeminate, given to astonishing feats of luxury. He was about thirteen when he came to the throne. Herodian describes his triumphal entry into Rome amidst a rabble of women, eunuchs and priests, the boy dressed in the silken robes worn by the priests of the Sun-god at Emesa. His cheeks were painted, his eyebrows were darkened, there were ropes of pearls round his neck, and he wore a jewelled tiara. He had a fondness for walking on carpets of lilies, roses and hyacinths, and fed his dogs on goose-liver, his horses on grapes. The Romans soon wearied of him: he was murdered when hiding in a latrine, and his body was dragged round the Circus Maximus.

The Romans feared the influence of the east, and they were glad when Alexander Severus, a first cousin of Elagabalus, came to the throne with the promise of redressing the balance. He was only sixteen, but he had the makings of a good emperor. He was deeply religious, and kept in his private chapel statues of Orpheus, Abraham, Apollonius of Tyana and Jesus. Elagabalus liked luxury; Alexander Severus liked a quiet severity. He read carefully Plato's *Republic*, surrounded himself with good advisers, and in his campaigns paid strict attention to the wants of his soldiers, and shared their food. Inevitably he led an army against Parthia, and when he returned to Rome he asserted to the Senate that of 700 war elephants belonging to the enemy he had killed 200 and captured 300, and of 1,000 Parthian scythed chariots he had taken 200. In A.D. 233 he conducted, says the chronicler, "a most splendid triumph". His triumphal chariot was drawn, not by snow-white horses, but by four elephants, and for some reason the emperor walked on foot in front of the chariot. Coins were minted to commemorate his triumph. They show him crowned by Victory with the Tigris and Euphrates at his feet. He was only twenty-nine when he was slain at the orders of the huge Thracian peasant Maximin, who had once been his bodyguard.

They said of Maximin that he was eight feet tall, and could crush rocks with his bare hands. He was a good soldier, and dealt the Germans across the Rhine such a blow that Gaul was made safe for another twenty years. Since he was in the field and never returned to Rome during his brief three-year reign, he ordered artists to make records of his victories and these paintings were exhibited before the Senate. He executed so many of his own soldiers that at last they rose against him, and his head was cut off one afternoon when he was resting in his tent.

This Thracian peasant, who spoke Latin only haltingly, was the first of a long series of usurpers—at least nine and possibly thirty emperors ruled for brief periods during the years A.D. 238 to 253. None enjoyed triumphs, though Gordianus the Younger, who ruled for six years and was proclaimed emperor when he was only twelve, was busily collecting wild beasts to decorate his Persian triumph when he was assassinated in Mesopotamia.

Gordianus was the exception to all the rules—a child emperor beloved by everyone. Julius Capitolinus says of him that he was "light-hearted, handsome, winning, agreeable to everyone, merry in his life and eminent in letters". He fought valiantly against the Sasanian King Sapor I, and with the help of his father-in-law recovered Antioch and Carrhae. A Persian triumph was decreed for him. A complete list of the beasts intended to decorate the triumph has been handed down. It included 30 elephants, 30 leopards, 19 giraffes, 10 hyenas, 10 tigers, 10 wild boars and 1 hippopotamus. All these beasts were slain during the celebration of the secular games held by his successor, Philippus, the only Arab ever to become a Roman emperor, to honour the thousandth anniversary of the city of Rome. Such anniversary celebrations were held with great magnificence by Augustus, by Claudius, by Domitian and Severus; but after Philippus no more were ever held.

It was the time of "the Thirty Pretenders", when all the generals were vying for power and many proclaimed themselves emperor for a few months, for a few days, for a few hours. The Goths were pouring across the Danube; Gaul was in revolt; Spain was attempting rebellion; the Alemanni were threatening Milan; and the Persian king was threatening the whole of the east. There was need for a strong emperor. Instead there arose two weak ones—the vain Valerian and the monstrous Gallienus. Valerian decided to attack the strongest of his enemies and led his army against the Persians. Captured by Sapor I, he spent the rest of his life in slavery. "Through all his remaining years," says the historian Orosius, "he was compelled to perform the menial service of helping the king mount on his horse, not in the usual way by giving his hand, but by bending to the ground and offering his back." On the cliffs near Persepolis in the heart of Persia there can still be seen the magnificent relief showing a distraught Roman emperor kneeling before the king of kings.

Valerian's son Gallienus gave every sign of being delighted by his father's capture. When he heard that his father was in the hands of the Persians, he said simply: "I knew he was mortal." He was a profligate, a writer of love poems—one, a good one, has survived—and an amused spectator of an empire in ruins. There were, however, times when he could exert himself. The Roman army in Byzantium revolted. Gallienus surrounded the city, promised not to punish the rebels, received their surrender and immediately massacred them. Then he returned quickly to Rome and celebrated a triumph.

This triumph, held in A.D. 263, was celebrated with great pomp and with some curious additions to the usual procedure. According to Trebellius Pollio, the procession took place at night and was led by women and slaves bearing torches. It was a wonderful circus parade, and a triumph only in name.

> One hundred white oxen went in front, all of them having their horns bound with gold cords, and they wore brilliant hangings of many-coloured silk; on either side of them went two hundred lambs of a blinding whiteness. At this time there were ten elephants in Rome, and they too took part in the procession, together with 1,200 gladiators decked up in great pomp, and matrons wearing golden cloaks, and 200 tame beasts of various kinds all decorated with the greatest splendour, and playcarts bearing mimes and actors of all kinds, and boxers who fought not in the usual way but with soft leather straps. There were clowns who performed Cyclopean dances with marvellous and stupendous success. The streets resounded with merry-making, loud cries and applause, and in the midst of it all came the emperor, wearing the *toga picta* and the *tunica palmata* accompanied, as I have said, by all the priests dressed in their bordered garments and by all the senators; and so they made their way to the Capitol.

(Trebellius Pollio, *Gallieni Duo*, VIII)

Trebellius Pollio tells the story of some amused bystanders who noticed that there were Romans dressed up to resemble Persian, Gothic, Sarmatian and Frankish prisoners; and one of these bystanders went up to the band of "Persian" prisoners and demanded loudly what had happened to the Emperor Valerian. Gallienus ordered the little group of bystanders to be rounded up and sentenced them to be burned alive. Afterwards this crime was remembered against the emperor, and Trebellius Pollio was of the opinion that this single act led to the murder of Gallienus by his own soldiers five years later.

Gallienus wrote to one of his generals: "You will not have done enough for me if you put to death only soldiers, for they are the breed that inevitably dies in war. You must kill all those with evil intentions, all those who have spoken against me. Tear, kill, exterminate—*lacera, occide, concide!*" They remembered his cynicism, his irony, the strange complexity of his mind. He had Nero's vices, but in him they were diminished until they became no more than occasional cruelties; and he had a curious passion for philosophy. He delighted to have philosophers in his court, and Porphyry says he was on the point of bequeathing a town in the Campagna to the philosopher Plotinus to see whether Plato's Republic could be realized on earth. He married a Christian wife, the Empress Salonina, whose memory is preserved in the ruins of the triumphal archway which can still be seen standing against the church of St. Vito in Rome. The inscription reads: GALLIENO CLEMENTISSIMO PRINCIPI CVIVS INVICTA VIRTVS SOLA PIETATE SVPERATA EST ET SALONINAE SANCTISSIMAE AVG—*To the most merciful Prince Gallienus whose unconquerable virtue was only surpassed by his piety, and to the most sacred Empress Salonina.* In such terms did an unwise emperor commend himself to posterity.

Perhaps it was a pity. If he had not aimed so high, if he had been a little wiser, if he had been a little less happy with the display of power and the enjoyment of military charades, he might have made a good emperor. The coins show a fine-cut profile with much strength, but there is an expression of settled melancholy: almost he might be a Flavian emperor. One of his gold coins has puzzled commentators. It shows the profile of the emperor, and round it the words more appropriate to an empress: GALLIENAE AUGUSTAE. The reverse shows him riding in the four-horse chariot of a *triumphator* with the words: PAX UBIQUE. *Peace everywhere.*

There was however very little peace during the unhappy reign of Gallienus. The Christian historian Orosius speaks of him sympathetically for having put an end to the persecution of the Christians, but adds a long catalogue of the disasters which occurred during his reign. It is an amazing and damning catalogue:

By God's will the nations stationed on the frontiers, placed there for this purpose, were suddenly loosed on every side, and they were no sooner released from guidance than they invaded all the Roman territories. The Germans made their way through the Alps, through Rhoetia and the whole of Italy as far west as Ravenna. The Alemanni roamed through the provinces of Gaul, and even crossed into Italy. An invasion of the Goths brought ruin to Greece, Pontus and Asia; Dacia beyond the Danube was lost forever. The Quadi and the Sarmatians ravaged the Pannonian provinces. The Further Germans stripped Spain and assumed control over it. The Parthians seized Mesopotamia and completely devastated Syria. Today, in various places in the provinces you will come upon poor and insignificant settlements on the ruins of once-great cities. . . .

(Orosius, *Seven Books to Confute the Pagan*, VII, 22)

Towards the end of his reign a host of usurpers assumed the purple and challenged the power of an emperor, who seemed incapable of ruling effectively. The legions elected emperors, and then killed them; and Gallienus continued to give orders which no one obeyed. *Roma triumphans* had become a small city given over to conspiracies. These were the darkest nights of Rome: the city and the empire might have foundered completely if it had not been for the hardy soldiers of Illyria, in what is now Yugoslavia. The Illyrians saved the empire.

II

THE SLOW DECLINE

LET us imagine we are watching the Roman triumph unfolding across one of those vast scrolls which the Chinese delighted in painting.

First we see Romulus marching peacefully and triumphantly at the head of a small band of outlaws, bearing a single trophy, accompanied by prisoners who are free men, soon to be admitted into citizenship. This part of the scroll is thick with low-lying clouds, and we can only vaguely discern the progress of this triumph. With the Tarquins comes the glint of armour, and the *triumphator* is seen standing on a chariot of chased metal drawn by four white horses. There is a long procession with all the panoply of conquest; for the first time the conquering general climbs the sloping pathway to the Capitol, to speak to Jupiter and acquaint him of his victories. The years pass, and the triumph becomes simpler and sterner, but the wars against the Samnites bring opulence back again. Silver shields are hung in the Forum. The soldiers sing taunting songs, and a slave holds a golden crown over the head of the conqueror. Then again the triumphs become sterner, as the long-drawn wars are fought against the Carthaginians, until at last with the triumph of Scipio Africanus we see opulence of a terrifying kind: opulence which moves at the slow pace of unchallenged majesty.

With the triumph of Scipio Africanus everything is clear at last. The procession occupies the foreground, and there are no hovering mists. We see the *triumphator* bearing the ivory sceptre and the laurel branch, riding in a golden chariot, while his sons and nephews ride gaily on the trace-horses. The historians have gone to work in the archives: they have produced a triumph which has all the elements of past triumphs, elaborately choreographed. The triumph becomes self-conscious. For the first time everyone has his clearly delineated place. For the first time, too, we see the triumph as an instrument of empire.

Unroll the scroll, and soon we come upon a triumph gleaming with the glitter of Greek bronzes and marble statues; and instead of the opulence of Carthage there is the opulence of the east. Julius and Augustus extend the triumph until it swells like a three-ring circus into a vast theatrical display, heavy with destiny. Actors perform; great paintings portray the valour of the Romans and the iniquity of the enemy; and the element of self-consciousness is almost lost in the dazzling entertainment. With Nero the mould is broken. The heart of the procession is a core of madness, with the emperor so seduced by his own glory that he loses control: the triumph has become fantasy. We see Nero cavorting and preening himself. He must triumph in all things. It is not enough to conquer empires: he must conquer the arts and even the gods. Elagabalus strides across the scene in a frenzy of self-worship, applauding his own divinity. And when the madness passes, it leaves a shuddering in the air. The element of fantasy persists; there is a sense of doubt, of aimlessness. The face of Hadrian is clouded by it, and only Trajan stands completely upright, the triumphal arch at Beneventum proclaiming his sense of imperial authority. But as we watch the Flavian emperors passing on parade, we observe a twitching of the lips and a strange fixedness of the gaze. They were philosophers or they consorted with philosophers, and asked questions, and must have known it was dangerous to question a triumph. Finally the triumph becomes a charade with Roman slaves wearing wigs disguised as conquered Germans, and the Emperor Gallienus is heard shouting: "Peace everywhere", while the world is in ruins. So in emptiness and horror the Romans went down to defeat.

Salvation came from Illyria, a land of hardy mountaineers and herdsmen, thick-set, bullet-headed men who had no patience with fantasies. Of all the conquered provinces this seems to have been the one where the inhabitants most closely resembled the original Roman settlers.

Almost the last act of Gallienus before being stabbed to death at Milan was to appoint as his successor the Illyrian commander of a detached army in the neighbourhood of Pavia, who assumed the name of Marcus Aurelius Claudius, though he was born a peasant in one of the provinces bordering on the Danube. He had all the virtues: he was tall and handsome, with flashing eyes and a broad full face, and he could knock out the teeth of a horse with a blow of his clenched fist, and at the same time he possessed unusual gentleness in a military commander. He was singularly chaste—Trebellius Pollio speaks of his *unica castimonia*—and he was not the kind of man who could ever be accused of treachery. When the Emperor Gallienus heard from his agents in the field that Claudius was discontented with his command, and might be expected to turn against the emperor, he simply sent presents to Claudius and told his agents to keep quiet: he had complete faith in his lieutenant. When Claudius came to the throne and found himself confronted by an invasion of Goths *en masse*—we hear of 320,000 Goths pouring into Roman territory—he wrote a letter to the Senate: "If I vanquish the enemy, your gratitude will be the reward of my services; and if I fail, remember that I am the successor of Gallienus. The whole Republic is exhausted and worn to the bone. We lack javelins, spears and shields. We shall perform greatly." In that spirit he attacked the Goths, defeating them decisively at Mount Haemus, and adding to his name the title Gothicus. He might have become as great as Trajan, but he ruled for only two years before dying of the plague at the age of fifty-seven. In the presence of his principal officers he named Aurelian, one of his generals, to succeed him. After his death, or perhaps even while he was living, his statue in gold was placed in front of the Temple of Jupiter Capitolinus, and on the Rostra a column was erected bearing his statue in silver, showing him in the *tunica palmata* of a *triumphator*, although he never celebrated a triumph.

No one doubted the essential goodness and sobriety of Claudius II, but his successor was a butcher. Aurelian was another Illyrian, tall, strong, bloodthirsty. The chronicler describes him as *severus, truculentus, sanguinarius*. The people loved him for his rough good-humour, but his soldiers and the Senate feared him. Aurelian was the gentlest of Roman names, but the man was capable of punishing one of his soldiers by tying his legs to two bent trees and then releasing the trees so that the soldier's body was split apart. Fighting against the Sarmatians he was credited with killing a thousand of the enemy single-handed, and the Roman schoolboys sang a rollicking song about "the thousand thousand thousand heads lopped off, one man lopped them all", and how no one in all Rome possessed as much wine as the blood shed by the emperor. They called him *Manu ad ferrum*—Sword-in-hand, and it was as good a name for him as any.

Twelve years before coming to the throne Aurelian had been appointed consul by the Emperor Valerian in an extraordinary ceremony which took place in Byzantium. Aurelian's quality as a general was so high that the emperor presented him with a quite exceptional number of honours. These included, according to the historian Flavius Vopiscus, four mural crowns, five rampart crowns, two naval crowns, two civil crowns, ten spears, four coloured banners, four red tunics such as were worn by generals in the field, two proconsular cloaks, a gold-embroidered toga, the *tunica palmata*, a long under-tunic and an ivory chair. The military honours were more extraordinary than the consular honours. From the second century onwards consuls were permitted to march in solemn procession to the Capitol dressed in the garments of a *triumphator*, even when they had won no victories. They were also permitted to sit on ivory chairs, wear the red tunic of a general and display golden crowns decorated with battlements, ramparts or the prows of ships. The consul represented in his own person the permanent triumph of Rome over the Mediterranean world, but he was not permitted to ride in the triumphal chariot or perform the sacrifice of the triumph in the Temple of Jupiter Capitolinus. That drama could be performed only by the emperors: they alone led the hordes of prisoners along the Via Sacra and gave donations to the soldiers and stood in the triumphal chariots. To the end the consuls enjoyed only the *simulacrum* of the real triumph.

Aurelian seems to have been perfectly content to act as consul for a year and then to return to his command. He was not consumed with ambition. When he became emperor, he fought a series of hard campaigns against the Vandals, the Alemanni, the Goths and the usurper Tetricus, a former senator who seized power in Gaul, but for the moment he claimed no triumph for these victories. The east summoned him. Zenobia, Queen of Palmyra, ruled over large areas of Mesopotamia and Syria. She defied Rome, occupied Egypt and sent her army sweeping through Asia Minor until she had occupied all the territory south of Ancyra. In A.D. 271 she minted coins in Antioch and Alexandria bearing the portrait of her son with the titles Imperator and Augustus. Such defiance demanded punishment. Aurelian marched against Palmyra. He was perfectly aware that he was confronting a woman of great beauty, considerable generalship and vast powers of intrigue.

No Roman had ever confronted a queen like Zenobia. She was dark-skinned, with flashing eyes and pearly teeth; she marched with her soldiers and drank with her generals. She spoke Latin, Greek, Syrian and Egyptian, and the philosopher Longinus was probably her Greek secretary. When Aurelian came up to Palmyra and prepared to receive her surrender, he discovered a wily opponent. He offered to spare her life and the lives of her children in exchange for her jewels, her gold, her silver, all her silks, her horses and camels. Zenobia reminded the emperor that she had no intention of surrendering. Did she not belong to the family of Cleopatra, who preferred to die a queen rather than remain alive as a slave? Aurelian laid siege to Palmyra. Supplies ran low. The Palmyrenes were in despair. At a meeting of the council of state it was decided to send the queen on a swift dromedary to Persia to seek help, but she was captured by the Romans while fording the Euphrates. Suddenly and dramatically there was an end to the brief Palmyrene empire. Zenobia was brought in chains to Rome to decorate the triumph in which Aurelian celebrated his victories.

This triumph took place in A.D. 273, ten years after that strange carnival procession with which Gallienus celebrated a victory over the rebels of Byzantium. A menagerie accompanied the procession. Flavius Vopiscus of Syracuse, our chief authority for the reign of Aurelian, tells the story of the triumph with some hesitation, as though he did not quite believe it. He says:

There may be some advantage in knowing the manner of Aurelian's triumph, which was a most brilliant (*speciosissimus*) celebration. There were three royal chariots. One belonging to Odaenathus[1] was most carefully and elaborately wrought of silver, gold and jewels. Another, of similar workmanship, had been given to Aurelian by the King of the Persians. The third Zenobia had made for herself, hoping to visit Rome in it. This hope was not unfulfilled, for she entered the city with it, but vanquished and led in triumph. There was another chariot with a team of four stags, said to have belonged to the King of the Goths. There are many who have handed down the memory of how Aurelian rode up to the Capitol, and there slaughtered the stags which he had captured with the chariot, thus fulfilling a vow to Jupiter Optimus Maximus.

In the procession there were 20 elephants, 200 tamed animals of different kinds from Libya and Palestine (which Aurelian at once presented to individuals to spare the state the expense of their upkeep). There were also 4 tigers, giraffes, elks and other such animals taking part in the triumph, together with 800 pairs of gladiators and prisoners from the barbarian tribes. These were Blemmyes, Axomitae, Arabs from Arabia Felix, Indians, Bactrians, Hibernians, Saracens and Persians, all bearing gifts. There were also Goths, Alans, Roxolani, Sarmatians, Franks, Suebians, Vandals and Germans—all prisoners with their hands tied. Among them were also some Palmyrenes, who had survived the capture of the city, and these were the most important citizens. There were Egyptians, too, brought to Rome on account of their rebellion.

There were also ten women who had been captured while

[1] Odaenathus was a Palmyrene prince who held senatorial rank and the title of Commander of the East. He was assassinated in 266 A.D., and his wife Zenobia succeeded him.

fighting in male costume in the ranks of the Goths: they had survived after many others had fallen. An inscription borne before them indicated that they were of the race of the Amazons —such signs were borne before all the captives, showing what nations they belonged to. In the procession was Tetricus, arrayed in a scarlet cloak, yellow tunic and Gallic breeches, accompanied by his son, whom he had proclaimed emperor in Gaul. There was finally Zenobia, decked with jewels and wearing golden chains which others carried. Then came the golden crowns presented by the cities, and these too were preceded by inscriptions. The Roman people followed, with the banners of the guilds and of the camps, the mailed cuirassiers, the wealth of the kings, the entire army, and lastly the Senate (though the senators came sadly enough, since there were senators being led in triumph)— all this added a great deal of pomp to the procession.

It was almost the ninth hour when the procession reached the Capitol, and when they arrived at the Palace it was very late.

(Flavius Vopiscus, *Divus Aurelianus*, XXXIII—XXXIV)

Gibbon, who seems to have believed implicitly in Vopiscus, says that no general since the foundation of Rome had more nobly deserved a triumph than Aurelian; nor was any triumph ever celebrated with greater magnificence. "Unfeigned joy, wonder, and gratitude, swelled the acclamations of the multitude," he wrote; and it may have been true. But there are serious objections to the account. According to the historian Zosimus, Zenobia died on her way to Rome. There is no particular reason why he should have invented the story, for he has recorded her life in great detail and might be expected to know the manner of her death. As related by Vopiscus, this account of Aurelian's triumph reads like the imaginary triumph which the emperor wished he had enjoyed, such a triumph as he might himself have recorded in the court annals for the benefit of posterity. It is too detailed, too accurate, and altogether too magnificent.

Trebellius Pollio fills in the details—there are too many details. He tells how the vanquished queen was weighed down with such a weight of jewels that she sometimes had to pause. Her feet were bound with shackles of gold, her hands were joined together with golden chains, and she wore another golden chain round her neck, the other end being held by a Persian buffoon. He records a letter written by Aurelian when reproached by the Senate for leading her in his triumph. The emperor justifies his action at considerable length:

I have heard, O conscript Fathers, that I am being reproached for having performed an unmanly deed by leading Zenobia in my triumph. The truth is that those who find fault with me now would find occasion to praise me greatly if they knew what manner of woman she is, how wise in her counsels, how steadfast in following out her designs, how firm towards her soldiers, how large-hearted when necessity arises, how stern when discipline demands. I might even say it was through her that Odaenathus conquered the Persians and then, when Sapor had fled, advanced right up to Ctesiphon. I could add that she was held in such fear by the people of the Orient and also in Egypt that neither Arabs nor Saracens, nor Armenians ever moved against her. Nor would I have spared her life, except that I knew how much she had contributed to the Roman state when she preserved the imperium for herself or for her children throughout the east. Therefore let those who are pleased with nothing hold their venomous tongues!

(Trebellius Pollio, *Tyranni Triginta*, XXX)

This letter, of course, was not intended to reproduce the actual words of the emperor, and we need not examine it too closely to discover the motives behind Aurelian's reasons for leading the queen in triumph. Augustus had hoped to lead Cleopatra in chains; Julius Caesar had actually led Princess Arsinoë in chains; and neither could be accused of unmanliness. There was in fact no reason why the Senate should complain against the introduction of a queen in the triumph, and this letter therefore, and all the circumstantial details concerning her presence in the triumph, must be regarded with suspicion.

So the mysterious and beautiful queen passes out of history, ending her days at sea or, as others say, in Hadrian's Villa at Tivoli where she lived out the remaining years of her life as a Roman matron, surrounded by her children, giving herself to good works, a gentle unassuming woman who demanded nothing of the emperor except to be allowed to live. The emperor demanded more. He especially demanded to be known as the successor of Augustus and inscribed on his coins: *Pax Augusti, Pax Aeterna, Restitutor Orbis*. He collected more titles than any other emperor: he was Gothicus, Sarmaticus, Armeniacus, Parthicus and Adiabenicus, as well as Germanicus. He was a hard prince, *durus princeps*, and ruled by the sword, and met the fate usually accorded to those who rule by the sword—he was murdered.

Probus, who succeeded him after the brief reign of Tacitus, the seventy-five-year-old senator who claimed descent from the historian, was made of the stuff of great emperors. He was another Illyrian, with the rough geniality which seems to have characterized all the Illyrian emperors of Rome. Heavy-set and handsome in his soldierly way, he was good to his soldiers and mitigated the severities of Aurelian when he was a general occupying important frontier posts. He seems to have spent most of his six-year reign fighting, but in A.D. 281 he returned to Rome to celebrate a triumph over the Germans and the Blemmyes, a warlike tribe which had invaded Upper Egypt from Nubia. He had made forays in Gaul, Parthia, Sarmatia and the territories of the Goths, and in his triumph there were companies, each consisting of fifty men, from all the countries he had invaded. He liked round numbers, and at the games which followed he presented 100 lions, 100 lionesses, 200 leopards and 300 bears. In honour of his triumph he minted coins showing him riding in a six-horse chariot with the legend: *Gloria Orbis*.

For once the legend seems to have been true. There was power and kindliness in this man, who once surprised his soldiers by declaring that there would soon come a time when the Roman empire would have no further need of soldiers—the whole world would be at peace. He died on his way to Persia during a halt in his native city of Sirmium (Mitrovicza). He was one of those men who cannot bear to be idle or to see others idle, and so he set his men to draining the marshes and building a canal with outlets flowing into the Save. His soldiers rebelled, ran him into a look-out tower and there killed him. Afterwards they were sorry and built an enormous tumulus and carved for him a marble monument on which they engraved the words: "Here lies the Emperor Probus, a man of probity, conqueror of all the barbarian nations and victor over tyrants."

In the brief reigns of Carus and his two sons Carinus and Numerianus no triumphs are reported. Numerianus was an amiable prince with a liking for rhetoric and some skill as a poet. During his reign he struck coins inscribed with the legend *Triunfu Quadorum*, showing himself and his father riding in a four-horse chariot with Victory in attendance and a crowd of prisoners.

These three emperors ruled for less than three years and left no impress on the Roman scene. They were succeeded by an emperor who profoundly changed the forms of Roman rule. He shattered the prism. Quite suddenly the world was confronted with an emperor who ruled, not from Rome, but from Nicomedia in Bithynia, on the Adriatic shore close to Byzantium. He did not rule alone, but with the help of a co-emperor and two assistant emperors who bore the title of Caesar. These emperors with their separate courts resembled oriental monarchs: they wore the diadem; their purple robes were of silk; their shoes were adorned with precious stones.

Bullet-headed Diocletian, with his close-cropped hair and look of a prize-fighter, began life as a servant in the house of a Roman senator. He became governor of a province, then consul, then commander of the Praetorian Guard; on the death of Numerianus he was proclaimed emperor. Brilliant and cultivated, he had the wit and fortitude to share the empire with his chief-of-staff, a former Illyrian peasant named Maximianus, who was given power over Italy and Africa, while Diocletian retained power over Thrace, Egypt and Asia. The outlying provinces were entrusted to the two Caesars, Galerius, a former herdsman from Dacia, and Constantius, a grandnephew of the Emperor Claudius II. In effect the empire was being ruled by a quadrumvirate of skilled and experienced soldiers, whose common bond was the close friendship which arose from their knowledge of war.

They were fighters, and there was something harsh and primitive in all of them. They were well-chosen, and they fought continually. Maximianus launched an expedition against Carausius, who had proclaimed himself emperor of Britain, and he put down a vast rebellion of poor peasants in Gaul. Diocletian threw his army against Egypt, which had revolted, besieged Alexandria for eight months, and when the Alexandrians begged for mercy, he put them to the sword. Galerius was sent into Armenia and was routed. Returning to Antioch he was greeted with the displeasure of Diocletian, who ordered him in penance to march behind the emperor's chariot, wearing the imperial purple, for the length of a mile. It was a punishment worthy of a captive king, and Galerius took care not to be routed again. In the following year, to clear his honour, he invaded Persia, attacked the Persian army commanded by Narses, the king of kings, and put it to flight. The Persian king was wounded, his wives and children were captured, and immense booty was captured. The story is told that after this battle a Roman soldier came upon a leather bag filled with pearls. He threw the pearls away and kept the bag, thinking it was more valuable.

Gifted men were making a stupendous effort to preserve the empire. They thought the greatest danger lay outside. In this they were wrong. The greatest danger to the state lay with the Christians who occupied a host of minor posts in the army and in government. Diocletian and Galerius gave orders to exterminate the Christian faith, and Christians were unmercifully persecuted. But it was already too late: the leaven was already working.

After a reign of nearly twenty years Diocletian decided to celebrate a long succession of victories with a triumph. The triumph
took place in Rome on November 20, A.D. 303. It was a modest
triumph, befitting a man who was about to perform a feat beyond
the power of any emperor before him—he was about to abdicate
and spend the remaining years of his life peacefully growing cab-
bages in a Dalmatian garden. Diocletian and Maximianus celebrated the triumph together. There were the usual trophies from
Africa, Egypt, Britain, Gaul, Germany and Persia. Narses was not
led in the procession: he had fled to the hinterland of Media. In
the procession there were effigies of the Persian king and his relatives. There were the usual massive paintings representing rivers,
mountains and provinces; the usual displays of captured weapons;
the usual long lines of prisoners. Yet there was no extravagance in
the procession: the triumph was sober, as Diocletian was sober.
Shortly after the triumph Diocletian announced his determination
to abdicate, and he forced Maximianus to abdicate with him.

Today the sole relic of those victories is the crumbling arch
erected by Galerius about A.D. 300 in Salonika to celebrate his victories in Persia. Once there were three archways, but only the
central arch has survived. Once it was covered with sculptured
reliefs even more plentifully than the arch of Trajan at Beneventum. But enough sculptures remain to suggest the original glory.
We see the emperor haranguing his troops, receiving the surrender
of captives, riding in state towards a city where the welcomers stand
at the gates. There is an exquisite tenderness in the portrait of the
emperor as he stands before the altar, surrounded by the priests,
while the white ox gazes impassively at the spectator, and there is
no knife in sight. Though the reliefs are in ruins, enough detail
remains to show that the hand of the sculptor is failing. There is
tenderness and a kind of limpidity, and at the same time the sculptures seem to have lost purpose and direction. The next great
archway to be built would show only illimitable confusion.

At the time the abdication of Diocletian must have seemed an
act of pure generosity; but it had an appalling effect. There was no
government: only a host of governors. The Roman armies were
now at the mercy of the generals who thought themselves worthy of
the purple: for a brief while six emperors claimed the allegiance of
the Roman people. In A.D. 306 Constantius died in York. About the
same time Maxentius, the profligate son of Maximianus, was proclaimed emperor in Rome by the Praetorian Guard. Galerius from
his headquarters in Nicomedia sent an army against Maxentius,
but the army deserted him. At this juncture Constantine, the son of

Constantius, marched into Italy and defeated Maxentius at the village of Saxa Rubra near Rome. Maxentius tried to escape over the Milvian Bridge, but perished in the river. His body was recovered, and Constantine entered Rome in triumph.

Gibbon says there were no more triumphs after the triumph of Diocletian, but in fact there were many more. Constantine entered Rome with all the trappings of a conqueror. He received a tumultuous welcome. The Senate conferred upon him the title of Senior Augustus and erected a golden statue of him, adorned with the attributes of a god. It decreed games and festivals, and voted the triumphal arch which still stands near the arch of Titus and the Colosseum.

Seen from a distance the arch of Constantine possesses a heavy magnificence; it has the virtue of being unmistakably triumphal. But on closer view it becomes almost a parody, a thing of many styles and many thefts, an improvisation erected to please an emperor's vanity. The arch is a composite of many arches. Whole panels, roundels and friezes have been stolen from other arches. Trajan and Marcus Aurelius are recognizably present on it. Trajan takes part in a boar-hunt, slays a lion, sacrifices to Apollo, harangues his soldiers, gallops on to the battlefield, receives the crown of victory and enters Rome in triumph. There are other panels showing Marcus Aurelius receiving gifts and departing for the wars. The carvings which belong specifically to the time of Constantine possess a uniform insignificance. It is not that they are bad art; it is simply that they are not art. There are thin friezes showing soldiers on parade or besieging a town, which might have been carved by a palsied child. There are meaningless roundels apostrophizing the sun and the moon. All nobility has vanished. Squat, tumescent figures like rudely carved chessmen march in procession or ride miserably on wooden horses, and vanish into stone. On the side of the arch nearest the Colosseum there is a disturbing inscription:

IMP. CAES. FL. CONSTANTINO MAXIMO
P.F. AVGVSTO. S.P.Q.R
QVOD. INSTINCTV. DIVINITATIS. MENTIS.
MAGNITVDINE. CVM. EXERCITV. SVO.
TAM. DE. TYRANNO. QVAM. DE. OMNI. EIVS.
FACTIONE. VNO. TEMPORE. IVSTIS.
REMPUBLICAM. VLTVS. EST. ARMIS.
ARCVM. TRIUMPHANS. INSEGNEM. DICAVIT. [1]

[1] It is possible that TRIVMPHANS in the last line should be read: TRIVMPHIS. The last line of the translation should then read: 'dedicate this noble arch adorned with triumphs.' The stone has worn away, and the word is not clear.

To the Emperor Caesar Flavius Constantinus Maximus,
the Pious, the Fortunate Augustus,
who by the inspiration of God and the greatness
of his mind, and with the help of his legions,
did with proper force avenge the Republic,
destroying the Tyrant and all his partisans,
the Senate and People of Rome
triumphantly dedicate this noble arch.

No one any longer knows what meaning was attached in Constantine's mind to the words *instinctu divinitatis*, but there is no reason to believe that they convey a Christian sentiment. The divinity that ruled Constantine was rarely Christian. A tall, heavy-set man, with a high colour and glittering eyes, given to sudden rages, he maintained almost to the last day of his life a protracted worship of the Sun-god Helios. His rages grew more violent as he grew older. He was fifty-four when he gave orders for the murder of his son Crispus and about the same time had his wife Fausta drowned in her bath. He tolerated Christianity, and in Constantinople, which became his capital, he is said to have placed his own statue in the Forum with the attributes of Apollo and Christ, only substituting the nails of the Passion for the rays of the Sun.

Constantius, his son, was a Christian, and perhaps the most forbidding of all Roman emperors, a cold, chaste, savage, watchful man, who wrote intolerably bad poetry and had the misfortune to find himself committed to the Arian heresy. He had dark, bulging eyes and shaven cheeks which were strangely glossy; a long, heavy body, tiny legs; the look of a man about to spring. Ammianus Marcellinus says of him that "no one ever saw him wipe his mouth or nose in public, nor spit, nor turn his head from side to side". After putting down a revolt by the Frankish usurper Magnentius, Constantius entered Rome in triumph, accompanied by his formidable wife Eusebia and his sister Helena, the future wife of the Emperor Julian. It was April 28, A.D. 357. The sun shone. Vast crowds gathered in the streets. The emperor was seated alone in a golden chariot, wearing military uniform. For some reason he particularly desired a very long and imposing procession. In front marched the legionaries bearing banners stiff with gold, shaped in the form of dragons. Beside him rode the Imperial Guard flying purple standards bound to the golden and jewelled tops of their spears. Constantius seems to have been consumed by pride. "He never so much as moved a muscle, but his countenance remained unchanged, and as if his neck were fixed he gazed straight ahead, turning neither to right nor left, like a statue, and even when he was jolted by the wheels of the chariot, he never moved his head or hands" (Ammianus Marcellinus, XVI, 10.10). It is, of course, the classic pose of the *triumphator*, and cannot have been unusual. What was remarkable was the ferocious fixity of his gaze, his doll-like composure, his assumption of the pose at a time when the world had almost forgotten the *tremendum maiestatis*. Constantius was determined to be imperial.

Once the triumphal ceremonies were over, Constantius stepped down a little from his exalted position. He made a public speech from his seat in the Forum, and later he spoke to the nobles in the Senate-house. The emperor was polite, if distant, and examined the civil honours of the Republic and the consular images of the noble families. So many people were acclaiming him that he permitted himself the observation that the entire human race seemed to be present to welcome him. There was thunderous applause. He presided over the equestrian games. He thought of building for himself a colossal equestrian statue like the one which stood in the Forum of Trajan, and he only desisted when Hormisdas, an exiled Persian prince, slyly observed: "Then you must have a stable as well." Instead he arranged to transport to Rome a vast obelisk, the most sacred in Egypt, which had once stood before the Temple of the Sun at Heliopolis. Some time later the obelisk was set up in the Circus Maximus. It is just possible that this same obelisk is the one which stands outside St. John Lateran, "the mother of churches". After thirty days in Rome the young red-headed emperor hurried to Illyria to put down an uprising, and then set out for Persia, never to return to Rome. He was only forty-four when he died of fever near Tarsus.

His successor was his nephew, the brilliant Julian, who was very short and wore a thick curly beard in imitation of the Athenian philosophers under whom he had studied. He thirsted after triumphs, but reigned for too short a time to receive one—he was killed during the Persian war, apparently by a javelin thrown by one of his own soldiers; and he spent his last hours quietly conversing about the nature of the soul. Julian was a pagan who derided Christianity; his successor, Jovian, a convinced Christian, a good soldier, a handsome and impatient hedonist, died after a reign of eight months.

With Julian the dynasty of Constantine came to an end. Jovian was an officer of the bodyguard. Valentinian, who followed him, was a Pannonian officer who made his headquarters in Treves, and gave to his brother Valens the task of defending the Danube and the east. He never visited Rome and died of a burst blood-vessel when in a rage after listening to the long-winded pleas of some barbarian envoys. When Valens fell fighting the Goths at Adrianople in A.D. 378, the Romans suffered their greatest defeat since Cannae with two-thirds of their army left behind on the battlefield.

The new emperor of the east was Theodosius, the son of a distinguished general, by origin a Spaniard, who fought a decisive engagement with the usurper Maximus at Aquileia in A.D. 388. Theodosius was a stern and choleric man with a deep feeling for Christianity. He was the first Roman emperor to embrace Christianity full-heartedly. On the occasion of his triumph the following spring he is reported to have assembled the Senate and demanded that the senators choose between the ancient pagan gods and the God of the Christians. Except for a brief mention by the Alexandrian poet Claudian no details of his triumph have survived. The Christian historian Orosius, who was born about this time and might therefore be expected to know what happened, says nothing at all—he is too busy recounting how, by the intervention of God, Theodosius was rewarded with bloodless victories. All we know for certain is that he made his triumph in the company of his son Honorius, then a boy of ten, and some time later erected in Constantinople the great Golden Gate, an arch of triumph gilded all over, in celebration of his triumph.

It was the time when the Goths were hammering at the gates. Only a few years before Ammianus Marcellinus had spoken of the Roman empire declining into a peaceful old age. Now quite suddenly the long years of peace, broken only by occasional years of civil war, came to an end with the invasion of the Gothic prince Alaric, who had been ravaging Greece and was determined to ravage Italy. In November A.D. 401 Alaric passed the Italian Alps and descended upon Aquileia. Soon all Venetia lay open to the Goths, and Alaric was ready to march on Milan, the capital of the young Emperor Honorius. For two years there were indecisive engagements; then at last in the spring of A.D. 403 the imperial forces under the command of Stilicho routed the Goths in two pitched battles and Alaric was forced to sue for peace. In the following year the Emperor Honorius entered Rome in triumph.

The poet Claudian, who was an eye-witness of the triumph, has described it in great detail. He tells how the court left Ravenna and crossed the Apennines, pausing on the banks of the Clitumnus where in ancient times the great white herds were found from which the most magnificent were taken and sacrificed at the Capitol; but they found no bulls. They reached Rome by way of the Milvian bridge, the emperor and his victorious general riding together in the triumphal chariot. Vast preparations were made to welcome the emperor. Triumphal gates and archways were erected in his honour, many of them bearing indiscreet references to the total destruction of the Gothic nation—Alaric was to find the gates still standing when he sacked Rome six years later. It was the custom in the past for the senators to walk before the triumphal chariot, but Honorius dispensed with this custom. Both emperor and general wore ornamental robes thickly covered with embroidery, but the embroidery was invisible under the heavy chains of jewellery they carried about their persons. The public applauded vociferously, filling the streets as far as the Capitol and the Palatine, and even covering the roof-tops. The emperor wore the diadem. Great bursts of applause greeted the appearance of the *cataphractarii* in their coats of chain-mail and the *draconarii* with peacock plumes rising from their helmets. They wore scarves of scarlet silk and carried long dragon-pennants which flapped in the wind. It was all a little too magnificent.

So the procession passed along the Via Sacra under the triumphal arches of ancient emperors, and there was a brief pause at the palace of Septimius Severus followed by a reception at the Circus, where all the public bodies were marshalled to greet the emperor. Then there were games: chariot races one day, hunting of wild beasts the next, with a military tattoo on the third day, the soldiers displaying their prowess at drill. Wherever the young emperor went he was greeted with extraordinary enthusiasm.

Claudian was a *protégé* of Stilicho, and we do not have to believe every word of his highly coloured account of the emperor's triumph which appears in *The Sixth Consulship of Honorius*. Yet he speaks as an eye-witness, with a sense of the glory of the event. He was the last of the pagan poets, and his poem forms a pagan swan-song.

Feasting on the admiration of the people, Honorius spent a year in Rome, living in a palace on the Palatine. Legend has been busy with his brief visit: it is said that an Asiatic monk named Telemachus jumped into the arena when the gladiators were fighting to protest against their bloodthirsty cruelty; and he was rewarded with a fatal shower of stones from the angry spectators. Later the spectators grew penitent, and demanded from the emperor an edict banning gladiatorial shows forever.

Alaric had been defeated below the walls of Verona, but it was no more than a temporary defeat. The Gothic prince seems to have believed it was his destiny to loot the greatest city on earth, and in October, A.D. 408, while Honorius was safely attending to his court at Ravenna, Alaric reached the walls of the city, and would have sacked it if he had not been bribed by 5,000 pounds of gold and 30,000 pounds of silver and 3,000 pounds of pepper. The next year Alaric came again. This time he was bribed with the title of Master of the Horse and the powers of a military governor. Still unsatisfied, he came to the city for a third time in August, A.D. 410, sacked it for three days, and departed as suddenly as he came. He died a few weeks later, and was buried royally in the bed of a stream which was diverted and then allowed to pass over him as he lay in state, with gold vessels heaped all round him.

Rome had seduced the Goths; the Gothic conquerors who came later derived pleasure from the Roman name, intermarried with the family of Honorius and became his lieutenants. The Visigothic chieftain Wallia restored Spain to the empire, and sent messages proclaiming his conquests to the court in Ravenna. A triumph was accordingly decreed for Honorius. This triumph, which occurred about A.D. 415, seems to have been graced with the same panoply as the former triumph, but there was no Claudian to celebrate the majesty of the young emperor. All we have is the brief record of the chronicler: *Romam triumphans ingreditur.* Eight years later the handsome and ineffective emperor died of the dropsy, having ruled with the utmost delicacy for twenty-eight years.

Long ago, in the time of Cicero, it was a common belief that the Roman empire was destined to last twelve centuries corresponding to twelve vultures once seen by Romulus. Now the twelve centuries were nearly over; and strange barbarian armies were gathering in all the provinces of the empire. The Vandals were in Africa. Gaul and Spain were being ravaged. Suddenly the Huns under Attila invaded Italy, and only a miracle saved Rome.

Only a few years separated the invasion of Attila and that of the Vandals under Gaiseric who arrived from Africa with a large fleet at the port of Ostia. Gaiseric professed himself a Christian. He was a short, swarthy man with a cruel mouth, who walked with a limp; and he listened intently to the pleas of Pope Leo I, who begged him to spare the lives of the Romans. Alaric had asked for gold and silver; statues had been melted down, and women had poured their gold chains and necklaces into the melting-pots. Gaiseric wanted the statues to grace his palace in Carthage, and he wanted the gold chains and necklaces of the Roman women for his own women. For fourteen days the spoils of Rome were methodically transported to the ships moored alongside the quay of La Marmorata. The gold and silver statues were lifted bodily from the Forum and out of the imperial palace on the Palatine. The Temple of Jupiter Capitolinus, which had presided over the destinies of Rome since the time of the last Tarquin, was plundered. The gold sheeting on the roof, which had cost Domitian 12,000 talents, equivalent perhaps to £3,000,000, was rolled up and loaded on to the waiting ships, together with all the statues and votive offerings in the temple. The golden table and seven-branched candlestick, which Titus displayed so ostentatiously in his triumph, went with them. The Pope melted down six silver vases, each weighing a hundred pounds, which had been presented to the Church by Constantine. Gaiseric had promised to spare the lives of the Romans; he had not promised not to enslave them; and thousands of young men and women accompanied the treasure-fleet to Carthage. Only one of the ships was lost at sea. Somewhere off the coast of Sicily there lies a sunken ship bearing all the treasure from the Temple of Jupiter Capitolinus.

St. Jerome was shaken to the depths by the invasions of the Goths. About the year A.D. 410, he wrote in his *Commentary on Ezekiel*: "Who could have believed that Rome, founded upon her triumphs which have blazed her name to the whole world, could fall to ruins?—that she, the Mother of Nations, should also be their grave?—that all the regions of the east, of Egypt and of Africa, should be filled with swarms of young refugees from the former Lady of the World?"

In time the theft of the Roman treasure was avenged, and the gold and silver statues which once decorated the Forum and the Palatine, and then graced an obscure palace in Carthage, found their way to Constantinople.

In A.D. 530 Gelimer, a great-grandson of Gaiseric, ruled over immense stretches of northern Africa. Justinian, the emperor of the east, was in no mood to allow the Vandal prince to remain on his throne and sent an expeditionary force under Belisarius, who had won important victories in Persia, against him. Belisarius landed in Africa, and after a hard-fought campaign he broke the Vandal army and forced it to scatter into the mountains. Gelimer himself was almost starving to death when he was captured. Brought before Belisarius he gave a strange strident laugh—it was the laughter of a man who has been stripped of his royal powers and has spent many months as a fugitive, expecting death at every moment. Belisarius carried off the spoils and the prisoners to Constantinople, and in A.D. 534 he was awarded a triumph. It was modelled on the Roman triumph, but there were important differences. It started from Belisarius's own house, wound through the streets of the city and ended before the thrones of the Emperor and the Empress Theodora in the Hippodrome. The historian Procopius, who was an aide to Belisarius and an eye-witness of the triumph, quite naturally tended to exaggerate the novelty of the occasion. He wrote:

Nearly six hundred years have passed since anyone enjoyed a comparable triumph, unless perhaps we include such emperors as Titus and Trajan and others who led their armies against the barbarians and won victories.

Belisarius displayed the spoils of war and his prisoners within the city, but he did not follow the ancient form of the triumph— he went on foot from his own house to the Hippodrome, and then he went to the place where the races start, and afterwards he marched up to the throne. The spoils consisted of royal treasure—golden thrones and those carriages which are used by the king's consort, and much jewellery fashioned from precious stones, and gold drinking-cups, and other things suitable for the royal table. There was also silver weighing many thousands of talents, and altogether the treasure amounted to an exceedingly great sum (for Gaiseric had despoiled the imperial palace in Rome, as I have already related).

Among these treasures were those which Titus, the son of Vespasian, brought to Rome from Jerusalem. There was a certain Jew who had the ear of the emperor, and he said: "It is wrong that these vessels should be installed in Constantinople. They should be in the place where Solomon, the king of the Jews, formerly placed them. It is because of these treasures that Gaiseric invaded Rome and the Roman army has conquered the Vandals." The emperor was alarmed, and arranged to send the spoils from the Temple of Solomon to the care of the Christian sanctuaries in Jerusalem.

There were many prisoners in the triumph, among them Gelimer himself and all his family, and as many of the Vandals as were tall and fair of body. Gelimer wore a kind of purple cloak over his shoulders, and when he entered the Hippodrome and saw the emperor sitting on his high throne and the people watching him from every side, he realized that he had fallen into an evil plight, but he neither wept nor cried out. Instead he kept saying over and over again the words of the Hebrew scripture: "Vanity of vanities! All is vanity!" Led before the emperor's throne, he pulled off the purple cloak and fell prone on the earth and did obeisance.

Belisarius also fell to the ground beside him, being a suppliant.
(Procopius, *History of the Wars*, IV, 9)

Belisarius had good reason to beg for mercy, for it had been
rumoured that when he entered Carthage he had sat on the throne
of Gelimer, and this was taken as a sign of his desire for the imperial throne. He was however pardoned. Gelimer, too, was
favoured by the emperor and even invited to enrol among the
patricians of Constantinople on condition that he abjured his
Arian faith; but this he refused to do. Justinian was so pleased with
his victory that he ordered the erection of a colossal statue, representing himself on horseback, in front of Sancta Sophia, and he re-
modelled his own palace until it shone with statues and mosaics
representing his triumph in Africa.

Justinian's aim was to win back the lands conquered from the
Romans by the barbarians. In this he was remarkably successful,
though he never led an army into battle. The agent of his conquests
was Belisarius, who having conquered Persia and Africa, went on
to invade Italy, with such effect that he captured the Gothic king
and all his treasure in Ravenna, and brought them in triumph to
Constantinople. But there was no triumph. Belisarius was in disgrace; Justinian was afraid; and the emperor, to rid himself of a
possible rival, sent the general who had reconquered the Roman
empire once more against the Persians. In the place of Belisarius,
as commander of the Roman armies on Italian soil, there was
Narses, a middle-aged Armenian eunuch, who had never before
commanded an army.

Narses was a man of immense courage, calculating, stern, possessed of a superb intelligence. He was very small, almost a dwarf,
but he possessed a commanding presence. He had been one of the
eunuchs in the palace, and had grown grey in the service of the
emperor: he was over seventy when he fought his decisive engagement against Totila. His troops formed a motley army of Huns,
Lombards, Gepids and Herulians, but they were nevertheless loyal
to the emperor in Constantinople, and they deserved the immemorial right of marching in triumph through Rome.

It was the last of all the Roman triumphs, and perhaps the
strangest, for no one taking part in the procession could be called
Roman, yet all of them by virtue of their oath to Justinian represented the power of the Roman empire. The Capitol was despoiled
of all its ornaments, and only a few bronze statues were left standing in the Forum. But the ancient temples and triumphal arches
remained; the Temple of Janus was still standing; so were the

great basilicas of Julius and Constantine. The mausoleum of Hadrian had been converted into a fortress. Yet Rome was still recognizably the towering city which had seen so many triumphs in the past. Only one thing was lacking for the enjoyment of the conquering general—a great audience. The population of Rome had dwindled until it was perhaps no more than 40,000.

On that day in A.D. 554 when Narses rode in triumph through the streets of Rome, the story of the Roman triumph comes to an end. There were to be other triumphs by other conquerors, but for the most part they were to assume the nature of carnival processions: the long unbroken chain had snapped at last. Narses rode in a chariot. His Ostrogothic prisoners with their allies, the Franks and the Alemanni, walked before him; trophies were carried; and the soldiers with garlands in their hands sang their paeans in honour of the conquering general. For the last time a triumphal chariot rumbled over the Via Sacra, and then it was over. Narses returned to Constantinople to receive the congratulations of his emperor: he lived to the ripe age of ninety-five. The last of the *triumphatores* was an elderly Armenian eunuch who had never fought a battle before.

Narses surprises us, but we have little reason to be surprised. The rulers of the Roman empire were no longer Romans: had not in fact been Romans for centuries. Tribal chieftains from Asia had assumed the purple, and the most powerful of them all began life as an obscure Slavonic princeling who bore originally the name of Pravda, meaning "truth" or "justice". He became Justinian, the founder of our laws and the author of the proudest boast of any Roman emperor. Looking back at the great victories won during his long reign, and the triumphs enjoyed by so many generals and emperors before him, he declared: "Only in our reign has God granted to the Romans to achieve such triumphs. God did not judge the ancients worthy of such accomplishments, which now at last are realized in our time."

12

THE CHURCH TRIUMPHANT

EVER since the evening of October 27, A.D. 312, when the *labarum* with the monogram of Christ was first raised by Constantine, the triumphal march of the Church was assured. The Church became a power, not always tangible, but robed in the majesty of conquest, protected by imperial favour, subservient to no earthly power. After the physical empire came the ghostly empire; and the Roman gods fell before the single god incarnate in Jesus, crucified by an obscure provincial governor in the reign of Tiberius.

The Roman gods did not, of course, fall at once. For a long while paganism and Christianity lived side by side. A calendar published in Rome in A.D. 354 lists the birthdays of the apotheosized rulers from Augustus to Constantius, the consuls from the year 510 B.C. and the pagan festivals throughout the year, noting that on December 25, there were games in the Circus to celebrate "the birth of the unconquerable sun" (*natalis solis invicti*). There followed a table of Easter Sundays, and the feast-days of the martyrs. Christianity and paganism walked side by side in apparent harmony; it seems not to have been impossible for a man to attend the feast of the Lupercalia in the morning and divine service in the evening.

Constantine himself appears to have lived quite satisfactorily in both worlds, offering prayers to the pagan and Christian gods with the same profound devotion. On occasion he wore the Cross on his helmet, and sometimes appeared with one of the Holy Nails set in his golden diadem. He protected Christians, but he also protected pagans; and during all his visits to Rome except perhaps the last he continued to offer public vows to Jupiter Capitolinus. On some of his coins were stamped the figures of *Sol Invictus* and *Jupiter Conservator*, while on others we see the *labarum* or an altar surmounted with a Cross.

No one has ever succeeded in discovering his true beliefs; perhaps he had none. To the bishops who assembled at Nicaea, he came as a Christian emperor, "resplendent as one of God's angels in heaven", wearing a purple mantle shimmering with gold and jewels. It was observed that he did not take his seat until the bishops requested

him to do so by a sign, and it was widely believed that his extreme
deference to the bishops sitting in council implied a greater deference to Christ, but it is possible that he attended the councils of
the pagan priests with the same humble air. In Constantinople he
raised to himself a statue bearing the nimbus of the sun-god: in
Rome, according to Eusebius, there was a statue of the emperor
bearing a crucifix on a lance, with an inscription saying he had
destroyed tyranny by virtue of his faith in Christ.

Constantine remains an enigma. That heavy face with its high
colour and fierce lion-like eyes, so florid, so awesome in its bland
majesty, suggests the conqueror to perfection. But sometimes
doubts arise. The statue of Constantine in the porch of St. John
Lateran shows a mysterious smile hovering about his lips, and we
see that smile again in the brown sardonyx gem now in the Penn-
sylvania University Museum which shows him riding in triumph,
attended by his lictors. He wears a laurel crown, while a winged
genius holds a crown of gold above his head. The reins hang slack
from his left hand, but in his right he displays the *tyche*, the mysterious symbol of his possession over the city. In front of him are
displayed the *fasces* and a sign with the ancient inscription: SPQR.
We see two slaves beside the chariot, two soldiers, a woman mourning, but they are no more than artistic decoration: the purpose of
the artist is to describe the triumph in Christian terms, and therefore he has shown the emperor gazing fondly upon the *labarum*,
which takes the form of a long pike bearing the monogram of
Christ. This gem supplies us with the first record of the Christian
triumph; there were to be many others.

Yet one should pause briefly over this gem and examine it a little
further. It is not quite what it seems to be. Remove the *labarum*,
and we have the Roman triumph almost as we see it on the Boscoreale cup. There is no Christian feeling in the design. One of the
slaves carries the triangular knife of sacrifice, and we are made
abundantly aware of a sacrificial victim, invisibly present. The
sharply-turned head of the helmeted Roman who stands in front
of the horses speaks with a purely pagan authority; the mourning
woman represents the long procession of prisoners marching in
front of the triumphal chariot. Here is the Roman triumph in all
its august solemnity at the point where it *dissolves* into the Christian triumph, which is august and solemn in an entirely different
manner. Gone is the ferocious severity on the face of the *triumphator*; gone too the sceptre and the laurels; gone the stately progress
to the Capitol. We are present at a triumph which is not a con-
tinuous procession, but an event outside time altogether. Almost

the *labarum* dominates the scene, yet in fact there is an uneasy balance between paganism and Christianity.

Though we shall never know how deeply that sardonic emperor was influenced by the religion which he tolerated and sometimes embraced, he left his permanent stamp on it. Without him there could have been no Council of Nicaea; and without his deliberate toleration of paganism, it is unlikely that pagan customs would have survived into Christian ritual. The ancient Roman festivals of the Saturnalia and Lupercalia were merged into the festivals of Christmas and Candlemas, while the festival of the Floralia, when the pagan temples were filled with flowers, deeply impressed itself upon the observance of Easter. The pagan priests were sometimes tonsured; they lit candles at the altars, burned incense, dipped their hands in holy water placed at the entrance of the temples, and carried idols gorgeously apparelled in processions through the streets, as the Roman priests do today. The Roman triumph and the person of the *triumphator* were not forgotten. In time the *tunica palmata* became the alb, and the *toga picta* became the dalmatic. Even to this day some vestiges of the triumph appear in the papal coronation. As the Pope emerges in his pontifical robes from the Chapel of St. Gregory, a master of ceremonies kneels before him, holding a golden wand tipped with burning tow, and three times he repeats the admonition: *"Pater sancte, sic transit gloria mundi."* Then the tow is extinguished, and the Pope proceeds to the high altar to receive the pallium.

Inevitably the Roman triumph, as the supreme act of human exaltation, continued under Christian auspices, if only because it was so deeply embedded in the consciousness of the Romans. Papal processions consciously imitated it. In time the Gothic churches were to have portals designed after the triumphal archways, while the Roman basilicas were decorated with royal archways of glittering mosaic before the altars. At a very early period the theme of the Church militant and triumphant was announced to a people who were perfectly willing to regard Christ as the *triumphator in excelsis*, the last of the deified Caesars, the first *imperator* to rule over Heaven and earth. Christ was King, and He marched in eternal procession accompanied by the angels and the faithful. Had He not in Jerusalem imitated the Roman triumph by entering the city in triumph, while the faithful saluted Him with palms? In the Middle Ages He was often regarded as a kingly warrior waging war against the hosts of darkness. So Hugo of St. Victor wrote in the prologue to *De Sacramentis Christianae Fidei*: "All the saints who were before his coming were as soldiers going before his face;

and those who have come and will come after unto the end of the
world are as soldiers who follow their king."

The earthly kings also continued to triumph under the protec-
tion of the Pope. When Constans II visited Rome in A.D. 663 he
was welcomed with elaborate ceremonial, the Pope himself await-
ing the emperor at the sixth milestone outside the city, while huge
crowds gathered along the road, and crosses, banners and tapers
accompanied the procession. A more impressive triumph, described at length in the *Liber Pontificalis*, was granted to Charlemagne on the occasion of his first visit to the city in A.D. 774, when
he was summoned by Pope Adrian I to defend Rome against the
Lombard Astolf. Just as the senators met the *triumphator* outside
the city, so now the magistrates and nobles together with the
crosses and banners of the Roman basilicas went out to meet him,
and the Flaminian Way was lined with Roman youths under arms
and children with palms and olive branches in their hands, chanting the praises of their deliverers. When he saw the crosses, Charlemagne dismounted from his horse and continued to St. Peter's on
foot; and when he reached the Vatican he climbed the steps on his
knees, as Julius Caesar once climbed the steps to the Capitol, kiss-
ing each step until at last he stood beside the Pope, who was waiting for him in the portico. It was the triumph of the Pope over the
earthly emperor, but the emperor also triumphed in his own way,
for he marched on the right hand of the Pope to the altar and
accepted the honours and titles showered on him as *defensor
ecclesiae* and saviour of the state.

Twenty-six years later there was another tumultuous welcome
for Charlemagne. A new Pope, Leo III, had come to the throne.
Leo III had been captured and thrown into prison; he escaped and
made his way to Paderborn, taking refuge in the court of Charlemagne; and in the autumn of A.D. 800 Charlemagne descended
upon Rome to stand in judgment over those who had threatened
the life of their Pope. In gratitude Leo III permitted him to be
crowned. On Christmas Day Charlemagne was conducted before
the tomb of St. Peter and there received the crown of the Holy
Roman empire from the hands of the Pope. The words used by
the celebrants at the coronation were believed to be very nearly
the same as those used to greet the election of a Caesar: *Carolo
piissimo augusto, a Deo coronato, magno, pacifico Imperatori,
Vita et Victoria.* "To Charles, the most pious Augustus, crowned
by God, the great and pacific Emperor, Life and Victory." The
theme of victory and triumph were never far from the imaginations
of the Romans.

In the time of Charlemagne the temple of Jupiter Capitolinus still stood on the Capitol. Most, if not all, of the ancient Roman monuments remained. Visitors to Rome saw the monuments of the church rising amid the still-gleaming monuments of the Caesars.

Paganism survived. Until the eleventh century the afternoon of Easter Saturday in Rome was marked by the festival of Coromannia, when the archpriests of the eighteen parishes summoned the faithful to church, while the sacristans adorned in white garments, with flowers in their hair and wearing two horns like the ancient Silenus, headed the processions. These sacristans waved wands covered with bells, and danced all the way to St. John Lateran, and the archpriests rode asses back to front. In the Lateran the Pope was presented with a clock and a doe, and gave branches of laurel, cakes and holy water in return. The Bacchanalian procession had been incorporated into the worship of Easter.

Even the triumph remained, though it was suitably disguised. The Caesars raised triumphal arches on the Via Sacra leading to the Capitol; the Popes raised them on the roads leading to St. Peter's, especially *ad pedes pontium*, at the foot of the bridges crossed by the pilgrims on their way to the Apostle's tomb. So we find the arch of Gratianus, Valentinianus and Theodosius in the Piazza di Ponte S. Angelo, and the arch of Arcadius, Honorius and Theodosius at the approach of the Pons Vaticanus, and the arch of Valentinianus and Valens beside the Ponte Sisto. All these archways have now vanished, but in their own day they testified to the papal triumph.

The *Ordine* of Benedetto Canonico written in the twelfth century describes the triumphal procession of the Pope as he rode from the Lateran to the Vatican for his coronation. Quite deliberately the Pope employed the triumphal progress for his own ends, and over part of the journey he travelled the same route as the ancient *triumphator*.

The Pope rode on horseback, on a horse with scarlet trappings. Cardinal bishops and cardinal priests, deacons and subdeacons, abbots and other prelates walked in front of him. Senators, judges and the *praefectus romanus*, the chief civilian authority in Rome, brought up the rear in token of their subservience to spiritual authority. The streets were decorated with arches of shrubbery, and innumerable thurifers from all the churches and monasteries of Rome were stationed along the route to sweeten the air. So the procession made its way past the Capitol, under the archways and across the bridge of Sant' Angelo, where the Pope was consecrated Bishop of Rome according to the usage of centuries and was then

crowned on the steps outside the Vatican. Then he made his ceremonial progress back to St. John Lateran, mounted on a white
palfrey. During this progress it was the custom of the newly-con-
secrated Pope to pause near the fortress called Monte Giordano
near the bridge of Sant' Angelo to receive from the Rabbi, who led
the Jewish community in Rome, a copy of the Pentateuch, which
the Pope held for a moment or two in his hands and then returned
upside down, saying that while he respected the law of Moses, he
disapproved of the stubbornness of the Jews. The Rabbi bowed
his head and held out his hands to receive the traditional twenty
pieces of gold (venti soldi provvisini) by which the differences
between Jewry and the Papacy were resolved. In addition the
Pope gave a formal blessing to the Jews, and was given six pounds
of pepper and cinnamon.

Such was the triumphal ceremony celebrated on February 22,
1198, when Pope Innocent III was crowned and at his consecration
delivered a sermon in which he claimed for himself a position
higher than that claimed by any *triumphator* before him. He
claimed that he was "the Vicar of Jesus Christ, the successor of
Peter, the anointed of the Lord God of Pharaoh, one whose place
was between God and man, acting as intermediary between God
and man, under God but above man, less than God but greater
than man". Not even the deified Caesar had claimed so high a
place in the economy of heaven.

The papal triumph continued through the years, becoming
more worldly as the time of the Renaissance approached. We hear
in the later Roman triumphs of strange carnival figures wandering beside the triumphal chariot—*lamiae* with pointed teeth, hor-
rendous creatures like the *petreia*, a misshapen drunken old
woman who led the procession, and the *manducus*, a giant whose
enormous jaws clacked open by means of a string. Mountebanks
seem to have escorted the triumphal chariot in the Silver Age, as
in the Middle Ages they escorted the papal triumph. Gregorovius
tells of the triumphal entry of Pope Gregory XI into Rome on
January 17, 1377:

> The Pope sailed up the Tiber to St. Paul's, where the whole of
> Rome came out to meet him. Horsemen in splendid array, carry-
> ing banners, pranced here and there amid the braying of trum-
> pets. The procession made its way through the venerable gate of
> St. Paul, through which a Pope had never entered before. He
> came with a force of scarcely 2,000 men under the command of
> Raymond of Turenne. . . .

A crowd of white-clad mountebanks, dancing and clapping their hands, preceded the Pope when he left St. Paul's. The magistrates of the city on horseback, the militia and the archers escorted and surrounded Gregory's triumphal procession. He rode a richly caparisoned palfrey, under the baldacchino, which was upheld by the senators and other nobles, while the banner of the Church was carried in advance by Juan Fernandez Heredia. The procession wound through that memorable quarter of Rome which leads between the Tiber, Monte Testaccio, and the Aventine, through the Marmorata to the Capitol and the church of St. Mark's, whence Gregory proceeded onwards by the Via Papalis through the Campus Martius to St. Peter's. The women, says the chronicler, wept with joy to see the heavenly sight.

In those days the Marmorata was completely forsaken except for the Arch of Lentulus, but there were ponderous towers on the Capitol and near St. Mark's. The Romans had veiled the streets with motley draperies, and even the roofs were covered with rejoicing crowds. It was afternoon when the procession reached St. Peter's, which sparkled with the radiance of 18,000 lamps.

(History of Rome, IV, ii, p. 481)

When the Pope threw himself down at last in prayer before the Apostle's grave, he was exhausted, but perhaps no more exhausted than the ancient *triumphatores* when they placed their laurels on the lap of Jupiter Capitolinus. In the continuing story of the triumph the prayer at the grave of St. Peter took the place of the sacrifice on the Capitol.

The papal triumph was not the only expression of the ancient Roman triumph in the Middle Ages. In the wars between the Italian city states, in poetry and painting and devotion the triumph remained, haunting men with visions of glory.

In the hearts of the Milanese there had always been a desire for independence, but the people continually quarrelled among themselves. Heribert, Archbishop of Milan, seems to have been the first to have pondered the problem of inventing a symbol to represent the unity of the people fighting for communal liberty. In A.D. 1037 he devised a battle-car, consisting of a low heavy wagon drawn by oxen, with a lofty pole bearing the image of the city's patron saint and the banner of the commune floating from the yard-arm. His inspiration was not originally the triumphal chariot; he was thinking of the Ark of the Covenant, which the Israelites led into battle. In time the *carroccio* was to fulfil the functions of a holy Ark, a movable Christian altar, a platform, a speaker's rostrum, a command-post, a rallying point and a triumphal chariot. Its uses were almost inexhaustible, and it became in time the most precious symbol of the embattled communes, the visible representation of the city they were sworn to defend. The procession led by the *carroccio* came to be known as a *trionfo*.

All over northern Italy the communes fought for freedom around the sacred *carroccio*, not always successfully. At the battle of Cortenuova between the Milanese and the armies of the Hohenstaufen Emperor Frederick II the *carroccio*, drawn by snow-white oxen, was at the heart of the fray. On the high mast stood a crucifix and there was a bell to summon the commune to arms. The *podestà* of Milan was the Venetian Pietro Tiepolo, who had refused to crown Frederick with the iron crown. In rage Frederick attacked the Milanese with all his strength and destroyed them. Tiepolo was punished by being roped to the lowered mast while the *carroccio* was drawn through the streets, the people shouting in derision at the plight of the once powerful *podestà* left dangling in mid-air. Trumpeters from the back of an elephant blew triumphal blasts. Frederick II went on to hang Tiepolo, the son of a Doge of Venice, on the shores of the Ionian Sea, and the sacred *carroccio* was removed to the Capitol in Rome to form part of his triumph.

This very solid *carroccio* rumbling across Italy to decorate a mediaeval Caesar's triumph demonstrated one aspect of the triumph: there were many others. Dante imagined the heavenly triumph of Beatrice. He saw her riding in stately progress in her triumphal chariot drawn by a griffin, "all gold in so far as he was a bird, but otherwise all white mingled with scarlet". This heavenly beast, representing the power of God, was accompanied by many other heraldic and theological emblems. Four angelic creatures crowned with leaves and plumed with peacock feathers guarded the two-wheeled chariot; and three angels danced around the right wheel of the chariot. They were the colour of flames, of emeralds, of freshly fallen snow. Four angels attended the left wheel, and these were robed in purple. There followed two aged and venerable men, who were perhaps St. Luke and St. Paul, and these in turn were followed by the four authors of the epistles and by "an old solitary man, walking as though in sleep, with sharpened features", who seems to have been St. John of the Apocalypse.

So Dante imagined his emblematic triumph in all the colours of the New Testament. "Neither Scipio Africanus nor Augustus ever rejoiced Rome with such a fair chariot," Dante comments in the *Purgatorio*, "and even the Chariot of the Sun were a paltry thing

beside it." In one of the drawings Botticelli made during the last
months of his life he describes this great chariot in its toils, with
Beatrice sitting enthroned, wearing a white veil, crowned with an
olive wreath and surrounded by a host of angels who scatter roses
in the air. We see the seven heavenly messengers hastening before
her with the seven candles of the Revelations; and all the assembled
figures suggest the slow procession of a ceremonial dance.

Beatrice had her triumph; so did the Pope; so did the city of
Milan. The Virgin also had her triumph. When Duccio di Buonin-
segna completed his famous altarpiece, the *Maestà*, it was removed
in solemn procession from his studio to the high altar of the
cathedral of Siena. An anonymous chronicler described the
triumphal procession which took place in the summer of 1311.

> On the day when the *Maestà* was carried to the Duomo the
> shops were closed; and the bishop conducted a great and devout
> company of priests and friars in solemn procession accompanied
> by the nine *signori* and all the officers of the commune and all
> the people, and one after another the worthiest with lighted
> candles in their hands took their places near the painting, and
> behind came the women and children with great devotion. And
> they accompanied the said painting as far as the Duomo, making
> the procession around the Campo, as is the custom, all the bells
> ringing joyously, out of reverence for so noble a painting. And
> this painting Duccio di Niccolo the painter made, and it was
> made in the house of the Muciatti outside the gate *a Stalloreggi*.
> And all that day they stood in prayer with great almsgiving for
> poor persons, praying God and His Mother, who is our advocate,
> that He may defend us in His infinite mercy from all evil, and
> keep us from the hands of traitors and the enemies of Siena.[1]

Vasari seems to have remembered this story when he came to
describe how the Rucellai Madonna was brought in triumph to
Santa Maria Novella in Florence. It was a story which was repeated
many times in the early days when painters of genius were painting
Madonnas.

These triumphant processions belonged to the delights of
religion: they were gentle and compassionate, far removed from
the armed might of the triumphant Church. For the Popes it was an
article of faith that the Church was triumphant, and the phrase is
repeated endlessly in the chronicles of the Middle Ages. When the

---

[1] Charles Eliot Norton, *Historical Studies of Church-Building in the Middle
Ages*, New York, 1880, pp. 144-145.

Pope offered the Golden Rose to whatever king had promised to defend the faith, there was always the accompanying formula: "Receive this Rose from Our hands. It stands for the joy of both Jerusalems, the Church triumphant and militant. Receive it that you may grow greater in the virtue of Christ." The same formula reappears in the sentence of excommunication. When the Bishop of Vasona pronounced his verdict on the saintly Savonarola: *"Separo te ab Ecclesia militante atque triumphante"* (I separate thee from the Church militant and triumphant), Savonarola answered with perfect calm that he denied the triumph of the Church—that triumph could belong only to God. He said: *"Militante non triumphante: hoc enim tuum non est"* (Militant, but not triumphant: for this is not yours). In his work *The Triumph of the Cross* he demonstrated his faith in the abiding works of the Church and gave the fullest expression of his own creed, but he made it clear that the triumph of the Church could also be a denial of the triumph of God.

Meanwhile the churchly triumphs continued, and the Italians especially seemed haunted by these vast processions which imitated from a great distance the processions of the ancient emperors. Whenever the Pope ventured abroad, he rode in triumph. So we find Aeneas Piccolomini, Pope Pius II, entering Mantua through flower-decked streets 'in the spring of 1459. At the head of the procession rode three Cardinals followed by twelve white riderless horses with golden saddles and bridles representing the twelve apostles. There followed three immense banners, one bearing the Cross, another the keys of St. Peter and the third the heraldic arms of the Piccolomini. Then came the clergy of Mantua, and another white horse bearing the Host in a golden box surrounded by candles, and then a host of nobles and ecclesiastics. Last of all came the little bent figure of the Pope resplendent in purple and jewels. A contemporary chronicler says he was a "rosy little man with red rims to his eyes, about sixty years of age. He is gouty, and cannot walk, and is therefore obliged to be carried". There was no doubt about the nature of his triumph: the Mantuan chronicler describes it as *magnificus triumphus*.

Pius II, half-pagan, the most gentle of Popes, and perhaps the most intelligent, had prepared a sophisticated triumph, and had no illusions about his own magnificence. He was sufficiently Christian to prefer a Christian triumph, unlike Leo X who visited Florence fifty-four years later and rode in a triumphal chariot painted by Pontormo, accompanied by seven other chariots bearing figures from ancient mythology. Among those figures was the golden boy, representing the Golden Age, who died in agony soon afterwards. Leo X was a very secular Pope, and the story of his Florentine triumph belongs to another chapter.

The papal triumphs reflected the peculiar sensibilities of the Popes, but they also reflected the preoccupations of the time. One might expect the coronation of the Borgia Pope Alexander VI to be accompanied by vast panoply; and so it was. The new Pope was a heavy-set man, very tall, possessed of great natural dignity, and he suffered from an affliction of the eyes which made him blink continually. Like Pius II, but for different reasons, he had no illusions about his own magnificence. His coronation procession included archers and horsemen dressed like Turks—the Turks had recently conquered Constantinople—and there was an escort of Palatine guards with long halberds and gleaming bucklers. The Pope rode on a snow-white horse with a silver bridle. Count della Mirandola brandished the papal standard, which showed a bull grazing, and everywhere in the procession and on the houses there were representations of that placid bull. On the Palazzo San Marco there was a colossal statue of a bull which spouted water from its horns, eyes, ears and nose, and from its forehead came wine.

A chronicler with a malicious turn of mind wrote that the Pope received more homage than Cleopatra received from Antony, and a prothonotary from the papal court designed a triumphal arch which curiously suggested that Alexander VI was God indeed. On the arch there was an inscription in gold letters, reading: *"Caesare magna fuit, nunc Roma est maxima. Sextus regnat Alexander: ille vir, iste Deus."* (Rome was great under Caesar, but now she is greater. Alexander VI reigns: Caesar was a man, but the Pope is God.) Alexander VI, who always suffered from the heat, showed an altogether ungodlike impatience with the weather. He fainted during the procession. He had chosen for his coronation the anniversary of the greatest of all triumphs—that of Augustus Caesar, who also suffered from the relentless heat of a Roman August.

Alessandro Farnese, Paul III, was a man of a different temper, generous and lighthearted, addicted to building and restoring churches. When the Holy Roman Emperor Charles V sent word after his successful invasion of Tunis that he proposed to visit Rome, the Pope decided to receive him as a *triumphator*, with all the proper panoply. There was no *Via triumphalis* leading to the foot of the Capitol: the Pope decided to make one. He ordered a wide street made out between the arches of Titus and Severus, flanked by a double row of elms. This entailed the demolition of many buildings and the destruction of vineyards, but the Pope's order was final. He could not, however, pay compensation to the owners, and only with the greatest difficulty was he able to send to Charles V, who was waiting impatiently at Naples, the vast number of mattresses and the stupendous requisition of wine and food demanded by the emperor. At the Pope's urgent request the entry of the emperor was delayed until the end of February 1536. While the Pope was debating what should be done, an interested spectator at the papal court was François Rabelais, who wrote in January:

> If I had as many gold crowns as the number of indulgence days with which the Pope would like to reward *proprio motu, de plenitudine potestatis* anyone who could get it put off for five or six years, I should be richer than Jacques Coeur ever was. They have started a lot of great schemes to receive him (the emperor) in this city, including by the Pope's order a new road for him to enter by, from the St. Sebastian Gate. To construct and level this they have demolished and knocked down more than two hundred houses and razed three or four churches to the ground, which many people think is a bad omen. . . . It is a pity to see the ruins of the houses. No payment has been made to the owners.

When at last Charles V arrived in Rome, the huge procession making its way through the St. Sebastian Gate and so past the Colosseum to the Capitol, and thence to the Vatican, he was greeted by the Roman people with a cry proper to a *triumphator*. He was called *"coronatus magnus et pacificus Imperator Romanorum"*—a strange description of the least pacific of emperors. The emperor knelt before the Pope, and was lifted up, and taken to pray at the tomb of St. Peter; afterwards there were fireworks and salvoes of artillery, and the Pope and the emperor between them discussed the future of Europe, but to little effect. The gaunt and serious Charles found little commendable in the nervous and smiling Pope, and soon with nothing accomplished he continued his northward journey.

Seven years later Paul III was still busily refashioning Rome, and about that year his stone-cutters destroyed the great arch of Augustus which had endured for more than fifteen centuries. An even more serious act of vandalism occurred in the late summer of 1546 when the ancient Regia was uncovered in the Forum. Pirro Ligorio, a Neapolitan who designed the Villa d'Este, was present when the graceful building emerged from the ground. It was as beautiful a building as he had ever seen, constructed of Greek marble in exquisite taste, and in a perfect state of preservation. On its walls were inscribed the list of consuls and *triumphatores*, ordered to be placed there by Augustus, and known as the *Fasti Consulares et Triumphales*. According to Ligorio it took only thirty days, from August 15 to September 14, to destroy the Regia completely, the marble blocks being surrendered to the lime-kilns or to the stone-cutters of St. Peter's. The greater part of the *fasti* was destroyed, most of the remaining fragments now in the Conservatori Museum being saved by Cardinal Alessandro Farnese, who removed them to his own garden.

In 1506, when the statue of Laocoön was brought to light in a vineyard, another Pope gave orders for it to be borne through the city on a flower-decked chariot. Michelangelo was present at the excavations and took part in the triumph of the statue.

Botticelli drew the Triumph of Beatrice out of his own flowering imagination, in an age before the full weight of antiquity had been felt. Titian belonged to the Age of Excavations, when every field in Rome revealed a treasure of Greek and Roman statues. His great woodcut of *The Triumph of the Faith* moves with august solemnity, the robust figures drawing their inspiration as much from ancient statues as from his own profoundly Christian faith. We see Christ in His triumphal chariot drawn by the doctors of the Church, preceded and followed by the patriarchs, the sibyls, the martyrs and the prophets. He depicts the triumphant Christ as a man of divine resolution, without menace, riding in the strange calm that precedes the storm. The storm came only a few years later, when a German monk, who had watched in pity and horror the pilgrims shuffling up the steps of the Scala Santa, rebelled against the Church. Luther came; and the long years of triumph were over.

The Church was never so triumphant as when she was most humble, never so serene as when she put aside her triumphal robes. Today the Pope goes to the prisons and speaks with murderers, and washes the feet of the poor, renouncing all roles except that of the Servant of God. He renounces, too, the earthly triumph with all its pitfalls, remembering that the great triumphal processions of the past did little more than feed the spiritual pride of the Popes. To imitate Caesar is especially dangerous; and it is most dangerous when it is done well.

Meanwhile the great processions continue, but no earthly king is borne in triumph. The festival of Corpus Christi, instituted in 1264 by Pope Urban IV, is still observed with pomp and solemnity. In Spain the great procession with the gilt and flower-decked altar moves with triumphal fervour; a rain of white rose petals falls upon the Real Presence as God is carried through the streets. Here and there in the procession we recognize survivals of the ancient Roman triumph—the standard-bearers, the mace-holders, the bearers of the heraldic arms of the city. Here, too, as in ancient Rome, we come across the figures of mockery, amusing themselves with phallic emblems. The *cabezudos* thwack the passers-by with their inflated pig-bladders on short sticks. The prisoners also march by, but they take the form of giants representing fierce Moorish kings and veiled queens conquered centuries ago; and there is no menace nor any strength left in the ten-foot high *gigantes* who waddle behind the Host. The form of the ancient triumph is preserved, but in the chariot is the Body of Christ.

13

THE ALLEGORY OF TRIUMPH

FOR hundreds of years the Church assumed the title to the Roman triumph, but the memory of the secular triumphs persisted. The Holy Roman emperors followed in the train of the Caesars and demanded the right to celebrate their own triumphs, and since most of the Holy Roman emperors were Germans, the *via triumphalis* was often the long imperial road between Germany and Italy, passing through Munich, Innsbruck, Bozen and Verona. From the Caesars these emperors borrowed their mysticism, their arrogance and their vocabulary. For them the Capitol, not the Vatican, was the most sacred spot on earth.

When Frederick II captured the Milanese *carroccio*, he sent it to Rome and mounted it on the Capitol. The chariot rested on five marble columns. "Augustus Caesar Fredericus II," read the amazing inscription, "bids Rome to accept this *carroccio* as a tribute to the glory of their city. Captured during the defeat of the Milanese, it comes as a trophy in the triumph of Caesar, whose love for the city prompted him to send it, where it may be a witness to the disgrace of the enemy and the honour of Rome."

Frederick II protests too much. The chilling inscription shows how little he understood the ancient Romans, who would have contented themselves with a brief lapidary inscription of ten or twelve words, without needless repetition. Frederick II was so pleased with his capture of the *carroccio* that he ordered it to be led in solemn procession through Italy. The inscription at the base of the monument was not his only encomium on his own conquests. He wrote to the Roman people a letter in which he complimented them on living in a time when the ancient triumphs were being revived. This strange and solemn letter reads:

If you should trace back the nature of the triumph to its inevitable origin, you would understand that We cannot exalt our imperial glory without exalting first the honour of the city which We have always regarded as the fountain-head of Our power. Thus We recall the ancient Caesars to whom the Senate and the people of Rome granted triumphs and laurel crowns for deeds of arms performed under the banners of victory, and so

We are following your wishes by following the ancients, and We offer you an illustrious example. We send you after Our victory over Milan the standard-bearing chariot of that commune as prize of victory and spoils from a conquered enemy.

Receive therefore with gratitude, O Quirites, the victory of your Imperator![1]

The strange gift must have puzzled the Romans, but there were more puzzles to come. The emperor, who saw himself as Caesar, began to assume all the panoply of the Caesars. He wore the triumphal costume, flew a gold banner inscribed with a Roman eagle, and called himself *Felix Victor ac Triumphator*. He assumed the titles of *dux, imperator* and *augustus*. He had already celebrated a triumph in Jerusalem, but this triumph wore the aspect of a sacrament, a mystical *Gloria in Christo*, "accompanied more by miracle than by valour". But no miracles followed his victory over the free commune of Milan: only disaster, and the proliferation of legends. In time the legendary Caesar merged imperceptibly into the legendary emperor.

Inspired by the example of the great *triumphatores*, Frederick gave himself the task of conquering the world. "His heart beat with no other purpose than to become lord and master of the whole earth," wrote Brunetto Latini. Frederick would have approved the statement. Once he wrote during one of his campaigns: "I fight in order that the power of Augustus should not lack for fresh triumphs." He saw himself as another Pompey or Julius Caesar: the Pope saw him as the Devil incarnate and excommunicated him five times.

In time the *carroccio* on the Capitol disintegrated: one by one the communes fell to the emperors or the *condottiere*. Freedom was snuffed out by little men who saw themselves as conquerors deserving a Roman triumph, glorying in the colourful processions which accompanied their brief conquests. So it happened that when the half-mad Castruccio Castracane entered Lucca in 1326, he deliberately modelled his entry on the Roman triumph, driving his prisoners before him, standing in a chariot, receiving in stern silence the applause of the awed citizens. It was a time when Italians were beginning to warm themselves at the ancient fires. Petrarch was writing *I Trionfi*, celebrating Time and Eternity, Fame, Death, Love and Shame, seeing these emblematic qualities as vast triumphal processions passing before his eyes, his *Trionfo della Fama* being hardly more than a catalogue of the Roman

[1] Ernst Kantorowicz, *Frederick the Second*, Richard R. Smith Inc., New York, 1931, p. 448-9.

TRIUMPH OF CHASTITY, FROM PETRARCH, *TRIONFI*,
VENICE, 1488

triumphatores. Frederick II had identified himself with Caesar, and now all Italy was beginning to identify itself with ancient Rome.

Petrarch's friend, Cola di Rienzo, saw himself as the man chosen by God to resurrect the ancient past. He claimed to be the divine agent of the *renovatio*, that mysterious regeneration of the earth which would bring about eternal peace under a single emperor— himself. On the fifth day of Lent in 1347, he hung from the architrave of the church of San Giorgio in Velabro a banner reading: *In breve tempore Romani torneranno al loro antico buon stato.* "Soon the Romans will return to their ancient state of glory." It seemed at first a harmless gesture, but it was to have astonishing consequences. All Rome cherished the thought of a revival of her long-lost glory: all Rome was prepared to follow in the footsteps of this son of an innkeeper and a washerwoman who proclaimed himself Tribunus Augustus and for a few months led the Romans in a frenzied effort to recapture their vanished greatness.

Cola di Rienzo seems to have believed that the *renovatio* would be brought about by performing the appropriate ceremonies, and the most appropriate ceremony of all was the triumphal march. In Catholic Rome he could not of course follow the pagan rite: it was necessary to pay tribute to the existence of the Church. Accordingly he arranged that the triumphal procession should proceed in reverse. It would begin at the Capitoline hill and end at the church of St. John Lateran, and the new *triumphator* would be arrayed in the robes of an earthly conqueror, but instead of the laurel wreath he would wear a golden crown which contained a fragment of the True Cross, and instead of the laurel branch in his right hand, he would carry a jewelled "sword of justice".

The triumph took place on the first day of August, 1347. The roads between the Capitol and the Lateran were strewn with roses. Everyone was in festive costume. First came a troop of horsemen, some beating drums and others blowing on silver trumpets. They were followed by the *triumphator* on a white horse, with the great banner of the Republic, showing the sun in the midst of a circle of stars, floating above his head. The wife of Cola di Rienzo followed, attended by a band of Roman matrons, and behind her came the ecclesiastical, civil and military orders under their own banners. At St. John Lateran he bathed and purified himself in a great basin of green basalt said to have been the one in which the Emperor Constantine had purged himself of his sins. Here too he received from the hands of a venerable knight the Order of the Holy Ghost, which he regarded as the necessary first step before the assumption of supreme power. That night he slept in the Baptistery, but the next morning he showed himself to the people, wearing a robe of purple and holding a sword in his hand. Already he believed himself to be the successor of Augustus, and in a loud voice he summoned kings and emperors to present themselves before the judgment seat. In particular he summoned Pope Clement VI, then in Avignon, and the Electors of Germany to appear before him "to inform us on what pretext they have usurped the inalienable right of the Roman people, the ancient and lawful sovereigns of the empire".

He had been a man of great promise, superbly handsome, well-liked by his friends—Petrarch admired him to the very end—and he was famous for his eloquence, so famous indeed that the Romans once sent him to Avignon to beg the Pope to return. He was also something of an archaeologist, always busying himself with old inscriptions. He had a deep feeling for ancient Rome and for the Roman people, who were suffering under the exactions of their rulers, the noble families of Colonna, Orsini and Savelli. His brother had been killed in a street-brawl, and the murderer was allowed to go unpunished. Cola di Rienzo therefore represented to an extraordinary degree the fierce resentments of the Romans against their rulers and against the weight of history. But resentment was turning into fantasy and then to madness.

Half-mad already, he debated with himself for two weeks before assuming the crown. At his coronation he was not content with a single crown, but permitted himself to be crowned six times with wreaths of oak, ivy, myrtle, laurel, olive and silver, which were held over his head by the most eminent of the Roman clergy, while he bore in his hand a crystal globe, emblem of his authority over the world. Exactly four months after his coronation, in a fit of weeping, he abdicated the government and fled to Naples.

It is given to some *triumphatores* to triumph twice, and seven years later he returned to Rome in the company of the papal legate, to receive a triumphant welcome from the people. Once again he took up his residence on the Capitoline hill and summoned the people by ringing the great bell. Once again he employed his eloquence to set the Romans against their noble rulers, who were banished from the city. Gradually he lost his power to deal with realities. Having raised an army to defend the Republic, he required money to pay his soldiers: the Romans refused to pay the taxes he imposed on them, marched to the Capitol and arrested him. At first they did not know what to do with the man who had so often addressed them brilliantly, encouraging them in their fight for freedom. They spent an hour thronging around him and gazing at him, hoping he would speak, hoping he would once more employ his eloquence to save his own life. But he was tongue-tied, gripped by fear, very pale, his face bloated, and after an hour someone struck a knife in his heart.

On the Capitoline hill, in the place where for centuries the blood of the sacred white ox had fallen, Augustus Caesar was himself being sacrificed.

The love for antiquity, which Cola di Rienzo fostered, was beginning to sweep through all Italy. The ancient legends and the sculptures which seemed to rise out of the earth as though the past had suddenly decided to disgorge its treasures, were cultivated and admired as never before. Not Rome only, but all the little princedoms scattered over Italy, claimed to be the inheritors of the Roman tradition. So it happened that the young Marquis of Mantua, Gian Francesco Gonzaga, inheriting his throne at the age of eighteen, summoned the painter Andrea Mantegna and ordered from him a painting of *The Triumphs of Caesar*.

For seven years—from 1485 to 1492—Mantegna worked on the painting, which is now in the palace at Hampton Court. Mantegna was a student of history, and he was determined to employ all the resources of art and scholarship to recreate the supreme event in Roman history. He would portray a triumph in all its multitudinous grandeur, and at the same time he would fill it with recognizable creatures of the flesh, so that the spectator would be drawn into the triumph, becoming part of it. Vasari says simply that this painting was "the greatest work to come from his hands".

There are nine panels, originally raised from the ground and separated from one another by painted columns. First come the trumpeters and the standard-bearers followed by youths holding up paintings of the captured cities—we see the flames and the battering rams and the dead hanging on the gallows, but these paintings arranged in registers are not intended to suggest the horror of war: they are no more than coloured banners waving above the procession. One figure stands out: a tall Ethiopian in a gold corslet minutely and exquisitely chased. He seems lost in dreams, looking over his shoulder towards the solitary *triumphator* far in the rear, with the expression of one who sees the world passing before him, but has removed himself from it: singularly alone, singularly detached. And so it is throughout the procession: here and there amid the motley crowds of litter-bearers, prisoners, pipers, musicians, holders of banners and trophies and urns filled with treasure, we come upon those dreaming figures who gaze over their shoulders, lost in a dream of splendour, until at last, at the very end of the procession, riding on his ceremonial chariot, motionless and silent amid the surrounding uproar, is Caesar himself, and he too has the air of a man dreaming impossible dreams.

It is an astonishing series of paintings, for Mantegna has somehow succeeded in conveying at one and the same time the headlong rush and roar of the procession and the glory which is conscious of itself. To an almost fantastic degree the painting represents the abstract quality of triumph. Such a triumph was never seen on land or sea; there is more splendour in it than Caesar ever dreamed of. Mantegna has accomplished this incandescent blaze of glory by presenting such a wealth of deliberate detail, so much sweeping drapery and embroidery, so many abstract designs all contributing to the general effect that the eye is unable to rest, but is carried forward with the movement of the procession.

Nothing quite like this painting was ever painted before, and none came after it. No one ever saw the triumph with such a profound conception of the nature of the triumphal journey, or with such pity. Here everything has its appropriate place—even the jewels hanging on the ears of elephants, and the little dogs and sheep which scuttle between the feet of the celebrants, and the wild-eyed dwarfs and hunchbacks who crawl beside the heroic youths. The prisoners pass, sunk in their misery, and Mantegna has deliberately emphasized the horror of their situation by painting a prison above them with the prisoners gazing unmoved at the plight of those who will soon join them. There are less than seventy figures in the canvas, but they give the impression of thousands.

Nearly all Mantegna's paintings demonstrate his abiding interest in antiquarian studies, but here he excelled himself. He had studied the Arch of Titus, read Appian's description of the triumph of Scipio, carefully followed Suetonius's description of the triumph of Caesar, and there is some indication that he read Flavius Josephus's account of the triumph of Vespasian. There was no slavish effort to depict the triumph with archaeological exactitude. He allows his imagination full play—it is not one triumph, but all triumphs, not the triumph of Caesar alone, but that of all the *triumphatores*. He paints the column of Trajan, the Arch of the Sergii in Pola and the pyramid of Cestius, and not one of these was in existence at the time of Julius Caesar, and he seems not to have cared. His figures do not move in any recognizably Roman fashion: they are creatures of the Renaissance, gay, impulsive, quick and feverish. He depicts the sacred white oxen with extraordinary care, giving them the pointed crowns which appear on the Boscoreale vase, and they wear the proper garlands and tasselled strips of cloth denoting that they are spotless and fit for the sacrifice, but his swords, pikes and halberds belong authentically to the Renaissance. Gian Francesco Gonzaga, Marquis of Mantua, himself appears in the painting with a scimitar at his side. The supreme irony is reserved for the last painting, where Caesar bears the recognizable features of Mantegna.

There are many mysteries about the painting. Vasari, who saw it some fifty years after it was executed, speaks accurately of the spoils, the incense bearers, the elephants, the victories, the infinite variety of helmets, corslets and armour, but he also speaks of the figure "casting abuse on the triumphant hero". It was permissible during a Roman triumph to abuse the *triumphator*, but there is no such figure in the painting, nor is there any figure corresponding to it in the engravings made by Andrea Andreani in 1598. Perhaps this figure appeared in the tenth or concluding painting showing the retinue following Caesar's chariot, but this painting has been lost.

Today the *Triumph of Julius Caesar* is slowly crumbling away. Originally sold by Duke Vicenzo II of Mantua to Daniel Nys, the agent of King Charles I of England, it was hung in the king's palace at Hampton Court. The Puritans offered it for sale, but there were no bidders. Cromwell, after his triumphal procession through the streets of London in 1651, lived at Hampton Court, and the painting was accordingly reserved for his pleasure. Later it was sent to the Mortlake Tapestry works to be cleaned; returned to Hampton Court; moved from room to room; restored by Louis Laguerre; and when examined recently by Roger Fry, declared to be "damaged beyond repair". Yet even now, when the colours are so faded that we can barely discern the features of many of the figures, with Louis Laguerre's hand only too evident, with whole sections of the paint flaking away, we can still recognize the passion which once informed these paintings. For the first and last time there appeared an artist who could paint a triumph worthily.

Mantegna painted a triumph with power and grave majesty, but the ceremonial triumphs of the European kings were delicate and pompous affairs, frivolous to the point of weariness. Froissart records the entry of Queen Isabel into Paris in 1339. There were decorated archways, *tableaux vivants,* children dressed as angels scattering roses in her path, and an immense confusion of mythological figures, Judaic, Christian, Greek and Roman. A rope was stretched from the highest house on the Pont St. Michel to one of the towers of Nôtre Dame, and a tightrope walker travelled across the rope bearing flambeaux which could be seen two miles away. At the Châtelet there was built a wooden castle filled with armed men. Set among them was a bed of justice with St. Anne lying upon it, while from a painted meadow there came first a lion, then a white hart, then an eagle to pay homage to St. Anne; and no one knew what it all meant, and perhaps no one cared. There were floral archways, banners, processions of jugglers, long retinues of servants bringing presents for the queen: it was a very French and very feminine triumph, and for two hundred years similar processions were held in France.

Occasionally there emerged an emperor with a deep and troubled feeling for antiquity, who hoped to assume the role of *triumphator*. Alfonso I of Aragon, King of Naples, was a patron of the arts, a student of antiquities, a devoted admirer of Roman history, a deeply religious and superstitious man. He knew the Bible almost by heart. He could recite long passages and whole books of Seneca and Livy, and when he obtained from the Venetians what he believed to be an arm-bone from the preserved relics of the historian Livy, he received it with solemn pomp and regarded it with more homage than he regarded the relics of the saints which filled the churches of Naples.

When he entered the conquered city of Naples in 1443, he chose to appear in the role of a *triumphator*, in a gilded chariot drawn by four spotless white horses, attended by an escort of elegant cavaliers, priests, musicians, city worthies. He made a breach in the city walls forty ells wide, and proceeded towards the cathedral where a solemn *Te Deum* was sung. The conquered Neapolitans offered him a laurel crown, but this he refused on the grounds that he dared not compare himself with Alexander the Great or Julius Caesar. His chariot was more sedate than the chariots of the ancient Romans, very high and covered with a canopy bearing the arms of Naples and Aragon. He rested on a chair upholstered with cloth of gold, bearing in his hands the orb of the world and warming his feet at the flames of his own genius. Twenty patricians carried the poles supporting the gold canopy. Before him, instead of prisoners, there rode the Seven Virtues on horseback and a chariot bearing the figure of Fortune, who wore only the hair on the front part of her head, while the back part was bald—Laurenzo Laurana, who depicted the scene in a magnificent relief which still adorns the Castel Nuovo, discreetly shows her with her head turned towards the spectator. There followed a troop of horsemen in the costumes of many nations, some dressed as foreign princes. A player, wearing

the toga and laurel crown of Julius Caesar, stood above a revolv-
ing globe and explained to the conqueror the meaning of the
allegories. The procession was arranged by the Florentines, and
there were sixty Florentines wearing purple and scarlet. There
were also Catalans on foot, engaged in mock combat with players
dressed as Turks. Finally there came a huge wheeled tower, the
door guarded by an angel with a drawn sword.

Alfonso's triumph partook of the nature of a solemn rite. How
successfully he married the spirits of ancient Rome and Renaissance allegory can be seen from Laurana's relief, which has been
remarkably well preserved.

Alfonso was fully aware of the implications of a triumph and
assumed the role of *triumphator* with commendable gravity. Borso
d'Este never knew when to stop. A fat, handsome, amiable bastard,
he delighted in triumphal processions and triumphal archways to
the exclusion of everything except eating. He had no sooner come
to the throne when he demanded and received from the citizens of
Ferrara a "marble triumphal pillar" in his honour. Eight years
later, in 1452, he had himself created Duke of Modena and Reggio
in return for an annual tribute of 4,000 gold florins to the German
emperor Frederick III, and immediately set out on a triumphal
tour of his two newly-created duchies. Once again we meet the
four Cardinal Virtues: they came in a triumphal chariot sent by
the people of Modena to welcome him at the gates. They were
"adorned in the likeness of Venus". Beside this chariot of nearly
naked girls came another bearing a statue of St. Geminianus
attended by angels in white robes, to preserve the equipoise between Christianity and classical mythology. It was the same at
Reggio. Once again there were two chariots, one bearing St. Pros-
pero, the patron saint of the city, surrounded by the inevitable
angels, languidly spinning in circles and singing the duke's praises.
The second chariot bore no Virtues; instead there was an empty
throne, with Regulus, Cato, Numa and Cincinnatus standing at
the four corners. There was a wooden trireme rowed by Saracens,
and still another drawn by unicorns. This chariot bore only a
single palm-tree, and in the branches of the tree sat Charity with
her blazing torch.

The craftsmen of Reggio who designed these triumphal chariots
had clear purposes in mind. They chose Charity amid the unicorns
for good reason. Borso d'Este was known for his partiality
towards unicorns, and they hoped for a charitable rebate in their
taxes.

The best was still to come, for as the procession moved to the church of St. Peter, the Prince of the Apostles himself descended from the western porch and placed a laurel crown on Borso's head. This tribute from Christianity was followed by a tribute from ancient Rome, for soon Caesar attended by seven nymphs offered his blessing, and then Charity descended from her palm-tree and chanted a prayer, while angels from the top of the Palazzo del Capitano sang a psalm. Borso was delighted with his triumph. He complimented Malatesta Ariosti, who designed the chariots, and remitted some of the more onerous taxes.

Borso d'Este deserves a special place in any history of the triumph. More than anyone else he reduced it to nonsense. He was already old and silly when he went out for his last triumph in the spring of 1471, summoned to Rome by Pope Paul II. He made the most careful preparations for his journey. There were valets in cloth of gold and grooms in silver brocade, huntsmen leading packs of magnificent hounds, falconers with falcons and goshawks, trumpeters, pipers, a procession of tame leopards, a train of mules carrying the baggage. Twenty days were occupied on the journey from Ferrara to Rome, and everywhere he went he was treated as a conqueror. He stopped at Ravenna, Cesena, Pesaro, Todi and Rignano. Altogether seventeen Cardinals, and innumerable ambassadors, came to meet the old duke. "He resembled," said his biographer, Francesco Ariosti, "rather another triumphing Caesar than His Borsian Serenity."

Reaching Rome, Borso scattered silver on all sides and was greeted everywhere with cries of "most worshipful emperor". Flowers rained down on him. Wine ran from the public fountains, everywhere there were triumphal arches and music. Calleffini in his *Chronicles* says that "it was commonly believed among the Romans that no king or emperor had ever entered Rome with such great triumph and honour as the duke". When he reached St. Peter's, two Cardinals took him by the arm and led him to the feet of the Pope. It was accounted especially auspicious that it rained that night for the first time since he left Ferrara.

Borso, so fat that he could hardly stand on his feet, so simple-minded that he hardly knew what to say to the Pope and stuttered continually, was given all the honours of the Papacy. He was permitted to hold up the train of the Pope's cope. He was given the Golden Rose, usually reserved for emperors, and a collar of jewels, and he was allowed to glance briefly at the Veronica. He died shortly after his return to Ferrara. The court chronicler, who had continually compared him with Caesar, was at a loss how to describe him when he was dead, but finally, coming upon an appropriate formula, he wrote: "It seemed that Our Saviour God has died a second time."

It is just possible that Borso himself wrote that final mortuary inscription.

Borso was a freak, his triumphs no more than charming improvisations on the theme of the unconquering conqueror. Real conquerors triumphed to greater effect. When the ferocious cut-throat Cesare Borgia, Duke de Valentinois, returned from the Romagna with Madonna Caterina Sforza-Riario as his prisoner-of-war, all Rome trembled. Hundreds of carriages, all covered with black draperies, preceded the soldiers. The troops marched in a savage silence: the only sound came from the tramp of marching feet, the clatter of horses' hooves on the cobbles and the rumble of artillery. The Swiss guards wore black velvet with the plumes of night birds in their caps: Cesare himself came riding in a black gown. Suddenly, when the army reached the Castel Sant' Angelo, the funereal gloom gave way to thunderous explosions of colour as fireworks were set off against the walls: the hushed Romans saw the flaming outlines of immense helmeted soldiers in red and gold. A few days later Cesare, with a bold allusion to himself, presented a spectacular triumph of Julius Caesar with a procession of eleven magnificent chariots.

Alexander VI, the terrible Borgia Pope, was on the throne. For him the Papacy was only an instrument for furthering the ambitions of his children, Lucrezia and Cesare; and Lucrezia too must have her triumphs. Cesare's triumph took place in February 1500, the year of the Jubilee. Lucrezia's triumph followed on the first two days of the New Year, 1502, in celebration of her marriage to Alfonso I, Duke of Ferrara and Modena. The people of Rome presented a procession of thirteen triumphal chariots setting forth the triumphs of Hercules, Caesar and the heroes of ancient Rome. According to the ancient custom, they were preceded by the gonfalonier of the city and the magistrates, but instead of moving from the Campus Martius to the Capitol they set out from the Piazza Navone to the Vatican, circling the great square. Later two more chariots appeared, one bearing Glory with the world at her feet, the other bearing an image of Rome. Musicians played; poems were delivered; later there were masquerades, dances, a bullfight and torchlight processions.

A month later Lucrezia Borgia entered Ferrara in triumph. It was February 2, the Feast of the Purification of the Virgin, the ancient day of the Lupercalia. Once again there were triumphal arches, presentations of costly gifts, performances of plays and recitations in Latin extolling her beauty and virtue. But the triumphal chariots were designed to be more in keeping with the spirit of Ferrara: instead of Roman heroes, they celebrated the triumphs of virtue, of agriculture, of love and music.

The triumphs of Rome and Ferrara were homespun affairs, lacking the grace of the Florentine *trionfi*. The Florentines were professional makers of triumphs, with a long history of triumphal spectacles going back to the fourteenth century. There had been vivid and brilliant triumphs during the reign of Lorenzo the Magnificent, but the best came after him. The greatest painters of the time were employed to design the triumphs, and their range was extraordinary. In 1512, when Florence still seemed prosperous, though disaster was only a few months away, Piero di Cosimo and Francesco Granacci designed a "Masque of the Triumph of Death". It was a powerful and terrifying triumph. First came an enormous triumphal chariot drawn by black buffaloes, covered with a black pall on which skeletons and crosses were painted. On the chariot stood a colossal figure of death with a scythe in his hand, standing amid open tombs and black-robed figures with bones painted on them in luminescent paint. Behind the chariot came a mournful procession of robed penitents with skeletons painted on them, the skulls painted in front and behind. As the procession passed, more skeletons rose from the open tombs, chanting lugubriously, reminding the spectators that all men must die. Afterwards there came a procession of decrepit horses, bearing the bodies of dead men.

Such triumphs perhaps owed much to Petrarch's *Trionfo della Morte*, but they owed more to the Tuscan character with its sharp awareness of life's brief splendour. Petrarch, lamenting the death of Laura, lamented the death of all felicity, and was sustained by the hope of seeing Laura in Heaven. Death's triumphal chariot offered no hope at all. It was a bleak and savage thing, a gruesome juggernaut drawn by buffaloes so intensely black, and with so much evil in them, that they seemed to have escaped from Hell. Sometimes the triumph of death was accompanied by the triumphs of love and chastity, for "love is greater than death" and "chastity is of the kingdom of heaven". But the Sienese and Florentine artists painted death with more passion than they painted either love or chastity.

Many representations of the triumph of death have survived, but the greatest of all reposes in the museum at Palermo. This immense painting, stretching across an entire wall, speaks in stark horror of the deaths which the unknown artist has seen. The skeletal horse, more savage than any real horse and sketched out with the barbaric precision of Picasso's horse in *Guernica*, rides triumphant over the world, its outflung legs forming a triumphal archway over the decaying bodies of Popes and prelates. The artist had seen a death-pit. He had seen, too, the agonized faces of those who watch as the bodies are tumbled from the death-carts. But what he has seen is less important than what he has grasped with his imaginative vision—the horse's hair in flames, the hounds of hell leaping through the forest, death quivering as he rides with upflung hand, and all the young and well-apparelled noblemen glacing slyly at the enemy they can never quite believe in. This Palermitan painter has seen it all with an unerring and steady eye, and himself peers out at his creation from the huddled group of prayerful folk on the left. *O Mors, Quam Amara Est Memoria*—"O Death, how bitter is the memory", reads the inscription along the bottom. The artist has made sure that we shall not forget.

When Piero di Cosimo and Francesco Granacci arranged a Masque of the Triumph of Death in 1512, they were depicting a triumph which was not typically Florentine, for the greater part of the Florentine triumphs were elaborately decorative and highly colourful. Later that year Giuliano de' Medici, Duke of Nemours, seized the government. There followed a brief period of prosperity under a stern and colourless despot, and the Florentines, who adored colour above all things, arranged a triumph in the following year to celebrate the elevation of the duke's brother to the Papacy. There were two *trionfi*, given by rival companies called the Diamond and the Branch. The task of designing the first triumph was placed in the hands of Andrea Dazzi, a professor of Greek and Latin, who simply devised a procession of three chariots representing the three Ages of Man, notable for the fact that the robes were designed by Piero da Vinci, the father of Leonardo, and Andrea del Sarto helped to design the chariots. The Company of the Branch was responsible for a more elaborate procession of chariots, which became famous for its beauty and was remembered long afterwards because a naked boy entirely covered with gold paint stood on the last of the chariots and shortly afterwards died in convulsions. He was the son of a baker, very handsome, and was paid ten *scudi* for taking part in the procession, and no one could understand why the golden boy had to die.

The second triumph was a Florentine version of a Roman triumph, pointing the moral that "out of evil comes good, and out of good evil"—*E muta il bene in mal e'l mal in bene*. Gone were the joyous cries celebrating the world renewed which accompanied the earlier *trionfi* of Lorenzo the Magnificent. This procession represented the Florentine imagination in its most sober mood: austerity mingled with magnificence. Vasari describes the seven chariots, and his description should be quoted in full, because this triumph represented a turning-point in the development of the Florentine triumph. Henceforward the invention of the Company of the Branch was to be imitated all over Italy:

The first chariot, drawn by oxen draped with grass, represented the Golden Age of Saturn and Janus. On top of the chariot were Saturn with his scythe and two-headed Janus holding the keys of the temple of Peace, with Fury bound at his feet, and countless things pertaining to Saturn, beautifully coloured by Pontormo. Twelve shepherds, naked except for the skins of martens and sables, accompanied this chariot. They wore shoes of antique shape, and on their heads garlands formed of many kinds of leaves. They rode on horses without saddles caparisoned with the skins of tigers, lions and lynxes, the gilded claws hanging gracefully at the sides. The cruppers had gold cord and the spurs bore the heads of sheep, dogs and other animals. The bridles were made of various kinds of verdure and silver cord. Each shepherd was attended by four boys disguised as herdmen who carried pine-torches.

The second chariot, drawn by two pairs of oxen draped with rich cloth, their heads garlanded, heavy beads hanging from their gilded horns, bore Numa Pompilius, second king of the Romans, surrounded by the tablets of the law and all the priestly trappings proper for the sacrifice, as he was the first of the Romans to regulate religion and sacrifices. Six of his priests accompanied the chariot on mule-back, wearing hoods of fine linen embroidered with ivy leaves of gold and silver. They wore ancient sacerdotal vestments with rich gold borders and fringes, some carrying a censer, some a gold vase or something similar. Their attendants wore the costumes of Levites and bore torches in their hands shaped like candelabras of an ancient time.

The third chariot represented the consulship of Titus Manlius Torquatus, consul after the end of the first Carthaginian war, and who governed in such a way that Rome flourished in virtue and prosperity. This chariot was decorated with many fine ornaments by Pontormo, and was drawn by eight excellent horses. In front rode twelve senators wearing togas riding on horses caparisoned with cloth of gold, attended by lictors who bore fasces, axes and other instruments of justice.

The fourth chariot was drawn by four buffaloes accoutred like elephants, and represented the Triumph of Julius Caesar over Cleopatra: his most famous deeds were painted on the chariot by Pontormo. Twelve men in rich and shining armour decked out with gold walked beside it, with lances and torches.

The fifth chariot was drawn by winged horses which had the form of griffins, and bore Caesar Augustus, lord of the universe. He was accompanied by twelve poets on horseback, crowned like Caesar with laurel and dressed according to their provinces. Each poet bore a scroll inscribed with his name.

The sixth chariot was drawn by six pairs of heifers richly caparisoned, and bore the Emperor Trajan. Before him rode twelve doctors of the law wearing long togas and capes of grey miniver such as were worn in ancient times. Their servants were scribes, copyists and notaries, with books and writings in their hands, and they carried torches.

Finally came the chariot representing the Golden Age, richly ornamented with many figures in relief by Baccio Bandinelli and beautiful paintings by Pontormo, among them an admirable painting of the Four Virtues. In the midst of the chariot was a great globe with a man lying over it face down, wearing armour thick with rust. The armour was split open, and from the place where it was cleft there emerged a golden boy, all naked, representing the Golden Age renewed by the creation of the Pope and the end of the Iron Age represented by the dead warrior.

Such was the procession, which brought immediate fame to the brilliant nineteen-year-old Jacopo da Pontormo, and remained for generations as an example of a Florentine triumph at its best.

The sixteenth century saw innumerable triumphs. Every emperor returning from a campaign, every queen making a state visit to an important city received a triumph. Thousands of triumphal archways were built, but no one ever troubled to preserve them. Triumphs had become impermanent, to be forgotten as soon as they were over. The pattern of the royal triumphs was nearly always the same. When Queen Margaret entered Edinburgh in 1503 she passed under a triumphal archway with angels singing from its towers and from a central window an angel presented the queen with the keys of the city, while poets recited verses in her honour. When Charles V entered Messina in 1536 there was a triumphal archway with hanging curtains depicting the emblems of the city and of the emperor, and he too was presented with the keys of the city, while poets recited verses in his honour. More archways were erected in his honour in Apulia, Naples, Rome, Mantua and Florence. For his reception in Rome Pope Paul III caused a triumph to be held and ordered Raphael to erect fourteen heraldic statues on the bridge of Sant' Angelo, and then sent him to Florence to prepare for the emperor's triumph there. In the space of five days Raphael erected two river-gods representing the Rhine and the Danube, each of them fifteen feet high.

The German emperor Maximilian I set his greatest artists to work to prepare, not a triumphal procession through the streets, but immense engravings unlike any that had appeared up to that time—engravings that would cover whole walls and reveal the splendour of imaginary triumphs. A whole college of designers was set up. The master design was put in the hands of the Professor of Astronomy in Vienna. Under him worked Albrecht Altdorfer, Wolf Traut, Hans Burgkmair and Albrecht Dürer. Three huge panels were projected. The triumphal arch, or *Ehrenpforte*, consisted of ninety-two separate blocks depicting a Roman arch which no Roman would ever have recognized, such an archway as might have appeared to a German emperor in his dreams. There were battlements, turrets and spires, inlays of Venetian detail, a vast gallimaufry of undigested and repetitive symbols. There were three gates dedicated to Honour, Praise and Nobility. There was a central tower bearing the genealogical tree of the Hapsburgs, and twenty-four compartments over the side-gates illustrated the notable events of the reign of the emperor.

Another engraving illustrated his wholly imaginary processional triumph. The engraving was 200 feet long and consisted of 138 separate blocks. The procession was heralded by a naked man on a griffin blowing upon a strange horn; this was followed by the Landsknechte leading horses supporting a great tablet intended to bear the name and titles of Maximilian. There followed musicians, falconers, hunters of deer, boar and bear, elks and bison dragging chariots of musicians, a boy riding on a dromedary, some jesters, and the court favourite, Conrad von der Rosen, drawn by donkeys in a cart. The endless Gothic pageant continues with jousters armed with flails, lances and halberds, and courtly knights apparelled in the utmost splendour. Then came the artillery, treasures, sepulchral statues, prisoners in chains, a man carrying statues and emblems of victory, trumpeters, timballers, heralds, arquebusiers, pikemen, savages from Calicut and wreathed camp-followers. This nightmarish procession occupied the energies of Albrecht Dürer almost exclusively from 1512 to 1527: no emperor was ever so honoured. Yet the total effect of the triumph, as

SCENE FROM *TRIUMPHUS CAESARIS*, BY JACOBUS
ARGENTORATENSIS

one turns the pages of the books reproducing Dürer's engravings,
is one of almost unbearable boredom. A confused chorus of Germanic monsters passes in review. Maximilian's triumph is a master-
piece of horror.

The crowded epic of Maximilian leaves the spectator breathless,
but the triumph of Julius Caesar engraved by Jacobus Argentoratensis (Jacob von Strassburg) dazzles the spectator with its charm.
These designs, completed in Venice in 1504, mingle the gaiety of
the Renaissance with the gravity of ancient Rome. Imperturbable
Caesar wears a triumphal garment decked out with stars; he holds
a sceptre in one hand and a laurel branch in the other. Walking
beside Caesar is a helmeted matron followed by a girl who seems
to have stepped out of Botticelli's *Primavera*. So, throughout the
eleven engravings, there is this joyous mingling of many styles,
and the most joyous design of all depicts a boy riding a majestic
unicorn, holding a laurel branch topped with a coloured ball,
while a monkey sits by his side.

In the portrait of the boy on the unicorn Jacob von Strassburg
accomplishes a miracle. He makes the triumph intelligible, by
reducing it to human terms. Naked pipers precede the boy; bells
ring on the harness; even the little wolf-hound caught between the
unicorn's feet is covered with bells. Jacob von Strassburg is say-

A TRIUMPH, FROM COLONNA, *HYPNEROTOMACHIA POLIPHILI*, VENICE

ing: "Here is the real triumph—a boy riding on a gaily capari-soned unicorn on holiday."

Jacob von Strassburg's designs are of the earth, earthy: though published in Venice, they betray their Germanic origin. About the same time, in 1499, there appeared a magnificent series of designs of allegorical triumphs by an unknown artist, printed in Venice by Aldus Manutius. These designs are among the formidable illustrations to the *Hypnerotomachia Poliphili*, at once the most beautiful of books and the most mysterious. Almost nothing is known of the author, Francesco Colonna, and no one has ever been able to trace the style of the artist who decorated the pages with such a profusion of majestic ornament. Nearly a hundred years after it appeared in Italy an unknown scholar in England translated Colonna's difficult text written in a strange jumble of Italian, Latin and Greek, and dedicated the work to the Earl of Essex. In its English dress it wears the title *Hypnerotomachia: The Strife of Love in a Dream*. Four allegorical triumphs are depicted, and here is the unknown translator describing the first of them:

I behelde the ymage of a fayre white and tame Bull, trymmed and dressed with flowers, in manner like an Oxe for a Sacrifice.

And uppon his large and broade backe did sit a princely virgine, with long and slender armes, half naked; with her handes she helde by his hornes. Her apparell was exquesite of greene silke and gold, marveilously woven, and of a Nymphish fashion, covering her body and girded about her wast, edged about with Pearl and stone, and a crowne of glittering golde upon her fayre heade.

This Triumph was drawne by six lascivious Centaures, which came of the fallen seede of the sausy and presumptuous *Ixion*: with a furniture of gold upon them, and a long their strong sides like horses excellently framed and illaqueared, in manner of a flagon chayne, whereby they drewe the Tryumph; such as Erichthonius never invented for Iwistnesse.

The delightful drawing does not quite follow the text, which is a reasonably accurate transcription of the original. The "princely virgine" is attired in voluminous robes which spread around her shoulders in the shape of wings, and she wears no crown on her head, though one is being offered to her. A boy rides on a Centaur, Flower-tipped standards and laurels are being lifted high above the procession. In another drawing Andromeda is in the arms of her swan, and the triumphal chariot is led by baby elephants. Francesco Collona speaks in dreams. He describes another triumph which shows "a goodly matron lying on a princely bed, beeing delivered of two egges in a stately Pallace: her Midwyves and other Matrons and yonge women, being greatly astonished at the sight. Out of one of the which, spronge a flame of fire, and out of the other egge two bright starres". We are far from the Roman triumph. We are already in the Triumph of the Renaissance, when it seemed that all things were possible—even matrons giving birth to eggs, which in turn give birth to fire and stars.

The triumph was changing direction. All the arts of the imagination were employed to decorate the procession, which was beginning to possess only the most tenuous connection with the ancient triumph which made its way through the streets of Rome. The triumph still represented the highest attainments of man, but the nature of desirable attainments had changed. Towards the end of *The Deeds and Heroic Sayings of Good Pantagruel* Rabelais describes an imaginary triumph of Bacchus. The god drinks from a huge bowl as he rides in a triumphal chariot festooned with sacred ivy from Mount Meru. The captured kings of India, fettered with gold chains, walk beside the chariot. Everyone is carousing and shouting, and the *thyrsi* are tipped with laurel: the ass of Silenus is crowned with laurel, and smothered under it. There are trophies and spoils and hymns of victory. Relentlessly, majestically the triumph goes on its way. "So they move forward amid heavenly pomp, ineffable joy and supreme exaltation," says Rabelais; and as he speaks, he seems to be standing at the turning-point between the Middle Ages and the Renaissance. He does not believe in the triumph of Bacchus, and he does not quite disbelieve.

We hear the new voice most clearly in Marlowe's *Tamburlaine*: a voice of absolute faith in man's power to rival the gods. So Tamburlaine describes his triumphal march through Samarcand after he has conquered the whole world:

> Thorow the streets with troops of conquered kings,
> Ile ride in golden armour like the Sun,
> And in my helme a triple plume shal spring,
> Spangled with Diamonds dancing in the aire,
> To note me Emperour of the three fold world . . .
> Then in my coach like Saturnes royal son,
> Mounting his shining chariot, gilt with fire,
> And drawen with princely Eagles through the path,
> Pau'd with bright Christall and enchas'd with starres,
> When all the Gods stand gazing at his pomp.

When all the Gods stand gazing at his pomp. . . . There, if anywhere, we hear the authentic voice of the Renaissance rejoicing in its own power over heaven and earth.

But we should be on our guard against the voice of Marlowe. That voice, so solemn and magnificent, carolling with the sound of trumpets, has something artificial and theatrical about it. We see the actor rather than the emperor; and sometimes we see the dramatist before we see the actor. In Elizabethan times the ultimate triumph was the triumph of the theatre, where human pageantry was boxed up on a small stage, and was no less bright for being circumscribed.

The stage indeed borrowed so heavily from the Roman triumph that we must regard it as the triumph's logical successor. Those elaborate Elizabethan archways, erected to greet the progress of the queen, the actors addressing her from the top of the arch or from sally-ports cut out of the supporting columns, were remembered when men began to design the first enclosed theatres; and the proscenium arch derives across the centuries from the Roman triumphal archway. We do not remember the Roman triumph when we go to the theatre; but it is present nevertheless.

The triumph became allegory and poetry, a thing to delight in, far removed from the bloody spectacle offered by the Roman *triumphator* on his way to the Capitol. In the theatre every man is permitted to become emperor or prisoner, as he pleases; and every dead soldier is permitted to rise and wipe the blood away. Instead of the emperor there is the imperial mind of man wandering through the landscape of his dreams:

> Your majesty shall shortly have your wish,
> And ride in triumph through Persepolis.

> And ride in triumph through Persepolis!
> Is it not passing brave to be a king, Techelles?
> Usumcasane and Theridimas,
> Is it not passing brave to be a king,
> And ride in triumph through Persepolis?

> O, my lord, 'tis sweet and full of pomp!

14

THE FAG-END OF THE TRIUMPHAL PROCESSION

THE days of the triumphs are over, perhaps forever. We no longer rejoice in the ancient way with parades of booty and captives in chains, with the conquering general riding high in his triumphal car. We may see the conqueror parading briefly along Lower Broadway amid a rain of ticker-tape, or like General de Gaulle walking bravely with a few of his chosen associates to the Arc de Triomphe, but the ancient ceremony is shorn of its splendour. We put up captured guns in the parks and build war-memorials and add a new sheet of stained glass to the church windows; but the guns tell us little and the war-memorials are strangely unconvincing. Today we no longer find consolation in pageantry, and too many triumphs remind us of too many defeats.

The white horses and the chariots have gone, but sometimes even in our own times we are presented with strange relics of the rituals of the past. When Lord Kitchener celebrated his victory of Atbara, he rode through Berber on a white horse with the young enemy commander walking behind him in chains, whipped by Sudanese guards whenever he stumbled. There are people now living who can still remember that day, and there are still more who remember the Durbar of 1903, which took on the colour of a victory celebration, though no victory had been won. The viceroy was Lord Curzon, one of those Englishmen to whom the opulence of India was more agreeable than the poverty of the Indians. He made his entry into Delhi seated upon an elephant at the head of a column of horsemen in chain armour, warriors on camels, fighting men on stilts, monks in dragon masks, with 30,000 of Lord Kitchener's troops in attendance; and for a week there were parades of pageantry, while Curzon beamed and sometimes men detected on his face the stern expression of a conqueror, though he had never led an army in battle. He resembled one of those ancient Roman emperors who triumphed over imaginary tribes after imaginary battles in imaginary territories: there were only the waving flags and the gaudy costumes and the knowledge of disasters to come.

Today we know those disasters well. We know, though we shall
go on fighting them, that there is nothing to be gained by wars.
Hitler was conquered, but there were only the most perfunctory
celebrations. The Russians celebrated. They even led a procession
of prisoners through the streets of Moscow with the Nazi generals
marching in front, but how different was this triumph to the panoplied processions of the past! This triumph took place on July 17,
1944, and the Russian authorities seem to have been a little
ashamed of it, for they announced simply that there would be a
transfer of prisoners of war from one camp to another. In fact it
was a deliberate triumph. Some 58,000 prisoners were assembled
from prisoner-of-war camps all over Russia. On that July day they
came in endless columns along the Sadovaya Boulevard, led by
high-ranking officers and nineteen full generals, most of the soldiers
in rags. There was no pageantry. The crowds were silent; they
simply watched with wonder and awe as the tattered remnants of
the once formidable Nazi war machine passed before them, reduced
to shuffling insignificance. So may the Romans have watched the
progress of the Carthaginian captives after the destruction of
Carthage, one of the few events in human history comparable with
the destruction of Hitler's army, but there was one important
difference. No Russian general marched at the head of the procession. No Russian soldiers sang songs of triumph. The conquerors were the people of Moscow, who had suffered so intolerably that they found no pleasure in victory.

Perhaps it has always been so; perhaps all victories were delu-
sions, and all the parades were no more than artificial devices by
which the real conquerors were defrauded. Again and again
through history we hear the cry of Tiberius Gracchus, who complained that the Roman generals called upon their soldiers to
defend their sepulchres and shrines, though they had neither
sepulchres nor shrines to their name.

For century upon century the Roman triumph rumbled through
the streets of Rome with a magnificent display of human effrontery
and pride, celebrating the glory of man and the greater glory of
Jupiter. It survived into the Renaissance. The papal coronations
still follow the essential rituals of the triumph, and many of the
Roman Catholic churches have their triumphal arches dedicated
to the Christ who was crucified by the Romans. Our proscenium
arch stems from the triumphal arch, and though our Capitol is no
longer a temple dedicated to Jupiter Optimus Maximus, it traces
its descent directly to the ancient temple overlooking the Forum,
where the *triumphator* slaughtered the white oxen of sacrifice and

left his laurels on the lap of a god. In a hundred ways we are still influenced by that strange, barbaric procession.

It is one of the laws of history that all great and powerful rituals must eventually die and be reborn in mockery; and so it happens that the Roman triumph has provided us with one of our few remaining occasions for riotous festivity. Carnival in New Orleans can be traced back step by step to the Roman triumphs, but in the process there have been remarkable changes. The triumphal chariots drawn by four white horses have been exchanged for flowered floats drawn by white mules borrowed from the city's garbage collection wagons; more recently the floats have been motorized. Zulu, the African king, rides along South Rampart Street to the accompaniment of Dixieland jazz. His float is decorated with palm-trees and surrounded by private guards, who strut about like Keystone Cops. He wears a rabbit skin and a grass skirt; smiles, bows, waves, autographs coconuts, accepts gifts of Bourbon, and guffaws in perpetual triumph until the solemn moment when he meets his queen and her handmaidens at the Geddes and Moss Funeral Home. All that is bawdy and human is concentrated in the figure of Zulu, the laughter-loving *filius terrae*, the son of earth, lounging among the leopard skins and the potted palms, dispensing among men the justice of mirth. From him, and from him alone, comes the freedom to do as you please. He is the most potent of *triumphatores*, for he gives happiness to men.

But Zulu is only the introduction to the triumph. Others come after him. Charlie Chaplin, dapper in baggy trousers and white gloves; Napoleon, too, surprisingly nimble with his four hands; a man dressed as an alligator with a cigar in his mouth; the hanged woman and the executioner dancing together; and after them come all the legendary characters of Louisiana, the duellists on their way to the duelling-ground, and Governor Claiborne drunk with absinthe.

We are far from the Roman triumph, and yet close to it. Zulu represents the victory of our common humanity, the hunger we all have to rise above the dust, to show ourselves as creatures of freedom. We need pageantry, as we need air; and Zulu is as much a part of our necessary pageantry as kings and presidents. That gentle and compassionate lord of misrule is closer to us than the Roman *triumphator*, who is himself closer to Zulu than he ever guessed. We have only to follow the history of the triumphs to know how easily and with what abandon the *triumphatores* claimed for themselves the right to do anything they pleased beyond reason: Zulu claims for himself only the right to do anything he pleases within reason, and does not fall from grace.

The moral significance of the triumph lies precisely here, for every earthly triumph implies a fall from grace. *Triumph, glory, fame, honour*—all those tainted words which the Romans elevated to positions of great prominence concealed within themselves their own destruction. The triumph was a poison flowing through the streets of Rome, and every new triumph only gave a greater tolerance of poison to the Romans. In the end there were only the starved cats howling at midnight in the deserted Forum, where once the bowed prisoners and the conquering general trod.

"Before miserable man all the ages of the world pass as in a manacled procession," wrote Hermann Melville in *Pierre*. Those words, wrung from him in grief and despair, also describe the presence of the permanent slave-drivers, who stand aloof and unpunished, the most grotesque of creatures because they are unable to share the common humanity of the prisoners. They shine with the brightness of the fallen angels, and are forever damned. So in the end the *triumphator* gives place to *Christus triumphans*; and at last the triumphal chariot bears, not the earthly conqueror, but the conquered Son of God.

For more than ten centuries the Roman triumph echoed through the streets of Rome. The white-robed senators walked gravely at the head of the procession; the trumpets blared; carts and wagons heaped with treasure rumbled over the flinty roads; the chained prisoners made gestures of despair to the mocking crowds; and in his gilded chariot the *triumphator* gazed impassively across their heads towards the flags and banners bearing the names of the conquered towns and the ravaged kingdoms, content to see all the evidence of his power gathered within the limits of a single Roman street. It was all there, down to the last broken spear, the last coin stolen from a foreign treasury. And sometimes he must have been aware of the odour of corruption in the air, the knowledge of guilt and shame, the sense that all these evils must be paid for in the end.

In the end, of course, they were paid for in the blood and suffering of the Roman people, who only a brief while before had cheered the procession. Not only the *triumphator* and the soldiers were incriminated: all those who crowded in the streets and watched and applauded were incriminated: the evil was endless, like the ever-widening ripples when a stone is flung in a pond.

The triumph is still with us. We no longer bear the bloodstained trophies through the streets or cheer at the panoplied conqueror, but we are still haunted by the memory of the great processional triumphs. We have learned painfully that all honours are vain, but from somewhere in the depths of our unconsciousness there arises a great yearning for them; and we are all Caesars. Sometimes we rejoice in our lesser virtues, like that Marcus Antonius Terens whose memorial was discovered in the last century on the Via Praenestina:

> TO THE MEMORY OF
> M. ANTONIUS TERENS OF MICENUM
> ELECTED TO THE HIGHEST OFFICES IN HIS CITY
> MOST CELEBRATED IMPORTER OF PIGS AND SHEEP.

The real triumph belongs to the human race, for having survived so many conquerors. We cannot count the number of people who were slain so that the Romans could enjoy their 500 triumphs. These triumphs were the badges given to murderers; and it is always strange when murderers are rewarded. So through the centuries we have watched them at their trade, some brave, some cowardly, all of them dedicated to the task of acquiring glory by uncommon acts of murder. They fought so that they could ride for a day in a triumphal chariot and wear silk robes and hold an ivory staff in their hands, but it was the anonymous slave standing behind the *triumphator*, whispering in his ear about the vanity of honours, who represents the greater triumph. The voice of the slave was the voice of humanity, never so desperate as when it passed unheard.

We do not know when the slave first rode in the triumphal chariot and held the golden crown over the conqueror's head, or when he stepped down for the last time. We do not know whether the *triumphator* ever spoke to him in reply, or even glanced at him. He appears only briefly in the history of the triumph, and only once do we see him plain—on the Boscoreale cup, where he is depicted as a youth who seems to be filled with a sense of compassionate duty. One wonders why the slave never stabbed the conqueror in the back.

In our own dangerous age we can no longer triumph. We have come to the end of the road which leads to the sacrifice. We are all victims—the slaves, the prisoners, the conquerors alike. We make war in peril of annihilating the human race, leaving no conquerors to ride in procession. The last triumph of all will be set against the blue spaces of heaven as the flaming earth rides in procession round the deathless sun.

Index